# A NOTE FROM THE AUTHORS

Congratulations on your decision to take the AP U.S. Government & Politics exam! Whether or not you're completing a year-long AP U.S. Government & Politics course, this book can help you prepare for the exam. In it, you'll find information about the exam, as well as Kaplan's test-taking strategies, a targeted review that highlights important concepts on the exam, and practice tests. Take the Diagnostic Test to see which sections you should review most and use the two full-length exams to get comfortable with the testing experience. Don't miss the strategies for answering the free-response questions: you'll learn how to cover the key points AP graders will want to see.

By studying college-level U.S. government and politics in high school, you've placed yourself a step ahead of other students. You have developed your critical-thinking and time-management skills, as well as your understanding of the way our government works. Now it's time to show off what you've learned on the exam.

Best of luck,

Ulrich Kleinschmidt

William L. Brown Jr.

# RELATED TITLES

AP Biology

AP Calculus AB & BC

AP Chemistry

AP English Language and Composition

AP English Literature and Composition

AP Environmental Science

AP European History

AP Human Geography

AP Macroeconomics/Microeconomics

AP Physics B & C

AP Psychology

AP Statistics

AP U.S. History

AP U.S. Government & Politics

AP World History

SAT Premier with CD-Rom

SAT: Strategies, Practice and Review

SAT Subject Test: Biology

SAT Subject Test: Chemistry

SAT Subject Test: Literature

SAT Subject Test: Mathematics Level 1

SAT Subject Test: Mathematics Level 2

SAT Subject Test: Physics

SAT Subject Test: Spanish

SAT Subject Test: U.S. History

SAT Subject Test: World History

# AP® U.S. GOVERNMENT & POLITICS

# 2011

Ulrich Kleinschmidt

William L. Brown Jr.

KAPLAN

PUBLISHING

New York

© 2010 by Kaplan, Inc.

Published by Kaplan Publishing, a division of Kaplan, Inc.

1 Liberty Plaza, 24th Floor

New York, NY 10006

Printed in the United States of America

10 9 8 7 6 5 4 3 2

ISBN 13: 978-1-60714-544-8

Kaplan Publishing books are available at special quantity discounts to use for sales promotions, employee premiums, or educational purposes. For more information or to purchase books, please call the Simon & Schuster special sales department at 866-506-1949.

# TABLE OF CONTENTS

# PART THREE: AP U.S. GOVERNMENT & POLITICS REVIEW

# PART FOUR: PRACTICE TESTS

# PART FIVE: AP U.S. GOVERNMENT & POLITICS RESOURCES

# ABOUT THE AUTHORS

**Ulrich Kleinschmidt** has been teaching AP U.S. Government & Politics since the early 1990s. He also teaches AP Economics and is the Social Studies Department Chairperson at I. H. Kempner High School in Sugar Land, Texas, a suburb in the greater Houston area. He has been a national grader of the AP U.S. Government & Politics examination since 1999. He also has presented economics seminars for the College Board and has become a national trainer for the AP program.

**William L. Brown Jr.** began teaching AP U.S. Government & Politics in 1990. He also taught American History and Sociology at Eureka High School in Eureka, Missouri, a suburb of St. Louis. He has been a national grader of the AP U.S. Government & Politics examination since 1995 and a table leader since 1999.

# KAPLAN PANEL OF AP EXPERTS

Congratulations—you have chosen Kaplan to help you get a top score on your AP exam.

Kaplan understands your goals and what you're up against—achieving college credit and conquering a tough test—while participating in everything else that high school has to offer.

You expect realistic practice; authoritative advice; and accurate, up-to-the-minute information on the test. And that's exactly what you'll find in this book, as well as every other in the AP series. To help you (and us!) reach these goals, we have sought out leaders in the AP community. Allow us to introduce our experts.

## AP U.S. GOVERNMENT & POLITICS EXPERTS

**Chuck Brownson** teaches AP U.S. Government & Politics and AP Economics at Stephen F. Austin High School in Sugar Land, Texas. He is currently a graduate student working on his master's degree in political science at the University of Houston. He has been teaching AP U.S. Government & Politics and AP Economics classes for four years. He has been a reader for the AP U.S. Government exam for one year.

**Melissa Janecek** has taught AP U.S. Government & Politics for the last five years: one year at Navasota High School in Navasota, Texas, and the last four years at George Bush High School in Richmond, Texas. She is currently teaching at Seven Lakes High School in Katy, Texas. She also has experience teaching U.S. Government & Politics at North Harris Montgomery County College District. She has served as a reader for the AP U.S. Government & Politics exam for the past four years.

**Anthony "Tony" Jones** has taught AP courses for the past ten years, including AP U.S. History, AP European History, and AP World History. He has taught at Houston County High in Warner Robins, Georgia, and Rutland High School in Macon, Georgia. He is a member of the World History Association and the National Council for Social Studies. He is a table leader and reader for the AP World History exam. Additionally, he has been a presenter on integrating technology into the social studies and AP classroom at several conferences.

# Part One

# THE BASICS

# CHAPTER 1: INSIDE THE AP U.S. GOVERNMENT & POLITICS EXAM

This chapter will introduce the basics of the AP U.S. Government & Politics exam format: topics covered on the exam, patterns of previous tests, how your exam will be scored, and registration issues. This guide will help you get started on your approach to study and will help you decide which basic themes to target.

## OVERVIEW OF THE TEST STRUCTURE

Most universities use the AP U.S. Government & Politics exam to give credit for a freshman-level, three-hour, introductory course. It is considered the equivalent of a university course final examination.

The College Board's test has two major parts: a multiple-choice section and a free-response section. Each section is worth 50 percent of your total score.

| Section | Number of Questions | Time Allowed |
| --- | --- | --- |
| 1 | 60 (five choices: A to E) | 45 minutes (¾ of a minute per question) |
| 2 | 4 (each a free-response) | 1 hour, 40 minutes (25 minutes per question) |

The time constraints of this exam are a challenge. Successful students are prepared to recognize key terms and meanings quickly. National graders often note some fatigue by the time the third and fourth free-response questions are addressed. If you gain a comfort level with the subject vocabulary and train yourself to save time on the free-response questions, you will be ahead of the game.

## TOPICS COVERED ON THE AP U.S. GOVERNMENT & POLITICS EXAM

The current structure of the multiple-choice topics is meant as a general guide for study of the different course units. The numbers of questions per topic are set about two years before the exam is administered, so the 2008 exam was assembled between 2005 and 2006. Percentage guides given by College Board are approximates only. At the time of this publication, the 2007–2008 course guide was the most recent version available. College Board has not announced any significant changes in this year's exam.

| Basic Topics | General Areas within the Topics | Percent of Exam | Approximate # of Questions |
|---|---|---|---|
| 1. Constitutional Underpinnings | A. Formation<br>B. Adoption<br>C. Federalism<br>D. Democratic Government | 5–15% | 3 to 9 questions |
| 2. Political Beliefs and Behaviors | A. Citizen's Beliefs<br>B. Citizen's Learning<br>C. Public Opinion<br>D. Voting and Participation<br>E. Beliefs and Behaviors | 10–20% | 6 to 12 questions |
| 3. Political Parties, Interest Groups, and the Mass Media | A. Parties and Elections: Functions, Organization, Development, Effects, Laws, and Systems<br>B. Interest Groups and PACs: Interests Represented, Activities, Effects, Characteristics, and Roles<br>C. The Mass Media: Functions, Structure, and Impacts | 10–20% | 6 to 12 questions |
| 4. Institutions: Congress, Presidency, Bureaucracy, Federal Courts | A. Major Formal and Informal Powers<br>B. Balances of Power<br>C. Linkages: Public Opinions and Voters, Interest Groups, Parties, Media, and Subnational Governments | 35–45% | 21 to 27 questions |
| 5. Public Policy | A. Policy Making in the Federal System<br>B. Formation of Agendas<br>C. Institutions and Enactment<br>D. Bureaucracy and Courts in Policy Implementation<br>E. Linkages: Institutions and Federalism, Parties, Interest Groups, Public Opinion, Elections, and Policy Networks | 5–15% | 3 to 9 questions |
| 6. Civil Rights and Civil Liberties | A. Development of Rights and Judicial Interpretation<br>B. Substantive Rights and Liberties<br>C. The 14th Amendment | 5–15% | 3 to 6 questions |

## FREE-RESPONSE QUESTIONS: TOPICS AND EXPECTATIONS

The test structure was revised in 1998 to include four free-response questions. Students are asked to answer all four of the questions, unlike earlier tests that allowed students to select questions from several choices. The following table shows what topics have been selected since 1998.

| 1998: 1 | Primaries and Conventions | Four effects of change: primaries and conventions |
| 1998: 2 | Bill of Rights and the 14th Amendment | Incorporation cases: *Gitlow* or *Wolf* or *Gideon* |
| 1998: 3 | War Powers, Impoundment | Describe and evaluate the two acts |
| 1998: 4 | Low Voter Turnout | Demographics, three institutional obstacles |
| 1999: 1 | Candidates and the Media | Two ways that the media affects candidates, ways media are used |
| 1999: 2 | Interest Groups and Policy | ID groups, group resources, characteristics |
| 1999: 3 | Oversight of Bureaucracy | Two methods of oversight, oversight explanations |
| 1999: 4 | Charts: Federal Budget | Mandatory, discretionary, entitlement, changes |
| 2000: 1 | Constitution versus Articles | Three problems of articles, policy tensions |
| 2000: 2 | Court "Above Politics"? | Three nominee characteristics, two ways of influence |
| 2000: 3 | Map: 1992, 1996 Votes | Regions for Dems or GOP, explain factors |
| 2000: 4 | Campaign Finance Reform? | Obstacles: select *Buckley*, soft money, incumbency |
| 2001: 1 | Formal and Informal Changes | Identify two formal and two informal, state why the changes were made |
| 2001: 2 | Chart: Incumbent Re-election | Patterns of elections, factors, consequences |
| 2001: 3 | Ratification of 14th Amendment | Significance in cases, due process |
| 2001: 4 | Enact Public Policy | Difficult: divided government, weak parties |
| 2002: 1 | Divided Government | Problems, ways the president can overcome this |
| 2002: 2 | Chart: Benefits for Children and Seniors | Changes in help, relevant factors, effects |
| 2002: 3 | Institutions and Minorities | Federalism, parties, electoral system |
| 2002: 4 | Lower Voter Turnout | Two factors in turnout, why is turnout higher in presidential elections? |
| 2003: 1 | Presidential Approval Ratings | Two factors (positive or negative) in approval of president and why |
| 2003: 2 | Non voting Participation | Two forms of participation in government other than voting, their advantages |

*(continued on next page)*

| 2003: 3 | Graph of Federal and State Employment | Trends of changes, block grants, mandates |
|---|---|---|
| 2003: 4 | Leaders and Committees | Specialization, reciprocity, logrolling, parties |
| 2004: 1 | Presidential Powers: Formal and Informal | Two formal powers and two informal, advantages |
| 2004: 2 | Interest Group Techniques | Litigation, contributions, grassroots, groups |
| 2004: 3 | Minor Parties | Obstacles to third parties, contributions to third parties |
| 2004: 4 | Decline: Confidence in Government | Divided government and decline in confidence in government, the costs, and why it occurs |
| 2005: 1 | Independent Courts | Two ways in which the courts are insulated, two ways in which they are not |
| 2005: 2 | Change: Federal Government versus the States | Tax and spend, elastic clause, commerce, acts |
| 2005: 3 | Federal Protection from States | Selective incorporation, cases that show federal protection |
| 2005: 4 | Campaign Finance Reform | Soft money, independent spending, limits on money |
| 2006: 1 | Interest Groups, Political Parties: Goals and Support Connections | Define goals of both groups, describe two ways interest groups support parties, describe two ways interest groups are helped |
| 2006: 2 | Social Security Receipts, Spending, Reserves Chart | Define entitlements, source of Social Security, threats to Social Security, demographic trends |
| 2006: 3 | Congress, President, Agency Powers to Make Policy | Why did Congress give agencies power to execute laws? Select agency and identify policy-making powers. Congress's checks? |
| 2006: 4 | Bicameral Legislature of House and Senate | Why two chambers? Unique powers of House and Senate, explain |
| 2007: 1 | Electoral College | Explain winner-take-all system |
| 2007: 2 | First Amendment, Freedom of Religion | Select a case, describe Supreme Court's decision |
| 2007: 3 | War Powers Resolution | Describe two provisions of War Powers Resolution, powers that Congress has |
| 2007: 4 | Federal System | Define federalism, how it has increased power of state and federal government |

As noted, all major topics of the government course are represented in recent free-response selections. The questions require that students understand how the U.S. government balances the needs of many different groups: how it changes, how citizens participate, and how power is shared. As will be discussed in much greater detail later, the free-response section also includes the key instructions to "describe" and "explain" each section of each question. This is where well-prepared students will gain critical exam points.

## HOW THE EXAM IS SCORED

Because section 1 has 60 questions and 60 possible points, the free-response questions are also converted to a possible 60 points, giving each section a 50 percent value of the final score.

### MULTIPLE-CHOICE SCORING RULES

Beginning with the May 2011 administration of AP exams, the method for scoring the multiple-choice section has changed. Scores are based on the number of questions answered correctly. **There is no penalty for incorrect answers.** No points are awarded for unanswered questions. Therefore, you should answer every question, even if you have to guess.

### FREE-RESPONSE SCORING RULES

Each of the four questions is graded using a "rubric" point system. Each question may have a different number of possible points. Recent free-response questions have contained from 6 to 7 points. It is usually very easy to determine the number of points that need to be addressed. Questions are written with this in mind. An example would be a question with two parts, listed A and B. In part A, the student would be told to "identify" and "explain" a particular item. In part B, the instructions to "identify" and "explain" might be repeated. The student and the grader will immediately look for 4 points, one for the identification and one for the explanation of each A and B.

Regardless of the individual points set for each free-response question, the four questions are converted to a total of 60 points, or 50 percent of the test.

### COMPOSITE SCORING RULES

The most important scoring issue to note is that each year's test scores are "relative" to national results of that year. There is no set number of points that results in a passing score. The College Board gives each student a final score of 1 through 5, with 5 being the highest. The national office uses careful sets of statistics to ensure that the appropriate number of students receive scores that correctly identify the levels of mastery appropriate for the universities. If a test is particularly difficult in a given year and overall raw scores are down, the number of 5s, etc., continues to be similar to that of past years.

## SCORING RESULTS, 2006

| Number of Students (Total = 143,980) | Exam's Final Score (College Board Description) | Percent of Total |
|---|---|---|
| 11,561 | 5 (Extremely Well Qualified) | 8.0 |
| 25,415 | 4 (Well Qualified) | 17.7 |
| 41,982 | 3 (Qualified) | 29.2 |
| 44,096 | 2 (Possibly Qualified) | 30.6 |
| 20,926 | 1 (No Recommendation) | 14.5 |

The chances of receiving at least a 3 are above 50 percent. Many universities will extend some sort of class credit for scores of 3 and above. Almost all universities accept scores of 4 and 5, and about 25 percent of all students qualify in that range.

Many students and teachers ask what kind of raw score will create the appropriate final score. Each year's scores differ based on the relative difficulty of the questions. Usually, a raw score of over 70 percent will place you near the top of the list with the 5s. A composite score above 60 percent is within the usual range of 4s. The test is challenging but manageable. If a student can manage 45 correct answers on the 60 multiple-choice questions and achieve 45 points on the free-response questions, a high final score can be achieved.

## RECEIVING SCORES

AP Grade Reports are sent to students' addresses, high schools, and requested universities in July. Students may also call for scores, but there is a fee for this service. Check the College Board website for test dates and fee information.

# REGISTRATION AND FEES

To register for the exam, contact your guidance counselor or AP Coordinator. If your school does not administer the AP exam, contact AP for a listing of schools that do. Registration occurs in the spring; most schools complete the papers in March. At the time of this printing, the fee for an exam is $83. Many possible deductions are available. For those qualified with acute financial need, the College Board offers a $22 credit. In addition, many states offer subsidies to cover all or part of the exam.

## ADDITIONAL RESOURCES

For more information on the AP Program and the U.S. Government & Politics exam, contact the following:

AP Services
P.O. Box 6671
Princeton, NJ 08541-6671
Phone: (609)-771-7300 or 888-225-5427
Email: apexams@info.collegeboard.org
Website: collegeboard.com/student/testing/ap/about.html

# CHAPTER 2: STRATEGIES FOR SUCCESS: IT'S NOT ALWAYS HOW MUCH YOU KNOW

## INTRODUCTION

As noted in the first chapter, the AP U.S. Government & Politics exam is divided into two major parts of equal value: the multiple-choice section of 60 questions and the free-response section of 4 questions. Each correct multiple-choice question earns a point toward the maximum of 60 raw score points for that section. Each correct free-response question is worth 12.5 percent of the total score but is graded on a rubric system unique to each question.

The College Board keeps statistics on the frequency of high and low scores between the multiple-choice questions and free-response sections. It is often reported at conferences that there is a strong correlation between the two parts of the exam. A student who answers most of the multiple-choice questions correctly often tends to earn a larger number of free-response points. On the other hand, it is unusual that a student who does a poor job on the multiple-choice section rescues his or her total score with superior free-response answers.

What does this mean to you? You need to balance your study time and preparation skills. The same strengths that will help you with the first part of the exam will serve you well in the second. What strengths do successful students bring to the AP U.S. Government & Politics exam? For this test, the keys are vocabulary, the ability to make connections, and an understanding of the test expectations.

## GENERAL TEST-TAKING STRATEGIES

Most students who take this exam are taking the AP class at their school. Many are also signed up for several other AP courses and may be attempting multiple exams in May. Be realistic with your choices and your time. These are university-level exams on which you can do very well, but you'll need extra preparation. Attend any study sessions that your teachers provide. Use this manual as much as possible. Focus on the unique language of the subject. Watch for extensions of logic and

### CLEAR YOUR HEAD

Avoid interference from other subjects by making U.S. History the one you study right before you go to sleep.

questions that go beyond simple identifications. Divide your time into manageable units and don't burn out. Be sure to rest before the exam.

## HOW THIS BOOK CAN HELP

Kaplan's *AP U.S. Government & Politics* contains precisely the information you will need to ace the test. There's nothing extra in here to waste your time: no pointless review of material you won't be tested on, no rah-rah speeches—just the most effective test preparation tools available.

1. **Test strategies geared specifically to the AP U.S. Government & Politics exam.** Many books give the same talk about process of elimination that's been used for every standardized test given in the past 20 years. We're going to talk about process of elimination as it applies to the AP U.S. Government & Politics exam and only to the AP U.S. Government & Politics exam. There are several skills and general strategies that work for this particular test, and these will be covered in the next two chapters.

2. **A well-crafted review of all the relevant subjects.** The best test-taking strategies alone won't get you a good score. As its core, this AP exam covers a wide range of topics, and learning these topics is necessary. However, chances are good you're already familiar with these subjects, so an exhaustive review is not needed. In fact, it would be a waste of your time. No one wants that, so we've tailored our review section to focus on how the relevant topics typically appear on the exam and what you need to know to answer the questions correctly. If a topic doesn't come up on the AP U.S. Government & Politics exam, we don't cover it. If it appears on the test, we'll provide you with the facts you need to navigate the problem safely.

3. **Two full-length practice tests on which to cut your teeth.** Few things are better than experience when it comes to standardized testing. Taking these practice AP exams gives you an idea of what it's like to answer government and politics questions for three hours. Granted, that may not be a fun experience, but it is a helpful one. Practice exams give you the opportunity to find out what areas are your strongest and what topics you should spend some additional time studying. And the best part is that it doesn't count! Mistakes you make on our practice exams are mistakes you won't make on the real test.

These three points describe the general outline of this book: strategies, review, and then practice. This chapter will help you learn some specific skills you can use on the AP U.S. Government & Politics exam.

## HOW TO APPROACH THE MULTIPLE-CHOICE QUESTIONS

Remember, there will always be five answer choices, and you have only 45 minutes to complete 60 questions. It is critical to recognize quickly any key words or terms in the question. Don't rush your reading of the question, because one important word may be the key to a correct response. The following table is a list of such words from recently released multiple-choice questions.

In the released test, there were 10 questions (16.7 percent) with the key word *best* in the question. There were another 10 questions (16.7 percent) with a phrase including the word *most*. A third of the multiple-choice test is based on recognizing the trend. There were also six charts, graphs, and cartoons that required students to make some interpretations of evidence, statistics, or trends.

## KEY MULTIPLE-CHOICE WORDS

| Terms Used | Meaning/Hints |
|---|---|
| best | This is used in the general instructions and hints that some answer choices may be close to correct but are not the "most" correct. |
| best describes *or* best illustrates *or* best supports *or* best explains | You should know historic patterns or watch for significant data. |
| most *or* most likely *or* most important *or* most substantially | Same as above. |
| clear evidence | Watch for specific patterns and overwhelming evidence. |
| generally true | Watch out for choices that are not always, but are generally, true. |
| NOT *or* EXCEPT | A negative question is often used, also with the term *least* or the phrase *least likely*. |
| usually | These questions will be similar in style to "best" questions. |

## TIME MANAGEMENT AND SCORING

Pace yourself. You have 45 minutes to complete 60 questions. You should spend no more than 45 seconds on any single question. As you're reading a question, try to predict the answer, keeping in mind any key words such as "least likely" or "best". Then try to eliminate at least two answer choices that are out of the scope of the question, and take your best guess. If you have no idea what the answer is and cannot eliminate any of the answer choices, guess. The no penalty scoring makes this a wise decision. Go through the easy questions first, answer as many of them as possible, and get all the easy points quickly. Don't get caught running out of time before answering the easy questions. After going through all of the questions first, go back during the remaining time and tackle the questions about which you have the most doubts.

### CHANGE IS GOOD

Don't be afraid to change your answer to a multiple-choice question. If you don't feel confident about your answer, trust your instincts and go back to it if time allows.

### PICK YOUR BATTLES

If a question deals with a topic you *know* is one of your weak spots, don't waste valuable time reviewing the question more than twice. Just guess.

# HOW TO APPROACH THE FREE-RESPONSE QUESTIONS

As national graders, we've noticed that the students make the same kinds of mistakes year after year. We've also observed the ways successful students gather points. One of the biggest issues is the number of questions answered. Even though students have equal amounts of time available for the four free-response questions, they tend to make one of two mistakes: either they spend too much time on one question, or they get tired after three good answers and essentially skip a final answer. The best students are careful to give equal time and effort to all of the questions. These students do so with a simple strategy. First, they make a brief outline of each question that focuses on the number of rubric points suggested by the question. Successful students also label their outlines to match the rubric. They include brief key words, or even phrases, in the outline that match the question. Once they've done this for all four questions, they go back and fill in sentences and explanations.

Remember, this section is officially called a "free-response" section. Many U.S. high school students immediately focus on writing a five-paragraph essay, with introduction, body, and conclusion. This is not needed, or even desired, on this exam. Well-written sentences and explanations will help the grader recognize that you have mastered the materials. However, introductions that do not address what the question asks or that restate the question are simply a waste of your time. You gain no points for these and only lose time. Concluding paragraphs that rephrase all of the items already listed are equally useless to both student and grader.

Perhaps the most egregious error is the response that summarizes the topic of the question but never answers the question. Wonderfully written essays have been produced that hint all around the issues at hand but never get to the specific items needed to score points. Remember, the questions must be graded on a rubric point system, and graders can only give points if the student hits the information for which the question specifically asks. See the sample question described later in this section.

The writing of the free-response must by very specific in listing, identifying, describing, or explaining what the question asks. If the question requires one or two examples, only give one or two as requested. If the question requires that a link between sections be made, state that link.

The following list restates the free-response sequence suggested above. This strategy is important enough, and successful enough, to warrant repetition.

## Steps to Answering the Free-Response Questions

1. Make a numbered outline for each section of each question. (See the following sample.)

2. Fill in all the key words and concepts you immediately remember for all parts of your outline. Do this for all four questions.

3. Go back and explain, in well-presented but concise sentences, the key terms and topics.

4. Check and see if you not only "listed" or "identified" but also "described" and "explained" as needed.

5. Don't waste time rephrasing the question in an introduction.

6. Don't waste time presenting a conclusion paragraph that restates the items you have already completed. Use the time to be thorough on all four questions.

## SAMPLE QUESTION AND STRATEGIES

The following question appears on the College Board website as a released question from 2006.

> Question #1:
>
> While interest groups and political parties each play a significant role in the United States political system, they differ in their fundamental goals.
>
> (A) Identify the fundamental goal of interest groups in the political process.
>
> (B) Identify the fundamental goal of major political parties in the political process.
>
> (C) Describe two different ways by which interest groups support the fundamental goal of **political parties** in the political process.
>
> (D) For one of the forms of support you described in (C), explain two different ways in which that form of support helps **interest groups** to achieve their fundamental goal in the political process.

Note that the question asks for three levels of answers: identify, describe, and explain. A description must go beyond a mere listing, and the question is specific in the ways the interest groups and parties must be connected. An explanation must go to the level of showing "how and why."

> You must first decipher the number of points expected. An outline approach would address this quickly and help the grader immensely in finding your points. Here is a sample of a possible outline:
>
> (A) 1 point: Give the fundamental goal of interest groups. Give only one goal. Students who listed more than one fundamental goal lost this point.
>
> (B) 1 point: Give the fundamental goal of political parties. Give only one goal. Students who listed more than one fundamental goal also lost this point.

### THERE'S NO "U" IN HISTORY

Don't include personal opinions in the essay. The reader is looking for your grasp of the history itself and your ability to write about it.

(C) 2 points: Describe how interest groups support the party goal in two ways. Make sure the interest groups' support you describe actually supports the "fundamental" goal of political parties you gave in (B).

(D) 2 points: Select one of the two items you listed in (C) and explain how the interest groups gain from their help of political parties. Make sure that you focus on one of your descriptions from (C). Students who used two parts from (C) and gave one explanation from each did not receive the second point.

Without tackling all the possible correct answers, a plan has been formed for the maximum credit. You now know what to answer and how to structure the answer with the correct connections being included. This outline also shows that the rubric will include 6 points. The command to "explain" in part (D) is very important; it is the key to superior scores. If you start with such an outline, you will not forget to answer any section, you organize your thoughts, you find the key connections, and you still have time to fill in answers to your satisfaction.

## STRESS MANAGEMENT

You can beat anxiety the same way you can beat the AP U.S. Government & Politics exam—by knowing what to expect beforehand and developing strategies to deal with it.

### SOURCES OF STRESS

In the space provided, write down your sources of test-related stress. The idea is to pin down any sources of anxiety so you can deal with them one by one. We have provided common examples—feel free to use them and any others that apply to you.

- I always freeze up on tests.

- I'm nervous about the domestic policy development section (and/or the legislative branch section, the political beliefs and behaviors section, etc.).

- I need a good/great score to get into my first-choice college.

- My older brother/sister/best friend/girlfriend/boyfriend did really well. I must match that score or do better.

- My parents, who are paying for school, will be disappointed if I don't do well.

- I'm afraid of losing my focus and concentration.

- I'm afraid I'm not spending enough time preparing.

- I study like crazy, but nothing seems to stick in my mind.

---

**DON'T STRESS**

Remember, if you write good essays and get ¾ of the multiple-choice questions, you will get a high score on the exam. Don't worry about missing a few multiple-choice questions along the way.

- I always run out of time and get panicky.

- The simple act of thinking, for me, is like wading through refrigerated honey.

## MY SOURCES OF STRESS

_____

_____

_____

_____

_____

_____

Read through the list you made. Cross out things or add things. Now rewrite the list in order of most stressful to least stressful.

## MY SOURCES OF STRESS, IN ORDER

_____

_____

_____

_____

_____

_____

Chances are, the top of the list is a fairly accurate description of exactly how you react to test anxiety, both physically and mentally. The later items usually describe your fears (disappointing Mom and Dad, looking bad, etc.). Taking care of the major items from the top of the list should go a long way toward relieving overall test anxiety. That's what we'll do next.

## STRENGTHS AND WEAKNESSES

Take 60 seconds to list the areas of U.S. government and politics in which you have a strong knowledge. They can be general (foreign policy) or specific (the Bill of Rights). Put down as many as you can think of and, if possible, time yourself. Write for the entire time; don't stop writing until you've reached the one-minute stopping point. Go.

## STRONG TEST SUBJECTS

_____

_____

_____

_____

_____

Now take one minute to list areas of this subject at which you're not so good, just plain bad, have failed, or keep failing. Again, keep it to one minute and continue writing until you reach the cutoff. Go.

## WEAK TEST SUBJECTS

_____

_____

_____

_____

_____

Taking stock of your assets and liabilities lets you know which areas you don't have to worry about and which ones will demand extra attention and effort. It helps a lot to find out where you need to spend extra effort. We mostly fear what we don't know and are probably afraid to face. You can feel more confident when you know you're actively strengthening your chances of earning a higher overall score.

Now, go back to the list of your strengths and expand on it for two minutes. Take the general items on that first list and make them more specific; take the specific items and expand them into more general conclusions. Naturally, if anything new comes to mind, jot it down. Focus all of your attention and effort on your strengths. Don't underestimate yourself or your abilities. Give yourself full credit. At the same time, don't list strengths you don't really have; you'll only be fooling yourself.

Expanding from general to specific might go as follows. If you listed "domestic policy" as a broad topic in which you feel strong, you would then narrow your focus to include areas of this subject about which you are particularly knowledgeable. Your areas of strength might include regulatory policies, grant programs, etc. Whatever topics you know well go on your expanded strengths list. OK. Check your starting time. Go.

### STRONG TEST SUBJECTS: AN EXPANDED LIST

_____

_____

_____

_____

_____

_____

After you stop, check your time. Did you find yourself going beyond the two minutes allotted? Did you write down more things than you thought you knew? Is it possible you know more than you've given yourself credit for? Could that mean you've found a number of areas in which you feel strong?

You just took an active step toward helping yourself. Enjoy your increased feelings of confidence and use them when you take the AP U.S. Government & Politics exam.

## VISUALIZE

This next group of activities is a follow-up to the lists of strengths and weaknesses. Sit in a comfortable chair in a quiet setting. If you wear glasses, take them off. Close your eyes and breathe in a deep, satisfying breath of air. Really fill your lungs until your rib cage is fully expanded and you can't take in any more. Then, exhale the air completely. Imagine you're blowing out a candle with your last little puff of air. Do this two or three more times, filling your lungs to their maximum and emptying them totally. Keep your eyes closed, comfortably but not tightly. Let your body sink deeper into the chair as you become even more comfortable.

With your eyes shut, you can notice something very interesting. You're no longer dealing with the worrisome stuff going on in the world outside of you. Now you can concentrate on what happens inside you. The more you recognize your own physical reactions to stress and anxiety, the more you can control them. You may not realize it, but you've begun to regain a sense of being in control.

Imagine there are TV screens on the back of your eyelids. Let images begin to form on those screens. Allow the images to come easily and naturally; don't force them. Visualize a relaxing situation. It might be a special place you've visited before or one you've read about. It can be a fictional location that you create in your imagination, but a real-life memory of a place or situation you know is usually better. Make it as detailed as possible and notice as much as you can.

Stay focused on the images as you sink further into your chair. Breathe easily and naturally. You might have the sensations of any stress or tension draining from your muscles and flowing downward, out your feet and away from you.

Take a moment to check how you're feeling. Notice how comfortable you've become. Imagine how much easier it would be if you could take the test feeling this relaxed and in this state of ease. You've coupled the images of your special place with sensations of comfort and relaxation. You've also found a way to become relaxed simply by visualizing your own safe, special place.

Close your eyes and start remembering a real-life situation in which you did well on a test. If you can't come up with one, remember a situation in which you did something that you were really proud of—a genuine accomplishment. Make the memory as detailed as possible. Think about the sights, the sounds, the smells, even the tastes associated with this remembered experience. Remember how confident you felt as you accomplished your goal. Now start thinking about the AP U.S. Government & Politics exam. Keep your thoughts and feelings in line with that previous, successful experience. Don't make comparisons between them. Just imagine taking the upcoming test with the same feelings of confidence and relaxed control.

This exercise is a great way to bring the test down to earth. You should practice this exercise often, especially when you feel burned out on test preparation. The more you practice it, the more effective the exercise will be for you.

## EXERCISE

Whether you enjoy jogging, walking, biking, mild aerobics, push-ups, or a pickup basketball game, physical exercise is a very effective way to stimulate both your mind and body and to improve your ability to think and concentrate. Lots of students get out of the habit of regular exercise when they're prepping for the exam. Also, sedentary people get less oxygen to the blood and, hence, to the brain than active people. You can watch TV with a little less oxygen; you just can't think as well.

Any big test is a bit like a race. Finishing the race strong is just as important as being quick early on. If you can't sustain your energy level in the last sections of the exam, you could blow it. Along with a good diet and adequate sleep, exercise is an important part of keeping yourself in fighting shape and thinking clearly for the long haul.

There's another thing that happens when students don't make exercise an integral part of their test preparation. Like any organism in nature, you operate best if all your "energy systems" are in balance. Studying uses a lot of energy, but it's all mental. When you take a study break, do something active. Take a 5- to 10-minute exercise break for every 50 or 60 minutes that you study. The physical exertion helps keep your mind and body in sync. This way, when you finish studying for the night and go to bed, you won't lie there unable to sleep because your head is tired while your body still wants to run a marathon.

One warning about exercise: It's not a good idea to exercise vigorously right before you go to bed. This could easily cause sleep-onset problems. For the same reason, it's also not a good idea to study right up to bedtime. Make time for a buffer period before you go to bed. Take 30 to 60 minutes to take a long hot shower, meditate, or watch TV.

## Stay Drug Free

Using drugs to prepare for or take a big test is not a good idea. Don't take uppers to stay alert. Amphetamines make it hard to retain information. Mild stimulants, such as coffee, cola, or over-the-counter caffeine pills, can help you study longer because they keep you awake, but they can also lead to agitation, restlessness, and insomnia. Some people can drink an entire pot of coffee and sleep like a baby. Others have one cup and start to vibrate. It all depends on your tolerance for caffeine. Remember, a little anxiety is a good thing. The adrenaline that gets pumped into your bloodstream helps you stay alert and think more clearly.

You can also rely on your brain's own endorphins. Endorphins have no side effects, and they're free. It just takes some exercise to release them. Running, bicycling, swimming, aerobics, and power walking all release endorphins into the happy spots in your brain's neural synapses. In addition, exercise develops your mental stamina and increases the oxygen transfer to your brain.

To reduce stress, you should eat fruits and vegetables (raw is best or just lightly steamed); low-fat protein such as fish, skinless poultry, and legumes (such as lentils and beans); and whole grains such as brown rice, whole wheat bread, and pastas (with no bleached flour). Don't eat sweet, high-fat snacks. Simple carbohydrates like sugar make stress worse, and fatty foods lower your immunity. Don't eat salty foods either. They can deplete potassium, which you need for nerve functions. You can go back to your diet of junk food and soda after you have finished the AP U.S. Government & Politics exam.

## Isometrics

Here's another natural route to relaxation and invigoration. You can do it whenever you get stressed out, including during the test. Close your eyes. Starting with your eyes—without holding your breath—gradually tighten every muscle in your body (but not to the point of pain) in the following sequence:

- Close your eyes tightly.
- Squeeze your nose and mouth together so that your whole face is scrunched up.
  (If it makes you self-conscious to do this in the test room, skip the face-scrunching part.)
- Pull your chin into your chest and pull your shoulders together.
- Tighten your arms to your body and then clench your fists.
- Pull in your stomach.
- Squeeze your thighs and buttocks together and tighten your calves.
- Stretch your feet, then curl your toes (watch out for cramping in this part).

At this point, every muscle should be tightened. Now, relax your body, one part at a time, in reverse order, starting with your toes. Let the tension drop out of each muscle. The entire process might take five minutes from start to finish (you can shorten it to a couple of minutes during the test). This clenching and unclenching exercise will feel silly at first, but if you get good at it, you will feel very relaxed.

## COUNTDOWN TO THE TEST

The following table is just one suggestion of a logical approach to preparation. The earlier in the year you are able to commit some study time, the easier the exam will become.

| | |
|---|---|
| Starting Early:<br>(Several months before the exam) | • Take a diagnostic test to determine your strengths and your weaknesses. Once or twice a week, spend about an hour reading a review chapter and tackling a few multiple-choice questions.<br><br>• Take notes on terms/topics you don't understand and ask your teacher about them. Read your text sections.<br><br>• As the test date approaches, take a full practice test. Score yourself on the multiple-choice section and have your teacher, or a peer, grade the free-response section.<br><br>• Before the test, go over charts and focus on the vocabulary, case names, political units, etc. |
| If You Start Nearer the Exam Date:<br>(A couple of weeks before) | • Take a diagnostic test to determine your strengths and your weaknesses.<br><br>• Be efficient with your study hours. Skim review chapters and focus on the vocabulary. Take one of the practice tests in its entirety and keep careful track of time constraints. Focus on the areas you don't know as well.<br><br>• Work with peers and help teach them topics they don't know.<br><br>• Just before the exam, make a list of terms you have had the most trouble learning and concentrate on those. |

### STUDY SCHEDULE

The schedule presented here is the ideal. Compress the schedule to fit your needs. Do keep in mind, though, that research in cognitive psychology has shown that the best way to acquire a great deal of information about a topic is to prepare over a long period of time. Because you may have several months to prepare for this exam, it makes sense for you to use that time to your advantage. This book, along with your text, should be invaluable in helping you prepare for this test.

**If you have two semesters to prepare, use the following schedule:**

**September:**

Take the diagnostic test in this book and isolate areas in which you need help. The diagnostic will serve to familiarize you with the type of material you will be asked about on the AP exam. Begin reading your textbook along with the class outline.

**October through February:**

Continue reading this book and use the summaries at the end of each chapter to help guide you to the most salient information for the exam.

**March and April:**

Take the two practice tests and get an idea of your score. Also, identify the areas in which you need to brush up. Then go back and review those topics in both this book and your U.S. government and politics textbook.

**May:**

Do a final review and take the exam.

---

**If you only have one semester to prepare, you'll need a more compact schedule:**

**January:**

Take the diagnostic test in this book.

**February through April:**

Begin reading this book and identify areas of strengths and weaknesses.

**Late April:**

Take the two practice tests and use your performance results to guide you in your preparation.

**May:**

Do a final review and take the exam.

## THREE DAYS BEFORE THE TEST

It's almost over. Eat an energy bar, drink some soda—do whatever it takes to keep going (but watch the caffeine). Here are Kaplan's strategies for the three days leading up to the test.

Take a full-length practice test under timed conditions. Use the techniques and strategies you've learned in this book. Approach the test strategically, actively, and confidently.

WARNING: *Do not* take a full-length practice test if you have fewer than 48 hours left before the test. Doing so will probably exhaust you and hurt your score on the actual test. You wouldn't run a practice marathon the day before the real thing.

## Two Days before the Test

Go over the results of your practice test. Don't worry too much about your score or about whether you got a specific question right or wrong. The practice test doesn't count. But do examine your performance on specific questions with an eye as to how you might get through each one faster and better on the test to come.

## The Night before the Test

DO NOT STAY UP LATE STUDYING. Get together your AP supplies containing the following items:

- A watch (with alarm sounds turned off)
- A few No. 2 pencils
- Black or blue pens for the free-response section. Do not write the free-response answers in pencil.

(Please be ready to write legibly. Undecipherable writing may result in significant loss of free-response points.)

- An eraser
- Your photo ID card
- Your ETS admissions ticket

Know exactly where you're going, exactly how you're getting there, and exactly how long it takes to get there. It's probably a good idea to visit your test center sometime before the day of the test so that you know what to expect—what the rooms are like, how the desks are set up, and so on.

Relax the night before the test. Do the relaxation and visualization techniques. Read a good book, take a long hot shower, or watch something on TV. Get a good night's sleep. Go to bed early and leave yourself extra time in the morning.

## The Morning of the Test

First, wake up. After that...

- Eat breakfast. Make it something substantial but not anything too heavy or greasy.
- Don't drink a lot of coffee if you're not used to it. Bathroom breaks cut into your time, and too much caffeine is a bad idea.

- Dress in layers so that you can adjust to the temperature of the test room.

- Read something. Warm up your brain with a newspaper or a magazine. You shouldn't let the exam be the first thing you read that day.

- Be sure to get there early. Allow yourself extra time for traffic, mass transit delays, or detours.

## DURING THE TEST

Don't be shaken. If you find your confidence slipping, remind yourself how well you've prepared. You know the structure of the test; you know the instructions; you've had practice with—and have learned strategies for—every question type.

If something goes really wrong, don't panic. If the test booklet is defective—two pages are stuck together or the ink has run—raise your hand and tell the proctor you need a new book. If you accidentally misgrid your answer page or put the answers in the wrong section, raise your hand and tell the proctor. He or she might be able to arrange for you to regrid your test after it's over, when it won't cost you any time.

## AFTER THE TEST

You might walk out of the AP U.S. Government & Politics exam thinking that you blew it. This is a normal reaction. Lots of people—even the highest scorers—feel that way. You tend to remember the questions that stumped you, not the ones that you knew. We're positive that you will have performed well and scored your best on the exam because you followed the Kaplan strategies outlined in this book. Be confident in your preparation and celebrate the fact that the AP U.S. Government & Politics exam is soon to be a distant memory.

Now that you have a strategy for your preparation, continue your exam prep by taking the Diagnostic test that follows this chapter. This short test will give you an idea of the format of the actual exam, and it will demonstrate the scope of topics covered. After the Diagnostic test, you'll find answers with detailed explanations. Be sure to read these explanations carefully, even if you got the answer correct, because you can pick up bits of knowledge from them. Use your score to learn which topics you need to review more carefully. Of course, all the strategies in the world can't save you if you don't know anything about U.S. government and politics. The chapters following the Diagnostic test will help you review the primary concepts and facts that you can expect to encounter on the AP U.S. Government & Politics exam.

# Part Two

# DIAGNOSTIC TEST

# HOW TO CALCULATE YOUR SCORE

This Diagnostic test is a brief multiple-choice exam to help you identify your strengths and weaknesses in the area of AP U.S. Government & Politics. The goal is to help you determine the areas that you should focus on while studying. The questions are drawn from all areas covered on the actual AP U.S. Government & Politics exam.

To compute your score for the Diagnostic test, calculate the number of questions you got right and divide by 20. If you got 15 questions right out of 20, divide 15 by 20. To set this equal to a score out of 100, set up a proportion:

$$\frac{15}{20} = \frac{n}{100}$$
$$20n = 1,500$$
$$n = 75$$

$11/20 = N/100$

$20N = 1100$

$55 = N$

The approximate score range is as follows:

**5** = 80–100 (extremely well qualified)

**4** = 60–79 (well qualified)

**3** = 50–59 (qualified)

**2** = 40–49 (possibly qualified)

**1** = 0–39 (no recommendation)

A score of 75 is a 4, so in this case, you're doing well. If your score is low, keep on studying to improve your chances of getting credit for the AP U.S. Government & Politics exam.

# DIAGNOSTIC TEST ANSWER GRID

1. Ⓐ Ⓑ ● Ⓓ Ⓔ
2. Ⓐ Ⓑ ● Ⓓ Ⓔ
3. ● Ⓑ Ⓒ Ⓓ Ⓔ
4. Ⓐ Ⓑ Ⓒ Ⓓ ●
5. Ⓐ Ⓑ Ⓒ ● Ⓔ
6. Ⓐ Ⓑ ● Ⓓ Ⓔ
7. Ⓐ Ⓑ ● Ⓓ Ⓔ

8. Ⓐ Ⓑ Ⓒ ● Ⓔ
9. ● Ⓑ Ⓒ Ⓓ Ⓔ
10. Ⓐ Ⓑ ● Ⓓ Ⓔ
11. Ⓐ Ⓑ ● Ⓓ Ⓔ
12. Ⓐ Ⓑ Ⓒ ● Ⓔ
13. Ⓐ ● Ⓒ Ⓓ Ⓔ
14. Ⓐ ● Ⓒ Ⓓ Ⓔ

15. Ⓐ Ⓑ Ⓒ Ⓓ ●
16. Ⓐ Ⓑ Ⓒ Ⓓ ●
17. Ⓐ Ⓑ ● Ⓓ Ⓔ
18. ● Ⓑ Ⓒ Ⓓ Ⓔ
19. Ⓐ Ⓑ Ⓒ ● Ⓔ
20. Ⓐ Ⓑ Ⓒ Ⓓ ●

# Section I: Multiple-Choice Questions

**Time: 45 Minutes 20 Questions**

**Directions:** Select the answer choice that best answers the question or completes the statement.

1. Which of the following statements concerning the attitudes of the founding fathers is true?

   (A) They were a cross section of that era's citizens—both rich and poor—who were proportionately represented.

   (B) They were really not all that concerned with maintaining an integrated system that provided for a separation of powers.

   (C) They were a group that was motivated by a disinterested commitment to the public good, with little desire to express their own economic and human opinions.

   (D) The founders were divided among themselves about the definition of what the concept of federalism really meant.

   (E) The founders were admirable because what they created really was original and was not borrowed from earlier governmental concepts.

2. Which of the following descriptions concerning the *Federalist Papers* is **NOT** correct?

   (A) Alexander Hamilton, John Jay, and James Madison used the pen name "Publius."

   (B) The names of the authors of the *Federalist Papers* were a secret at the time of their publication.

   (C) The *Federalist Papers* probably played only a small role in securing ratification.

   (D) These essays have had a long-lasting value as an authoritative and profound explanation of the Constitution.

   (E) The *Federalist Papers* were almost exclusively printed in the Philadelphia newspapers.

3. Which of the following statements best describes the term *silent majority*?

   (A) The silent majority consists of those people who uphold traditional values no matter what their economic status, especially against the counterculture of the 1960s.

   (B) The silent majority refers to a group of mostly liberal, progressive thinkers of the 1950s.

   (C) The silent majority was a popular term utilized by the founding fathers to describe the people they believed they were representing.

   (D) The silent majority later organized into a political group that founded the "Bull Moose Party," one of the most successful third parties in American politics.

   (E) The silent majority was first used to describe those citizens opposed to the Supreme Court ruling in *Roe v. Wade*.

4. Which of the following statements concerning political participation in the United States is **NOT** correct?

   (A) The motor-voter bill was designed to make it easier to register to vote.

   (B) In the United States, the entire burden of registering to vote falls on the individual voters.

   (C) The real source of the voter participation problem in the United States is that a relatively low percentage of the adult population is registered to vote.

   (D) In the United States, a majority of the voting-age population is registered to vote.

   (E) The vast majority of registered American voters do not vote in elections.

GO ON TO THE NEXT PAGE

5. In the United States, voter turnout is highest for presidential elections among which of the following groups?

   (A) Unionized workers motivated by the union leadership

   (B) Eighteen to 25-year-olds enthused about voting for the first time

   (C) Citizens lower on the socioeconomic scale dissatisfied with their living conditions

   (D) Those U.S. citizens with college educations, no matter their ethnic or social standing

   (E) Women, who are motivated by gender-centered issues

6. Most research shows that voters base their decisions on how they are going to vote in presidential elections upon which of the following factors?

   (A) Party platforms created at the conventions

   (B) The competence of the candidate's chosen running mate

   (C) Party identification or single issues and which party the voter tends to perceive favorably on these issues

   (D) Effective television advertising developed by professional advertising personnel

   (E) The effectiveness of a candidate during the televised debates

7. Which of the following statements best describes the role of today's party convention?

   (A) They are important gatherings where decisions are made for long-term party goals.

   (B) They allow for important fund-raising by selling the television rights to networks.

   (C) Delegates perform an important function by establishing important party policies for the election at hand.

   (D) They are mostly symbolic pep rallies used to give their candidate a popularity boost.

   (E) They are the presidential candidate's forum for considering and choosing his running mate.

8. Which statement is **NOT** true concerning political parties in the United States?

   (A) The founding fathers of our country generally disliked the concept of parties, considering them to be motivated by ambition and self-interest.

   (B) Originally, parties were called by the labels *Republicans* and *Federalists*.

   (C) The party system as reorganized during the Jacksonian period was organized from bottom to top, rather than from the top down.

   (D) The party system was always intended to be a two-party system, and this concept is established in the Constitution.

   (E) The development of the convention system was in part a reform allowing for some local control of the nominating process.

9. Political parties have been declining in influence for which of the following reasons?

(A) Candidates and voters act more independently today.

(B) Sponsorship of the parties under the Constitution has been amended in the last 50 years.

(C) Candidates in the last half of the 20th century were mostly self-funded.

(D) Because candidates try to take popular views, there really is very little difference in the two parties.

(E) Parties have lost the ability to raise funds because of changes in regulations dealing with "soft money."

10. Which statement is most correct concerning third parties?

(A) Third parties are encouraged by our election system today because they act as important outlets for voter participation.

(B) Their existence is protected under the Bill of Rights in the U.S. Constitution.

(C) The emergence of third parties has led to a rise in straight ticket voting as a backlash to their influence.

(D) They benefit equally with the existing parties under federal campaign financing laws.

(E) In our political system, they have occasionally changed the outcome of presidential elections.

11. Which of the following is **NOT** correct concerning the House of Representatives?

(A) Unlike the Senate, it contains a very powerful rules committee.

(B) House members are not limited in the length of debate on bills.

(C) It is known as a noncontinuous body.

(D) The length of a representative's term is shorter than that of a senator.

(E) The House is generally based upon the Virginia Plan from the Constitutional Convention.

12. Which of the following is true concerning redistricting in the House of Representatives?

(A) The process of redistricting takes place every 20 years according to the Constitution.

(B) Redistricting is usually based upon the voter turnout in the previous elections.

(C) Partisan politics never plays a role in the redistricting process.

(D) Redistricting is handled by the legislatures in each of the states.

(E) The process can only add seats in the House and can never reduce the number of representatives.

13. The system of checks and balances between Congress and the executive branch is illustrated in all **EXCEPT** which of the following?

(A) The House and Senate overriding a presidential veto

(B) The Senate confirming a Supreme Court Justice nominee of the president's

(C) The Senate using its power of cloture to consider a bill

(D) Congress voting on a declaration of war requested by the president

GO ON TO THE NEXT PAGE

(E) The Senate confirming a presidential nominee to the cabinet

14. Which of the following terms concerning Congress is incorrectly described?

(A) Congress has a power known as the *franking privilege* that allows representatives to keep their constituents informed by using the mail system free of charge.

(B) The *filibuster* is a process that often bottlenecks legislation in the House of Representatives.

(C) The term *pork-barrel legislation* refers to bills passed that give tangible benefits to constituents in hopes of winning voters.

(D) *Gerrymandering* is a process of drawing a House district in an erratic manner to favor one party over another.

(E) A *rider* is a provision added to a piece of legislation that is not consistent with the bill's purpose.

15. Which of the following statements concerning the presidency is correct?

(A) Presidential vetoes are overridden in the vast majority of instances.

(B) The inauguration date for presidents was changed from March to January.

(C) Presidential succession always provided for the replacement by the vice president upon the death of a president.

(D) Presidential term limitations were addressed in the Bill of Rights.

(E) The president is no longer required to be a native-born American; naturalized citizens are also eligible.

16. Which of the following Supreme Court decisions dealt with the rights of an accused criminal in the United States?

    I. *Gideon v. Wainwright*
    II. *Mapp v. Ohio*
    III. *Korematsu v. U.S.*
    IV. *Miranda v. Arizona*

(A) I only

(B) I and IV only

(C) I, II, and IV only

(D) II, III, and IV only

(E) I, II, and III only

17. Often identifiable small groups benefit from policies that are paid for by a large part of society—this type of politics is known as?

(A) Majoritarian politics

(B) Client politics

(C) Entrepreneurial politics

(D) Interest group politics

(E) Progressive politics

18. The economic theory that assumes inflation occurs when too much money is chasing too few goods goes by which of the following labels?

(A) Supply-side economics

(B) Communism

(C) Keynesian economics

(D) Monetarism

(E) Gold standard

GO ON TO THE NEXT PAGE

*Use the chart provided to answer the questions that follow.*

| Supreme Court Losing Favor<br>Favorable Opinion of Supreme Court | Jan<br>2001<br>% | June<br>2005<br>% | Change |
|---|---|---|---|
| Total | 68 | 57 | −11 |
| Republican | 80 | 64 | −16 |
| Democrat | 61 | 51 | −10 |
| Independent | 69 | 62 | −7 |
| Conservative Republican | 78 | 59 | −19 |
| Moderate-Liberal Republican | 84 | 72 | −12 |
| Conservative-Moderate Democrat | 66 | 52 | −14 |
| Liberal Democrat | 54 | 51 | −3 |
| White Protestant | 71 | 57 | −14 |
| Evangelical | 73 | 51 | −22 |
| Mainline | 69 | 63 | −6 |
| White Catholic | 74 | 64 | −10 |
| Secular | 58 | 52 | −6 |

Source: Pew Research Center for Religion and Public Life

19. According to the chart, which of the following groups showed the **LEAST** amount of change in their favorable opinion of the Supreme Court?

    (A) Conservative Republicans
    (B) Moderate-liberal Republicans
    (C) Conservative-moderate Democrats
    (D) Liberal Democrats
    (E) None of the above

20. According to the chart, which of the following statements is **NOT** correct?

    (A) In January 2001, moderate-liberal Republicans had the most favorable view of the Supreme Court.

    (B) In June 2005, the favorable opinion of the Supreme Court by white Catholics had decreased 10 percent from January of 2001.

    (C) The white protestant evangelical group showed the greatest amount of change in their opinion of the Supreme Court during the period surveyed.

    (D) Overall favorable opinion of the Supreme Court is lower in the Democratic Party than the Republican Party.

    (E) Only mainline white Protestants showed an increase in their favorable opinion of the Supreme Court.

STOP

# ANSWERS AND EXPLANATIONS

**1. D**

The founding fathers themselves were in some disagreement over what the term *federalism* was really supposed to mean. This caused some of the best-known names of that period either to oppose or at the very least to have considerable reservations about their new form of government.

**2. E**

The role of the *Federalist Papers* is believed to be relatively small in importance as far as ratification was concerned. Their value has been in explaining the deeper meanings of the Constitution as interpreted by the three scholars who wrote the *Federalist Papers*—Alexander Hamilton, James Madison, and John Jay. The *Federalist Papers* were printed in New York papers, not in Philadelphia papers, because New York was a pivotal state for ratification purposes.

**3. A**

The *silent majority* was a phrase popularized by the Nixon administration to describe the multilayered socioeconomic group that upheld traditional values. This group was particularly prominent in the mid-to-late 1960s and early 1970s.

**4. E**

Statistics show that the vast majority of registered voters do vote in American elections. The debate has been in the difficulty of registering individuals so that they are eligible to vote.

**5. D**

Perhaps the single most telling factor in voter participation is the level of education. Higher educated Americans across all racial, ethnic, and gender lines are the most likely to vote.

**6. C**

Party identification continues to be a very strong factor in voter habits. Single issues about which voters care deeply have also gained in importance in recent years. Despite the media circus surrounding them, research has shown that the televised debates are not as critical to voter's decisions. Party platforms, running mates, and television advertising have been shown to have minimal impact as well.

**7. D**

It is widely agreed that today's conventions are little more than symbolic pep rallies that are used to "spike" the approval ratings of the candidates. Networks do not pay parties for television rights, and this has led to less and less network television coverage of recent conventions compared to those of the 1950s and 1960s.

**8. D**

It is not true that the party system was always intended to be a two-party system and that this concept is favored in the Constitution. There is no sanctioning of parties in the Constitution. The evolution of a two-party system is something that happened completely by circumstance. While today's election statutes favor a two-party system, third parties can still make a significant impact on U.S. elections.

**9. A**

Parties are declining in influence because candidates and voters act more independently today. There is little argument that today's politicians and voters act more independently than ever before in U.S. history. Straight-ticket voting is almost unheard of, and "coattail effects" are minimal at best. Many states vote for one party for president but elect governors, senators, and congresspeople of the opposite party.

**10. E**

Third parties have definitely changed the outcome of some presidential elections. Theodore Roosevelt, Ross Perot, and George Wallace were all third-party candidates who had an impact on a presidential election.

**11. B**

Because of the logistics and practicality of the issue, House members are limited in the length of their debate on bills. The length of debate on a particular issue is something that is decided by the extremely important Rules Committee.

**12. D**

Redistricting of federal House of Representative districts is handled by the various state legislatures every 10 years after a census is taken. While there are guidelines to this process, the final decisions are left up to those in state legislatures, and it has always been a partisan, highly contested issue.

**13. C**

The power of cloture has nothing to do with the system of checks and balances between the legislative and executive branches. Overriding vetoes, confirming judicial and cabinet appointments, and declarations of war are all considered a legislative check on the executive branch.

**14. B**

The filibuster does not bottleneck legislation in the House of Representatives. In fact, members of the House of Representatives do not possess the ability to filibuster; the Senate exclusively holds this ability.

**15. B**

The 20th Amendment to the U.S. Constitution changed the presidential inauguration date from March to January. This was done, in part, as a result of the time lag following the 1932 presidential election, which many believed deepened the Depression.

**16. C**

*Korematsu v. U.S.* was a court case concerning internment of Japanese-Americans during World War II. The other three cases all deal with various rights of an accused criminal. These include the right to a lawyer (*Gideon v. Wainwright*), the freedom from unreasonable search and seizure (*Mapp v. Ohio*), and the obligation to have your rights read to you at the time of your arrest (*Miranda v. Arizona*).

**17. B**

Client politics is defined as the politics of policy making in which some small group receives the benefits of the policy and the public at large bears the costs.

**18. D**

Monetarism is an economic philosophy that assumes inflation occurs when too much money is chasing too few goods. Monetarism proposes that the correct course for the government is to have a steady, predictable increase in the money supply at a rate about equal to the growth in an economy's productivity.

**19. D**

The chart shows that the change in the favorable opinion toward the Supreme Court among liberal Democrats fell only 3 percent. This is only half as much as the next lowest change.

**20. E**

The chart very clearly shows that from January 2001 through June 2005, the favorable opinion of the Supreme Court fell in every category surveyed.

# HOW TO MAKE THIS BOOK WORK FOR YOU BASED ON THE RESULTS OF YOUR DIAGNOSTIC TEST

If you have completed the 20-question Diagnostic test, you should now consider the results. What have you learned about the question structures? What have you gained from experiencing the kinds of topics covered on the AP exam?

Note that this sample was constructed with the course description in mind. The questions are arranged in the same sequence as the College Board's suggested outline. Questions 1 and 2 cover Topic 1 (Constitutional Underpinnings), Questions 3 and 4 cover Topic 2 (Political Beliefs and Behaviors), and so on. Key terms and phrases were chosen, such as asking you to find the answer that is "not correct" or the one that is "most correct." Focus on those key instructions, and you will have a much better level of understanding the demands of the multiple-choice section.

## CONVERTING A RAW SCORE TO THE AP SYSTEM

The Diagnostic test is only one-third of the length of the full test and, therefore, of limited use in predicting your final score. If you take this sample after you have completed the school course, your expectations should have been high. But because there is no set number of points that guarantee certain scores in any given year, you cannot directly match the percentage you got correct on the Diagnostic with the AP scoring system. However, the Diagnostic test will give you a general idea about your strengths and weaknesses, which will enable you to organize your study time for maximum effectiveness.

| Number of Diagnostic Questions Answered Correctly | Percent That Represents | Comments |
|---|---|---|
| 15 to 20 | 75% and higher | You are well on the way to earning a 4 or 5 if you do this well on the full test. Keep up the same level of success on the free-response questions! |
| 10 to 14 | 50% to 70% | Focus on vocabulary. Watch for the ways questions are phrased. You will need to score well on the free-response questions. |
| 0 to 9 | Up to 45% | Study and review time is here! Focus on the topics that gave you the most trouble. Build a stronger mastery of terms and concepts of government. |

| Part Three |

# AP U.S. GOVERNMENT & POLITICS REVIEW

# CHAPTER 3: THE DEVELOPMENT OF THE U.S. FEDERAL SYSTEM

## IF YOU ONLY LEARN SIX THINGS IN THIS CHAPTER . . . .

1. The Declaration of Independence stands as a list of freedoms and rights that the U.S. government continues to further and protect.

2. Many features of the U.S. Constitution were designed to be direct corrections of flaws in government found under the Articles of Confederation.

3. The Constitutional Convention of 1787 was a contest between political groups favoring central power and political groups favoring regional power. It was also a contest between states with large populations and those with small populations.

4. The ratification process created a need for a federal Bill of Rights. It also produced the *Federalist Papers*, a collection of essays explaining our system of government.

5. The two-party system of the United States solidified quickly after the Constitution was adopted, focusing around Hamilton's calls for a strong central government versus Jefferson's emphasis on local controls.

6. These two early parties began the history of U.S. political groups being split by their overall vision of controls versus freedoms.

## STEPS FROM THE DECLARATION OF INDEPENDENCE TO THE CONSTITUTION

The creation of the current system of government for the United States was inventive and daring yet couched in ancient political arguments and real cultural problems. The result of the Convention of 1787 was a new form of federal republic, but the Constitution of 1787 was vague in its descriptions of power or daily functions of the government. There were intense debates in several key states, especially the more populated New York and Virginia, where opponents to the new plan held early leads. Even after adoption, the nation continued to debate various interpretations of the levels of federal powers. These debates continue into the 21st century.

We can begin our discussion of the development of the U.S. Constitution by discussing the goals of government presented by the Declaration of Independence of 1776. Thomas Jefferson and the committee of leaders of the Continental Congress agreed on a statement that explained the need for attempted separation from the United Kingdom. However, the list of charges against King George III also had a significant effect on the goals of the Articles of Confederation and then on the Constitution itself. The Declaration of Independence lists many abuses brought about by bad leadership. Using the philosophical arguments of John Locke and others, this list is a blueprint of what government should not be allowed to do. It enumerates what freedoms government must provide for citizens and how citizens should control the government. Using Locke's "Second Treatise of Civil Government" (1690) as a model, Jefferson emphasized that the government was a form of social contract between citizens and leaders. Jefferson wrote that government exists to provide liberties and freedoms for those who agree to the rules and limits. He also wrote that the natural rights given to people by God cannot be removed by any government. He used Locke's phrase "life, liberty, and pursuit of property" to emphasize the fundamental goal of the country's governmental structure. The Declaration of Independence remains a key guide to the rights maintained in a limited government.

When the United States gained independence in 1781, a plan for rule—the Articles of Confederation—had already been debated and accepted. The Articles of Confederation included many features aimed at allowing for the goals of the Declaration of Independence to be put into place. Drafted by a committee headed by John Dickinson, the Articles of Confederation allowed for the dominance of local and state authority, control of taxes at the regional level, and a form of voluntary union by the states. This "free" government could not effectively deal with threats from foreign nations, disagreements between states, or the resulting financial chaos. The national leadership would now attempt to balance the needs for a more forceful and organized government with the fresh memories of the struggle for independence.

## SPECIFIC WEAKNESSES OF THE ARTICLES OF CONFEDERATION

Under relatively free and locally controlled government, no national executive branch was established, nor was there any separate judiciary. The central government could not collect taxes, but states were expected to volunteer extra funds. Because the states themselves were bankrupt, no national payments could exist. A final, major flaw was the inability to create any needed amendments without unanimous votes of all states. Any independently minded state (Rhode Island, for example) could instantly stop possible adjustments in powers. Alexander Hamilton predicted that the Articles of Confederation would fail and called for their removal almost every year of their existence. The shocks of European banks refusing to accept U.S. credit applications and the chaos of Shay's Rebellion (in late 1786) finally goaded other leaders into action. As a result of these weaknesses, the years of 1781 to 1787 saw very few advances. The passage of the Northwest Ordinance helped push some expansion plans, but states continued to feud over tariffs, the English continued to scoff at our military miseries, and regional disputes between merchants and planters deepened.

## Continuing Importance of the Declaration of independence and Articles of confederation

The goals of the Declaration of Independence and the faults of the Articles of Confederation were key to the debates over the creation of the Constitution. Many of the governmental items missing in the Articles of Confederation were added in the new plan. Many who later objected to the Constitution made sure the basic freedoms listed in the Declaration of Independence were added in the form of a federal Bill of Rights.

**Key items missing from the Articles of Confederation were the following:**

- No separate executive branch was established.

- No methods for the central government to collect taxes were present.

- No federal judiciary was created to settle interstate disputes.

- No amendments could be added without unanimous state approval. (None ever were.)

**As a result...**

- Only two major pieces of legislation were passed—the Land Ordinance of 1785 and the Northwest Ordinance of 1787.

- Disputes over trade and taxes raged between states, and no central authority could settle the problems.

- Veterans from the Revolutionary War were not paid, except through credit certificates.

- The central government had no funds.

- State governments were generally bankrupt and had no place to turn for help.

- National credit in key European banks collapsed.

- There were no agreements on tariff attempts, trade negotiations, or key issues such as support from France or the United Kingdom.

- Growing disputes began between northern and southern states.

- Shay's Rebellion panicked enough leaders to call for a convention to confront the growing economic and political crisis.

(Memorization of all of the problems of the Articles of Confederation years is not needed for the AP test. However, knowing how the Constitution corrected such difficulties will give a fuller understanding of the structure of the new government's powers.)

## THE DIFFICULT CONVENTION

It is important to remember how difficult the creation of the Constitution turned out to be and how close the debates came to collapsing. Several important leaders, such as Patrick Henry, refused to participate. Rhode Island refused to allow any representatives to attend. Delaware warned other states that it would not participate in a treasonous "coup." The main leaders who did attend were Alexander Hamilton, James Madison, Benjamin Franklin, George Washington, Governor Morris, and James Wilson. Summer heat made the meetings agony. The New York delegation was so divided that all three members left in disgust and two (John Lansing and Robert Yates) would try to defeat the ratification effort. Governor Edmund Randolph of Virginia, the other key state, refused to sign the document and also campaigned against it. Both New York's and Virginia's meetings would struggle for long periods before ratification.

## FORMATION OF CONGRESS

The biggest challenge of the convention became the issue of the formation of Congress. States with large populations were determined to have greater representation than those with smaller populations. Under the Articles of Confederation, each state had an equal vote, no matter what its population. But smaller states refused to create a system where they could be swallowed by growing regions. The final compromise, which created the current House of Representatives and Senate, took weeks to settle. These competing plans were later named for the states that sponsored their discussions.

The larger, more populated states were led by Virginia and Pennsylvania with the Virginia Plan. Drafted by Madison and presented by Governor Randolph at the very beginning of the summer, this plan based representation in Congress on the relative populations of the states. This plan, passed quickly, which also included a Senate selected by members of the House, a "president" selected by Congress (a parliamentary system), and a federal court selected by Congress.

Only the ability to call for multiple votes allowed the smaller states to keep asking for reconsideration and then led them to produce the New Jersey Plan. Drafted by William Paterson, this plan called for a single-chamber congress (unicameral), where each state would have the same number of representatives. This return to the system of the Articles of Confederation was not acceptable to the populated states. After weeks of heated debate and several prior rejections, the Connecticut Plan or "Great Compromise" was passed. This plan, by Roger Sherman, gave us a

House of Representatives dominated by populated states and a Senate with every state having an equal number of seats.

Other difficult points included the creation of a single executive elected by special "electors." This alone had to be put to a vote about 60 times. Other issues were often divided by those who favored a more "nationalist" approach of central powers versus the "localist" approach of state authority. Nationalists and localists were forerunners of the coming splits between Federalists and Anti-Federalists. This would be the central division between the first party leaders, Hamilton and Jefferson. The state of Pennsylvania finally requested to get its meeting room back. This left the delegates tired and frustrated, contributing to a limited debate over the structure and powers of the new federal court system. The delegates also deadlocked on the issue of slavery. The only compromise available was the horrible precedent of counting every five slaves as three free men and setting a 20-year limit on slavery restrictions.

Some Federalist arguments for the new Constitution included the following:

- Time for action had run out, and the country was collapsing.

- The Articles of Confederation could not provide for the following:

  - Federal taxes to stop national bankruptcy

  - Federal courts to stop interstate disputes

  - Federal powers to execute federal laws

  - Fairer balances between populated and "small" states

  - Federal powers to deal with foreign threats

- The Constitution would balance state and central powers.

- The Constitution only applied to federal laws, not state's rights.

- There were sufficient checks, separations, and balances to keep the federal government in line.

- Citizens controlled the House of Representatives, and states controlled the Senate.

- Limits to the legislative powers were included and carefully listed.

- The new, single executive held powers that were shared or checked at almost every level.

Some Anti-Federalist arguments against the new Constitution included these:

- The new plan gave too many controls to a "distant" and centralized government.

- The new "executive" was too powerful and "kinglike."

- The federal power to tax was a dangerous control over citizens and states.

- The legislative powers were long and detailed. Where was the list of limits?

- What were the basic, civil freedoms that the federal government could not remove? States had presented such "Bills of Rights"; why didn't the Constitution?

# RATIFICATION ISSUES

When states began to debate the new plan, the arguments in favor of adoption were assisted by the need for immediate economic reforms and by some panic concerning growing international threats. However, opponents could focus on the need for more structure in defining the national freedoms of citizens. Only with key promises of a federal Bill of Rights did many agree to put the new Constitution into force. Only 9 of the 13 existing states were required for ratification, and 9 states completed this by the summer of 1788. However, opponents held up the process in New York and Virginia. The nation understood that if either of these key states rejected the Constitution, the other nine votes would be relatively meaningless. Proponents called for giving the new system a trial, knowing that time for further discussions was being eliminated by foreign threats.

Opponents were stuck with warning about the reduction of state powers and creating a distant dictatorship, but they admitted that crises were at hand. During the months of state meetings concerning the possible adoption of the new Constitution, many essays were written in newspapers that defended or attacked the plan. New York became the focus area, with hundreds of pamphlets printed. The most famous sets were written by Madison and Hamilton and were later collected as a book under the title the *Federalist Papers*. Historians note that the readership of the *Federalist Papers* was relatively limited at the time of its original publication. Often, these essays were aimed only at those who had already decided to support or oppose ratification. However, the *Federalist Papers* became more valuable later. To attract some moderate or undecided readership, the writers did not list their own names. They collectively used "Publius," a reference to Roman debates about good government.

The essays stand as great explanations of how the U.S. government balances power, protects different political factions, settles disputes, and runs the diverse nation. Madison's essay "Number 10" is regarded as a definitive essay about regional political divisions. He used the word *factions* to describe how local governments could not handle minorities without the dangers of abuse by local majorities. This essay also explains that "factions" should have greater national access, a prediction of lobby groups and early party organizations. Essay "Number 51, " probably written by Madison, is known as the great defense of the balance and separations of power within this new plan. Hamilton's "Number 78" is still used to study the role of a powerful and critical federal judiciary.

Anti-Federalists had critical points to make about having a single executive leader, the excessive powers to potentially tax, and the lack of a list of power limits. Even though at that time, each state had a "Bill of Rights" in its state constitution, Anti-Federalists successfully forced Federalists to agree to add more definitions of rights as amendments.

When the first Congress convened in 1789, Representative James Madison led the effort to create 12 proposals, and 10 were adopted as the new Bill of Rights.

# THE DEVELOPMENT OF PARTIES UNDER THE CONSTITUTION

Most sources agree that the early Federal republic also saw the creation of political parties under the leadership of Hamilton and Jefferson. Both worked in Washington's administrations and were temporarily guided by the president's neutrality and abhorrence toward such organizations, yet they could not stop from creating opposing approaches to the meaning of the new government. The political coalitions that eventually formed under the names "Federalist" and "Democratic-Republican" did not exist without histories. Federalists held views similar to Tories in the English government. They wanted stronger leadership, especially economically and militarily. They were reacting to the memories of the chaos of the English Civil War and the weak leadership of the Articles of Confederation.

## THE FORMATION OF PARTIES

Democratic-Republicans reflected the beliefs of early liberals, where tolerance, freedoms, and independent actions were primary. Jefferson wanted to reinforce the values of the revolution and build the most free government in the world.

Hamilton wanted strong financial controls. Jefferson distrusted the eastern elites. Washington tried to counsel neutral positions on parties and international affairs. John Adams built on the Federalist ties with English industry, banks, and more conservative politics. Jefferson would prevail on Madison to join the more liberal approach, and both men would lead the dominance of Democratic-Republican goals of the early 1800s.

The Federalist Party would not be successful nationally after 1800, but the centralized approach to stability remains. These fundamental biases toward power still dominate the two-party system of the modern United States. Current liberals and Democrats have an agenda very similar to that of the Federalist's agenda. Conservatives and Republicans hold views similar to the goals of Jefferson. (Please note that although Thomas Jefferson is listed by the modern Democratic Party as one of its founders, this is only true in a strictly historical sense. The goals of the Democratic Party changed dramatically after the Great Depression.)

## EARLY DEVELOPMENT OF POLITICAL PARTIES

Prerevolution influences were the English Civil War and the Glorious Revolution of the 1600s. Conservative and liberal leadership were well entrenched in England. The first major step toward the two-party system in the United States came during the Washington administration.

The first great split was between Jefferson and Hamilton. Jefferson became the leader of the "liberal/radical" opposition, and Hamilton became the main spokesperson of the "conservative" Federalist government. Adams took on Federalist leadership during his presidency. Washington tried to remain above partisan politics during his terms. Madison started as a great defender of the Constitution but ended as a supporter of Jefferson's approach, favoring weaker government.

The election of 1800 is considered the first major turning point of political power. The Federalists, under Adam's leadership, gave up power without a civil war to the hated Democratic-Republicans under Jefferson's leadership. Federalists would not win again.

## EARLY POLITICAL DIVISIONS IN THE UNITED STATES

| General Time Period | Groups that favored "Nationalism": Stability, safety through good government, and centralization (more conservative at the time the Constitution was being drafted): | Groups that favored "Localism": Liberty, choices, and limited government (more liberal at the time the Constitution was being drafted): |
| --- | --- | --- |
| Colonial Development | • Anglican Church Leaders<br>• Catholic Church Leaders<br>• Monarchists<br>• Tories | • Protestant Church Leaders<br>• Parliamentarians<br>• Whigs |
| The Early U.S. Republic | • Nationalists<br>• Federalists<br>• Centralists<br>• Washington's Party<br>• Federalist Party (Hamilton, Adams, Washington) | • Localists<br>• Anti-Federalists<br>• States' Rights<br>• Jefferson's Republicans<br>• Jefferson's Democrats<br>• Democratic-Republican Party (Jefferson, Madison, Monroe) |
| Early to Mid-1800s | • Federalists (remnants)<br>• Whigs<br>• Republican Party<br>• Unionists | • Jacksonian Democrats<br>• Democratic Party<br>• States' Rights |

# REVIEW QUESTIONS

## MULTIPLE-CHOICE QUESTIONS

1. The Constitutional Convention of 1787 included all of the following issues **EXCEPT**

   (A) those who wanted a significantly stronger government argued with those who wanted to retain the Articles of Confederation.

   (B) leaders from states with large populations argued with representatives from states with small populations over the new form of Congress.

   (C) leaders from Rhode Island refused to attend.

   (D) localists feared the creation of a new dictatorship.

   (E) Virginia's leaders initially wanted a parliamentary system.

2. The *Federalist Papers* were

   (A) aimed at convincing readers that the Constitution would properly limit the powers of the new federal system.

   (B) aimed at convincing the public that Jefferson and Adams would support the Constitution once they returned from Europe.

   (C) not successful in keeping opponents from demanding a Bill of Rights.

   (D) key in swaying state votes in Virginia and New York.

   (E) critical of how the new government could organize itself.

3. The development of political parties in the early republic

   (A) can be traced to the leadership of Washington.

   (B) was developed independently by early American politicians.

   (C) was dominated by the conflict between Adams and Hamilton.

   (D) was rooted in English traditions of liberal and conservative views.

   (E) gave the Federalists a long period of dominance.

4. Madison's role in the early political development of the United States included all of the following **EXCEPT**

   (A) drafting the bulk of the Constitutional plan.

   (B) leading the debates supporting the new plan.

   (C) staying loyal to the Federalist program.

   (D) helping create the goals of Jeffersonian Democratic-Republicans.

   (E) writing the great essay on the powers of the central government.

5. Early Nationalists supported _____.
   Localists supported _____.

   (A) a conservative agenda; a liberal agenda

   (B) Jefferson; Hamilton

   (C) Washington; Adams

   (D) a liberal agenda; a conservative agenda

   (E) trade with our ally, France; trade with England

## FREE-RESPONSE QUESTIONS

1. The government under the Articles of Confederation was collapsing, yet political leaders still feared a new form of republic.

   (A) Identify and describe two reasons the leaders feared the new plan.

   (B) Give two specific examples of how the fears you identified in part (A) were alleviated in the compromises reached at the Constitutional Convention.

2. The two-party system was already well entrenched in early years of the United States as a republic.

   (A) Identify the two major viewpoints concerning governmental controls and give one label used to identify the groups.

   (B) Explain how the early split into two political camps shaped any two of the compromises that were reached during the writing of the Constitution.

# ANSWERS AND EXPLANATIONS

## MULTIPLE-CHOICE ANSWERS

**1. A**

Almost immediately, it was agreed that the Articles of Confederation were beyond revision. The Constitutional Convention of 1787 included disagreements between leaders from states with large populations and states with smaller populations over Congressional representation; leaders from Rhode Island who refused to attend; Localists who feared the creation of a new dictatorship; and Virginia's leaders, who initially wanted a parliamentary system. However, none of the delegates advocated retaining the Articles of Confederation.

**2. C**

In almost all states, supporters gave in on the idea of a federal Bill of Rights. Choice (A) is not the best answer because the papers focused on how the new government could function well and not necessarily be limited. Although Adams and Jefferson were both in Europe at the time, choice (B) is not true because the *Federalist Papers* were not aimed at convincing the public that Jefferson and Adams would support the Constitution once they returned. Choice (D) is incorrect because the essays probably did not sway votes in Virginia and New York; Hamilton seems to have carried New York, and Madison's pleas for a new system helped in Virginia's convention. Choice (E) is incorrect because the *Federalist Papers* were not criticisms about how the government could organize itself.

**3. D**

The development of political parties in the early republic was rooted in English traditions of liberal and conservative views. English traditions of Whigs and Tories influenced our leaders greatly. Washington did not trust party conflicts; Hamilton opposed Jefferson, not Adams; and the Federalists lasted only two administrations.

**4. C**

Madison's role in the early political development of the United States included drafting the bulk of the Constitutional plan, leading debates supporting the new plan, helping create the goals of Jeffersonian Democratic-Republicans, and writing the great essay on the powers of the central government. Choice (C) is the best answer because during the Jefferson presidency, Madison left the Federalist Party; he did not stay loyal to the Federalist program.

**5. A**

Early Nationalists supported a conservative agenda. Early Localists supported a liberal agenda. These were the labels given at the time.

## FREE-RESPONSE ANSWERS

1. **4-point Rubric:**

   **2 points in part (A): (any two reasons)**

   - Fear of a loss of state authority
   - Fear of a loss of tax authority
   - Fear of a too-powerful executive
   - Fear of a loss of many basic civil rights from state constitutions
   - Fear of national control of military powers
   - Fear that the goals of the Declaration of Independence would be abandoned

   **2 points in part (B): (any two from the Constitution)**

   - Specific mentions of state powers in sections such as Article 4
   - Restrictions on tax legislation, it only being originated in the publicly elected House
   - Many checks on the executive, such as override or approval
   - The limits of powers listed in Article 1 (protections of Writs of Habeas Corpus)
   - Promises of a Bill of Rights
   - Control of the military by the House and Senate (selected by states)
   - Promises of the proper goals in the Preamble

2. **5-point Rubric:**

   **3 points in part (A): (identify two, label one)**

   - A desperate need for better central controls and organization versus an emphasis on local freedoms and civil freedoms
   - Locke's views versus those of Hobbes or Montesquieu, who favored more central powers
   - Whigs or Tories
   - Nationalists or Localists
   - Federalists or Anti-Federalists
   - Federalists or Jeffersonian Democratic-Republicans

   **2 points in part (B): (explain the two sides shaping the Constitution)**

   - More central powers to tax
   - More central powers to control interstate trade
   - More central powers over a military
   - More central powers with a federal court system
   - Retained local powers of states
   - Retained local control of selecting the Senate
   - Retained local controls over selecting the executive

# CHAPTER 4: THE FEDERAL CONSTITUTION OF 1787 AND THE AMENDMENTS

## IF YOU ONLY LEARN SIX THINGS IN THIS CHAPTER . . . .

1. Our basic use of "federalism" as a political concept has changed dramatically since its inception. The Civil War, the Great Depression, and World War II were major events that lead to this change.

2. The original U.S. Constitution is short, mostly focused on Congress, and designed to guide the development of the national government. The writers did not intend to describe all possible powers and interpretations.

3. The Preamble lists six basic goals of the new government.

4. Article 1 contains the most details and descriptions, covering the organization and powers of Congress. Critical powers are the Commerce Clause and the Elastic Clause sections.

5. Almost all executive powers listed in Article 2 are vague and checked by Congress. The remaining descriptions of judicial and state powers are even less detailed.

6. After the Bill of Rights ratification in 1791, only 17 additions have been created. Many are governmental procedures, and only a handful of important civil liberties changes have been created in over 200 years.

## BASICS OF FEDERALISM

The definition of *a federal system* has changed over the centuries, even beginning with its use by supporters of the Constitution. Prior to the Convention of 1787, many in the country used the word to describe a government where states had general control of rights and powers, with interstate problems being settled by a central authority. Supporters of the Constitution hijacked the word for propaganda purposes; they could have easily used the word *nationalist* to compare the new plan with the Articles of Confederation. By using the word *federalist*, supporters of the Constitution could seem to deflect the charges that they were creating an overly centralized national government. Changes in federalism were extensive in the 20th century, especially after the Great Depression and World War II, leading to new demands for controls by the national government. Federalism came to mean basic rights guaranteed in all states by the Bill of Rights, economic leadership from the national capital, and financial controls under federally funded mandates.

## FEDERALISM

Federalism did come to stand for a stronger central government, yet early leaders such as Jefferson made sure that state controls remained intact. This was most clearly reflected in judicial questions, where the Bill of Rights was defined as applying only to federal laws. State laws, and their inclusion of civil liberties, could differ from federal laws. The most glaring example of this was the right of states to claim to hold "citizens in bondage" (slavery).

# THE CONSTITUTION OF 1787

The original Constitution contained eight basic parts: an introductory sentence explaining the goals and seven articles defining the powers of the new government. The majority of the descriptions concern the legislature, which was considered the primary branch of government by the founders. Evidence from the Constitutional Convention shows that the most time was spent designing this branch. The founders wanted legislative officials to be closely connected to the citizens. Almost half of the document is concerned with Congress. Almost all details of specific powers are about Congress. Congressional officers, such as the Speaker of the House and President of the Senate, are specifically listed. Congress must keep a journal, control its own members, and hold powers over the executive and courts. Congress is given a list of 17 duties, covering items such as interstate commerce, regulating money, creating courts, declaring war, taking care of roads, awarding patents, counterfeiting, and making rules for the military.

Even when a president can step in and veto legislation, the entire legislation must be rejected, and Congress can vote to override the president's objections.

Congress also faces a "mini Bill of Rights" in Section 9. Congress cannot suspend certain rights without declaring emergencies, cannot tax exports, and cannot grant titles of nobility.

## THE EXECUTIVE BRANCH

As a point of immediate comparison, most of the description of the executive branch covers details about the Electoral College, and much of that has been amended. The job description of the president is minimal; in addition, his or her powers are often directly checked by Congress and somewhat open to interpretation.

The president oversees the cabinet departments, but no other descriptions or duties are included. The president is commander of the military but must allow Congress to fund and manage the military rules. The president appoints and negotiates, but both powers require Congressional approval. The current use of the "recess appointment" power is a rare event where Congressional approval is not immediately needed. Presidents can also be removed from office by Congress.

## THE JUDICIARY BRANCH

The section of the Constitution describing the judiciary is even less detailed, with minimal descriptions of how courts can be created and what their general scope of jurisdiction includes.

Lower courts can exist to help the federal courts' workload, if Congress creates them. Federal judges and justices serve for life, unless they are impeached and removed. Federal courts have jurisdiction over cases involving state's suing or being sued. The rest of the article covers the issue of treason, a crime defined very broadly in other nations. In the United States, treason can only exist if someone is "levying War against them [the United States], or in adhering to their Enemies, giving them Aid and Comfort."

Articles 4, 5, and 6 describe how states relate to other states, describe how amendments can be created, and establish the legal status of the new government. Article 4 has states give "Full Faith and Credit" to the laws of the other states. States must return fleeing criminals to other states upon extradition requests from governors. No states can be created from lands inside existing states without the states' permission. Article 5 lists the ways Congress and the states create possible amendments. Article 6 gives the promise that debts from prior times will be honored by the new government. Also, a definition of the "supremacy" status of the Constitution is given. Finally, government officials of the country cannot be required to give religious oaths as conditions of office.

Article 7 concludes the four large pages with a call for ratification by 9 of the 13 states; this was completed in 1788.

## 5 BASIC FORMS OF POLITICAL AUTHORITY

The Constitution establishes the five basic forms of political authority that are central definitions of the government of the United States: leadership through representatives that serve at the will of the voters (republic), national and local levels of authority (federalism), different areas of authority for different leaders (separations of powers), forms of limits of power by having leaders control each other (checks and balances), and strict freedoms that cannot be removed from the public (civil liberties). The interpretations of the extent of these powers make up the basic political debates of our system.

# INTERPRETATIONS AND ADJUSTMENTS

## THE PREAMBLE

With the first sentence of the Preamble to the Constitution, the writers explained that this new plan was aimed at correcting the problems of the Articles of Confederation. The call for a "more perfect Union" showed that the existing government was a less-than-perfect union. The other goals of "justice," "domestic Tranquility," "defence" (defense), and "general Welfare" were clearly practical issues that were not being addressed during the turmoil of the early 1780s. The final call for "Blessings of Liberty" is a return to the goals of the Declaration of Independence.

## ARTICLE 1

The original primacy of the Congress is demonstrated by the length and care given to this portion. Congress is given leaders, rules for organizing, and at least 17 duties. Furthermore, Congress is given instructions to "make all Laws which shall be necessary and proper." This sentence has been given the title the "Elastic Clause" and has become one of the most important points of constitutional interpretation in the history of the United States. Clearly, the founders anticipated change and new challenges for this government. They did not intend to leave the national Congress with no powers to adapt to the times. However, the scope of such adaptations is still debated.

Conservatives can point to two other important phrases. In the first sentence of Article 1, Section 1, the key words "herein granted" could be interpreted as an indication that the founders felt that Congress must focus only on those powers listed in the Constitution, specifically the list in

Section 8. Also, the Elastic Clause contains the phrase "for carrying into Execution the foregoing Powers," suggesting that Congress can do what is necessary and proper for the other powers listed but not anything else. Modern liberals emphasize Congress's authority over "Commerce … among the several States" and the phrase "all other Powers vested by this Constitution" to argue that the founders did see the need for necessary expansions of power over issues that the early country could not even imagine.

Even though the descriptions in Article 1 are lengthy, many current practices have been created beyond the original framework. Congress has developed the complex committee and debate systems from traditional practices. Agencies and their powers are separate inventions. These parts of government were not included in the original plans. Even the portion of Article 1 that lists some limits to Congress's powers has been at the center of some controversies.

In Section 9, referred to in some sources as a "mini Bill of Rights," Congress is prohibited from suspending the "Writ of Habeas Corpus" rights. Citizens cannot be seized without being able to answer to charges, unless "the public Safety may require it." Under what circumstances could Congress make such a declaration? What happens when Congress needs to make such a declaration and can't or won't? This happened in 1861, and Abraham Lincoln used the powers given in Article 4 to suspend such writs. Should this Article 1 power be available to the executive?

## ARTICLE 2

Much of this portion of the Constitution is given to the selection process known as the Electoral College. Most of this section was amended by the 12th Amendment. What remains is an outline of a presidential office of key powers, but limited and checked powers. As will be discussed in detail in Chapter 13, the Constitution allows the president to command the military, deal with foreign nations, and have "Heads of Departments" but gives the office almost no fully independent powers. The founders did not trust individual leaders. They did not let them be selected directly by the public. Congress has an impact or control at almost every turn. The history of the U.S. presidency is, therefore, a history of stretching the limited Constitutional powers. Major events like the War with Mexico, the Civil War, the Great Depression, World War II, and the Cold War have all been steps in the development of an executive leader at the forefront of government and public awareness. During times of crisis, it is often impossible for the country to wait for group consensus. Citizens, and the Congress, have given presidents new levels of authority over a vast bureaucracy, the running of economic policies, and national security.

## ARTICLE 3

Article 3 states that there will be federal courts, that Congress can create them, and that judges' salaries are guaranteed, and it carefully defines treason. These are the basics covered in the article, and little else is present. The power of judicial review was given to the judiciary by the court case of *Marbury v. Madison*. Courts do have jurisdiction of cases "under this Constitution," and special cases go directly to the Supreme Court. The histories of court powers, court interpretations, and court attempts at policy have been major points of controversy historically and are at the center of recent struggles between conservatives and liberals. Conservatives favor a judiciary that resolves cases and leaves other powers to the legislative branch or the states. Liberals turn to the courts for resolution of problems that have not been solved by the states and to give guidance about how rights are created.

## ARTICLE 4

According to Article 4, states must give the various laws of other states "Full Faith and Credit," return fleeing criminals to other states, and give approval for new states to be carved out of their state properties. Some controversies have occurred when states strongly disagree about certain laws, such as the legality of gay marriage or the extradition of criminals to face the death penalty.

The last portion of Article 4 has been a source of large-scale controversy in the past. States are guaranteed protection by the federal Congress, but the sentence also contains the directive to presidents to step in if "the Legislature cannot be convened."

Presidents since James K. Polk have used this clause to expand powers. Polk ordered troops into disputed areas of Texas, knowing hostilities would begin and that Congress wanted more time for negotiations. Lincoln went so far as to reach for Article 1 powers of the possible suspension of Habeas Corpus rights in order to protect Maryland under Article 4. Other presidents have expanded these requirements of the federal government.

## ARTICLE 5

Amending the Constitution can occur in four possible ways. Both the federal government and states must be involved. Congress can propose amendments with two-thirds of the votes, or two-thirds of states can request that Congress call for a national convention for that purpose. Ratification occurs with the approval of three-fourths of state legislatures or three-fourths of the states approving through conventions called for that amendment. All amendments except the 21st have been created by Congress proposing and state legislatures approving. The 21st Amendment was passed by Congress proposing it and state conventions being called for ratification. No amendments have been proposed by states requesting a national convention.

## ARTICLE 6

The "Supremacy Clause" is the label for this brief description of the "supreme Law of the Land" covering "this Constitution, and the Laws of the United States…and all Treaties…" This clause also contains the promise to honor prior debts of the nation, which was important for the ratification debate. Leaders also are protected from having to make religious oaths as part of their duties to the government.

## ARTICLE 7

Once 9 of the 13 states ratified the Constitution in 1788, the document was completed and in effect. The nation did wait for Virginia and New York to vote for ratification to hold elections for the new Congress and executive. Later, North Carolina reversed a previous no vote, thus making for 12 states under the new laws. The new officers took their positions in the spring of 1789. Rhode Island, the one state that did not approve the Constitution in 1789, held a meeting to ratify the Constitution in 1791.

# THE BILL OF RIGHTS AND OTHER AMENDMENTS

Anti-Federalists fought the approval of the Constitution, especially in New York, Virginia, and North Carolina. The major debate point centered on the lack of a clear list showing the limits of power for this new federal system. The Federalists agreed to add a series of amendments as soon as the new Congress could form, and this was done in 1789. Madison, then a member of the first House of Representatives, led the development of the first set of amendments, which became the Bill of Rights. The section on civil liberties in chapter 15 will further explore the debates about the amendments; however, the chart at the end of this chapter provides an overview of the amendments. Note the key legal concepts connected to specific amendments as listed in the table.

It is remarkable how little the Constitution has been changed since 1791, when the Bill of Rights was added. Only 17 other changes have been adopted. Of these, deal with substantial civil rights, and the other 10 are about procedures of government. The seven rights are as follows:

1. Ending slavery
2. Due process and equal protection
3. Voting rights for all men
4. Senators elected by citizens of states and not state governments
5. Voting rights for women
6. Voting without fees
7. Voting rights for those age 18 to 20

All other amendments cover issues of lawsuits against states, changing electoral votes, income tax, prohibition and its repeal, the earlier start date for the federal government, two-term limits for presidents, electoral votes for the District of Columbia, required presidential succession, and timing restrictions on members of Congress changing their pay.

Congress has now included time limits to proposed amendments, especially because the 27th Amendment took 203 years to ratify. Since 1917, Congress has added a seven-year time limit to each proposed amendment, and this contributed to the failure of changes like the Equal Rights Amendment.

# OUTLINE OF THE CONSTITUTION

## BASICS OF THE CONSTITUTION

- Preamble: The goals of this new government
- Articles: Seven major pieces, each describing the government and its duties
- Sections: Organizing portions of the articles
- Clauses: Paragraphs within the sections

There were 55 leaders who worked on the document, 39 who signed it, and 3 who stayed through the Convention but refused to sign: Edmund Randolph and George Mason of Virginia, along with Elbridge Gerry of Massachusetts.

Following are the five political themes of the Constitution:

1. Representative government/indirect democracy
2. Federalism
3. Separations of powers
4. Checks and balances
5. Civil liberties via limited government

## OUTLINE AND KEY TERMS OF THE CONSTITUTION (NOT INCLUDING ITEMS REMOVED/AMENDED)

### THE PREAMBLE

*The basic goals of the new government of 1787:*
- "form a more perfect Union"
- "establish Justice"
- "insure domestic Tranquility"
- "provide for the common defence"
- "promote the general Welfare"
- "secure the Blessings of Liberty"

## ARTICLE 1: LEGISLATIVE BRANCH

*Sections 1, 2, 3: The Organization of House and Senate*

- There is a bicameral legislature (two bodies: House and Senate).

- House members serve for two years and must be 25 years old and seven-year citizens, and reside in their states.

- The Speaker of the House is the leader.

- New apportionment or reapportionment of districts and seats occurs after the 10-year census.

- The House has the power to impeach/bring charges against the president.

- Senate members serve for six years and must be 30 years old and nine-year citizens, and reside in their state.

- The President of the Senate is the vice president of the United States.

- The President *"Pro Tempore"* (*pro tem*) serves if the vice president is not available.

- The Senate has the power to remove those impeached by the House.

*Sections 4, 5, 6, 7: Workings of the Congress*

- An annual session of Congress is required.

- Congress has power over members, attendance, and qualifications.

- Congress must keep a journal *(The Congressional Record)*.

- Congress sets its own salary (limited by the 27th Amendment).

- Members are immune from arrest during a session.

- Members may not hold double political offices.

- Revenue bills must initiate in the House.

- Removal powers require a two-thirds vote.

- Congress can override a veto with a two-thirds vote.

*Section 8: The Powers of Congress "Delegated," "Enumerated," "Implied," "Necessary and Proper"*

- There are 18 clauses that give specific lists of federal powers.

- Key examples:

  - Clause 2: "To borrow Money…"

  - Clause 3: "To regulate Commerce…" (the Commerce Clause)

  - Clause 9: "To constitute Tribunals…" (create lower federal courts)

  - Clause 11: "To declare war…"

  - Clause 18: "To make all Laws which shall be necessary and proper…"
    (the Elastic Clause)

*Section 9: "Powers Denied to Congress" (the "mini Bill of Rights")*

- *Writ of Habeus Corpus* may not be suspended unless "the public Safety may require it."

- No "Bills of Attainder" may be created.

- No "*ex post facto*" laws may be created.

- No tax may be levied on exports from states.

- No titles of nobility can be given.

## ARTICLE 2: THE EXECUTIVE BRANCH AND THE ELECTORAL COLLEGE

*Section 1*

- The president's term will be four years, and the Electoral College will select the president.

- The president must be 35 years old, a U.S. resident for 14 years, and a "natural" (native-born) citizen "together" with the vice president.

- Electors will be "equal to the whole Number of Senators and Representatives to which the State may be entitled."

- Presidents will receive salaries set by Congress.

- Note: Much of this section has been amended by the 12th and 25th Amendments.

*Sections 2, 3: Powers and Duties of the President*

- Is commander in chief.

- Makes/negotiates treaties.

- Nominates ambassadors and judges.

- Works with "Heads of Departments" (Cabinet).

- Fills "Recess" appointments, lasting until the end of Congress's next session.

- Gives the "State of the Union" message.

- May adjourn Congress if they can't agree on a time.

- Receives foreign ambassadors.

- Takes "Care that the Laws be faithfully executed".

- Commissions "all Officers" of the military.

*Section 4: Removal of the President, Vice President, or "all civil Officers of the United States"*

- Impeachment (House)

- Removal trial (Senate)

- Upon "Conviction of, Treason, Bribery, or other high Crimes and Misdemeanors"

## ARTICLE 3: JUDICIAL BRANCH

*Section 1, 2: The Federal Courts*

- There will be one Supreme Court, and inferior courts if created by Congress.
- There will be life terms for federal judges, whose salaries are set by Congress.
- The jurisdiction of the Supreme Court will be cases under the Constitution.
- The Supreme Court has original jurisdiction in certain cases and appellate jurisdiction in cases from lower courts.

*Section 3: Treason*

- Treason "shall consist only in levying War against them (United States), adhering to their Enemies, giving them Aid and Comfort."
- Two witnesses are required in open court.
- Congress can set the punishment if convicted.
- No punishment extends to families (no "Corruption of Blood").

## ARTICLE 4: STATES

*Sections 1, 2, 3, 4: "Relation among the States"*

- There is "Full Faith and Credit," meaning states give credit to laws from other states that might be different from their own laws.
- Provides for extradition of criminals back to from another state seeking the criminal.
- New states can be created by Congress but only with the permission of the state from which the land came.
- Congress remains in charge of federal properties.
- All states are guaranteed a "Republican Form of Government" and protection provided by Congress or the president.

## ARTICLE 5: AMENDMENTS

- Congress proposes amendments with a two-thirds vote.
- State legislatures ratify with a three-fourths vote.

  or

- Two-thirds of state legislatures call for Congress to create conventions.
- Three-fourths of state conventions vote to ratify.

### ARTICLE 6: STATUS OF THE CONSTITUTION

*Supremacy Clause*

- The Constitution, laws of the United States, and treaties, "shall be the supreme Law of the Land…"
- Leaders are bound by oath to support the Constitution.
- No religious tests can be given as a condition or qualification for a government office.

### ARTICLE 7: RATIFICATION

- Nine of 13 states were needed to ratify the Constitution for it to take effect.
- This was completed in 1788.

## AMENDMENTS AND KEY TERMS

| Amendment and Topics | Key Issues/Terms (see Chapter 15) | Related Legal Issues/Terms (see Chapter 15) |
|---|---|---|
| 1) Religion<br>Speech<br>Press<br>Assembly and Petition | Establishment Clause versus Free-Exercise Clause Abridging? Just Speech? Peaceably, Redress | Which to Emphasize?<br>• *Lemon Test*<br>• *Clear-and-Present-Danger Test*<br>• *Pure Speech*<br>• *Symbolic Speech*<br>• *Community Standards*<br>• *Incitement*<br>• *Prior Restraint*<br>• *Libel and Slander* |
| 2) Right to Bear Arms | Regulated Militia versus Rights of the People | Which to Emphasize? |
| 3) Quartering of Troops | | |
| 4) Search and Seizure | Unreasonable search versus Probable Cause | *Exclusionary Rule, Good Faith Exception,* Privacy?, Reasonable? |
| 5) Indictments, Double Jeopardy, Just Compensation | Compelled, Due Process | *Self-Incrimination, Eminent Domain* |
| 6) Speedy and Public Trial, Confront Witness, Counsel | Speedy, Impartial Jury | What Levels of Courts? |
| 7) Jury in Civil Trials | | |
| 8) Excessive Bail Cruel and Unusual Punishments | | Death Penalty? |
| 9) Rights Retained by the People | | Privacy and How Much? |

| | | |
|---|---|---|
| 10) Rights to States | Reserved Powers | How Broad? When in Conflict with the 14th? |
| 11) Rules for Lawsuits against States | | One State Cannot Be Sued in Another State |
| 12) Separate Votes for President and Vice President | Reforms of the Electoral College | Corrections for the Elections of 1796 and 1800 |
| 13) Abolition of Slavery | | |
| 14) Citizenship State Limits Due Process Equal Protection (See chapter 15 for further details.) | Application to States | *Incorporation* "Congress shall have the power to enforce, by appropriate legislation…" |
| 15) Voting Rights and Race | No Denial on Account of Race, Color… | |
| 16) Federal Income Tax | | |
| 17) Direct Election of Senators | | |
| 18) Prohibition | | In Effect Only 1920 to 1933 |
| 19) Women's Vote | | Suffrage |
| 20) New Start for Federal Terms | Congress = January 3 President = January 20 | |
| 21) Repeal of Prohibition | | Left to Local Votes for Alcohol Purchases |
| 22) Two-Term Limit for the President | Two Full Terms or Maximum of 10 Years | |
| 23) Number of Votes for president for Washington, D.C. | No Fewer Electoral Votes than the Least Populated State (= 3) | |
| 24) No Poll Tax | | Jim Crow Laws |
| 25) Succession | If the President Dies or Becomes Incapacitated, the Vice President Must Assume the Presidency; If There Is No Vice President, Then the President Must Appoint One and Congress Must Confirm the Appointment. | Procedures for Succession? What Constitutes the State Where the President Can No Longer Serve? |
| 26) Voting Rights to Age 18 | | |
| 27) Acceptance of Pay Raises | Congress Should Wait Until after the Next Election. | Did Congress Avoid This by Tying Their Pay Increases to Social Security COLAs? Cost-of-Living Adjustments |

## CONSTITUTIONAL "CLAUSES"

Main Constitution's Text

Major Examples/Common Names

ASC = Article, Section, Clause (Paragraph):

| Name | ASC Location | Meaning |
|---|---|---|
| Admissions Clause | A4S3C1 | Congress admits new states. If parts of an existing state are involved, the state must give permission. |
| Advice and Consent Clause | A2S2C2 | Treaties and nominations: President starts, Senate approves with two-thirds vote. |
| Appointments Clause | A2S2C2 | Congress can give permission for "inferior" officers to be set without the Senate's approval. |
| Arisings Clause | A3S2C1 | "The judicial Power shall extend to all Cases, in Law and Equity, arising under this Constitution,…" |
| Comity Clause | A4S1 | Congress can determine the "Effect thereof" of state laws if they conflict with laws of other states. |
| Commerce Clause | A1S8C3 | Congress can "regulate Commerce with Foreign Nations, and among the several States…" |
| Compact Clause | A1S10C3 | "No state shall, without Consent of Congress…enter into any Agreement or Compact with another State…" |
| Contract Clause | A1S10C1 | No state may "pass any…Law impairing the Obligation of Contracts…" |
| Elastic Clause | A1S8C18 | (Congress) "To make all Laws which shall be necessary and proper for carrying into Execution…" |
| Exceptions Clause | A3S2C2 | Supreme Court has appellate jurisdiction in cases "with such Exceptions…as Congress shall make." |
| Full Faith and Credit Clause | A4S1 | States must give different laws and rules of other states the "Full Faith…" |
| Guarantee Clause | A4S4 | Each state shall be guaranteed a republican form of government by Congress or the president. |
| Origination Clause | A1S7C1 | Bills raising revenues (taxes) must originate in the House of Representatives. |
| Presentment Clause | A1S7C2 | Bills must be presented to the executive for final processing or veto. |
| Subscription Clause | After A7 | The list of the original signers of the Constitution (39 of the 55 delegates in Philadelphia; 3 refused to sign) |
| Supremacy Clause | A6S2 | The Constitution, laws of the United States, and treaties: "shall be the supreme Law of the Land…" |

# REVIEW QUESTIONS

## MULTIPLE-CHOICE QUESTIONS

1. *Federalism* originally meant that

   (A) the national government would protect minimal rights in states.

   (B) state governments would have relatively equal sets of rights.

   (C) the national and state governments would protect similar rights.

   (D) layers of government could have unique forms of rights.

   (E) states would join the union only if they adopted the Constitution.

2. All of the following are evidence of the original dominance of Congress **EXCEPT**

   (A) presidential veto powers.

   (B) the length and detail of Article 1.

   (C) checks on presidential appointments.

   (D) presidential "recess appointment" powers.

   (E) All are examples of Congressional dominance.

3. Which power was **NOT** included in the Constitution?

   (A) The vice president's position in two federal branches

   (B) Congress's power to declare the punishment for treason

   (C) Congress's power to filibuster bills to death

   (D) Congress's power to suspend *writs of habeas corpus*

   (E) Congress's ability to tax products sold from states

4. A major point of power disputes between presidents and Congress centers on

   (A) presidents assuming powers given to Congress in Article 1.

   (B) presidents acting without actual Constitutional authority.

   (C) Congress's unwillingness to allow presidents to be a real "commander-in-chief."

   (D) Congress's giving presidents power to control rules of the military.

   (E) Congress's refusal to protect the states in times of crisis.

5. Congress has all of the following powers **EXCEPT**

   (A) the right to set salaries for its members.

   (B) the right to remove members of Congress.

   (C) the right to create a huge national debt.

   (D) the power to serve temporarily as members of the Electoral College.

   (E) the right not to pay the military.

## FREE-RESPONSE QUESTIONS

1. Federalism is a form of layered governmental powers.

   (A) Identify two ways in which federalism developed under the U.S. system of government.

   (B) Explain two ways this transformation of federalism occurred.

2. The Preamble of the Constitution promises the country certain goals of government.

   (A) Identify any two of the goals.

   (B) Identify and explain where these goals are addressed in the Constitution.

# ANSWERS AND EXPLANATIONS

## MULTIPLE-CHOICE ANSWERS

### 1.  D

*Federalism* originally meant that layers of government could have unique forms of rights. For example, rights granted by the federal government can be very different than those granted by the states. The national government would protect "republican" governments in states, but not all rights. States could, and did, have vastly different sets of citizens' rights. Approval from only 9 of the original 13 states was needed for ratification and implementation of the Constitution.

### 2.  E

Presidential veto powers, the length and detail of Article 1, checks on presidential appointments, and presidential "recess" appointments are all true powers of Congress. If the president vetoes, Congress can still override. "Recess appointments" must be approved after a year.

### 3.  C

Congress's power to filibuster bills to death is tradition. Choice (A) is incorrect because the vice president is also president of the Senate. Choice (B) is incorrect because the Constitution clearly states Congress's power to declare the punishment for treason. Choice (D) is incorrect because according to the Constitution, Congress can suspend *writs of habeas corpus* in emergencies. (Congress can also declare emergencies.) Choice (E) is incorrect because Congress can't tax exports from state ports.

### 4.  A

A major point in power disputes between presidents and Congress comes from presidents assuming powers that were granted to Congress in Article 1. President Lincoln started many power trends when he got away with suspending *writs of habeas corpus* in the emergency of 1861. He claimed that Congress could not act, thus allowing him to take on Article 1 powers. Sometimes presidents use of listed powers is controversial in interpretation. Congress has never attacked the president's leadership role as civilian commander.

### 5.  D

Congress does not have the right to serve temporarily as members of the Electoral College. All of the other rights listed are granted by the Constitution except this dual role. Members of the Electoral College may not hold elected office.

## FREE-RESPONSE ANSWERS

1. **4-point Rubric**

   **2 points in part (A): (identify the two forms)**

   - States and federal government are separate and relatively equal.
   - State rules apply to states; federal rules and the Constitution apply to federal areas/jurisdiction only.
   - National laws come to dominance.
   - National rules and rights apply to states.
   - The Bill of Rights applies to states.

   **2 points in part (B): (explain the change)**

   - Supreme Court makes interpretations of federal authority.
   - Great Depression changes demand for federal authority.
   - WWII changes demand for federal authority.
   - Civil rights movement and Cold War make demands (discussed in later chapters).

2. **6-point Rubric**

   **2 points in part (A): (identify any two goals)**

   - A more perfect union
   - Justice
   - Domestic tranquility
   - Common defense
   - General welfare
   - Blessings of liberty

   **4 points in part (B): (2 for identifying in the Constitution, 2 for explanations)**

   - Stronger central powers, such as federal tax powers, courts, and executive, make a more perfect union.
   - Some limits of Congress and state powers in Articles 1 and 4, along with federal courts, give justice.
   - *Writs of habeas corpus,* no bills of attainder, no *ex post facto* laws, no taxes on exports, and guarantees of republican governments would create domestic tranquility.
   - Congress's power to regulate the military and the president's powers to be commander in chief would provide defense.
   - Congress's powers to regulate trade and commerce and the court's ability to solve conflicts would help with general welfare.
   - The immediate creation of a Bill of Rights furthered the blessings of liberty.

# CHAPTER 5: FEDERALISM AND THE U.S. GOVERNMENT

## IF YOU ONLY LEARN SIX THINGS IN THIS CHAPTER . . . .

1. Federal powers are listed in the Constitution or directly implied by the Constitution. All powers not listed in the Constitution are considered to be reserved to the states.

2. Federalism has shifted in meaning from a general notion of relative isolation between federal and state authority to the domination of federal standards. The inability of states to protect basic rights, such as citizenship, has contributed to this shift.

3. Within federal powers, the issues of separations of powers and checks and balances continue to limit our government.

4. Judicial review was not part of the Constitution but created by the Supreme Court decision in *Marbury v. Madison*.

5. Control of money has been a major way the federal government extends its rules and powers.

6. The scope of federal powers has shifted back and forth during the history of the United States.

## BASIC STRUCTURE OF THE FEDERAL SYSTEM

Federalism is the core idea behind the union of governments in the United States. Both national and state levels of authority exist and have unique duties. Also, some powers are shared between the federal government and the state governments. Some political scientists have classified the powers of these national and state governments in seven general ways:

1. Powers given to the government by the people are delegated to the national realm by the Constitution.

2. Those duties explicitly listed in the Constitution are enumerated. The bulk of these are found in Article 1, Section 8, showing the various jobs of Congress.

3. Some powers have been deducted from the "necessary and proper" powers listed at the end of Article 1, Section 8. These "Elastic Clause" powers are implied to be the proper adaptation of duties of Congress to be able to fulfill the other powers enumerated.

4. Some governmental powers are so basic that they exist without being listed or described in the Constitution. These inherent powers are held when the government must protect itself or keep itself organized. The Supreme Court has been called upon to help define the scope of such inherent powers.

5. Those powers that are very specific to only certain political units are known as "exclusive powers." For example, only Congress can declare war; this is an exclusive power.

6. "Concurrent powers" are those governmental functions that both the federal government and the states can wield. There is no specific list of the range of concurrent powers, but items such as taxation, borrowing, and budget expenditures are usually classified as concurrent.

7. Those powers retained by the states and people are labeled as "reserved." The 10th Amendment is the basic guide, listing the possible range of such powers and freedoms as "The powers not delegated to the United States."

## THE "SUPREMACY CLAUSE"

Article 6 of the Constitution states that the document, laws of the United States, and treaties under its authority shall be "the supreme Law of the Land." All officials of the country must give oaths to support the Constitution. States cannot use their powers to override the national powers.

## THE ORIGINAL SCOPE OF FEDERALISM

The original 18th-century view of U.S. federalism centered on the federal government and the state governments being considered relatively independent in their political powers. This structure of powers is known as *dual federalism*. The states had their own sets of judicial rights, Bills of Rights, and definitions of citizenship. Federal laws applied to federal actions, federal officials, or federal courts. The U.S. Bill of Rights held in federal cases but not in cases of state jurisdiction. The most obvious, and the most contentious, issue in dual federalism was states' holding some "citizens in bondage" (slavery). Dual federalism was also criticized as being too fragmented to handle the emergence of industrial centers, population shifts and expansions, and massive immigration.

## CHANGES IN U.S. FEDERALISM

One of the most fundamental and important changes in the government of the United States has been the gradual, but significant, redefinition of the federal system. The rapid expansion of the country to new lands, the upheaval of the Civil War, the creation of an industrial and international power, the collapse of world economies in the mid-20th century, the struggles of world wars, and threats of expanding communism have all significantly changed the public's expectations of central powers. Congress has turned to commerce and elastic powers clauses to deal with interstate travel and civil rights. Presidents have become the focal points of international events that require rapid and powerful decision making.

Initially, leaders of states and the central government usually agreed that federalism for the United States was a "dual" system of relatively independent powers for states. Constitutional restrictions were applied to federal law and federal controversies; state laws took care of the rest. The removal of the institution of slavery through warfare changed the scope of federalism as it applied to citizenship, and this was the springboard for applying other federal rights to state laws. The Great Depression caused the country to turn to central guidance in areas of jobs and money.

As the federal government expanded its responsibilities, money distribution has become a central feature of its power. When the federal government helps distribute tax dollars to states, it attaches rules and regulations to those monies. States are left to decide whether they want to accept the needed funds and bend to federal rules or whether they would prefer to attempt to do without the cash and maintain their own legal priorities. Even conservative administrations, such as that of George W. Bush, use such tactics to pressure states to follow their guidelines in issues such as the "No Child Left Behind" education standards. The modern interpretation of this evolving form of federalism has come to be labeled "fiscal federalism."

The discussion of federalism must include the courts. Supreme Court challenges concerning federalism have been around since the early 1800s. The Supreme Court has defined federalism as the power of the national government to create a national banking system, control economic commerce in many ways related to "interstate trade or commerce," and build vast transportation and communication networks. Details of such cases will be covered in chapter 15.

## Cooperative Federalism

The changes mentioned above have created a new definition of our form of federalism. Congress's control of issues surrounding interstate trade came to include the civil rights of citizens involved with interstate businesses and any businesses receiving federal funds. The "due process" requirements of the 14th Amendment have created many cases where federal rights in the Bill of Rights have been incorporated into states' powers. Expansion of the dependence on federal money to build infrastructure and support state programs has meant that federal rules apply to the uses of those monies by states. All of these examples are versions of a modern form of government known as *cooperative federalism*.

# EXAMPLES OF U.S. FEDERALISM: SEPARATIONS OF POWERS

Congress has the main authority to create legislation for the federal government. The executive branch can prioritize and attempt to veto, but Congress can ignore priorities and override objections. The Supreme Court might declare legislative acts of Congress unconstitutional but only if judicial challenges are formed, work their way up to the Supreme Court, and are accepted by the Supreme Court. Even then, Congress can propose amendments that will change the way the court can interpret such disputes in the future. If states ratify such amendments, Congress's powers are re-established.

Congress is divided into a bicameral legislature (House and Senate), with each having unique systems of creating legislation. The chambers have different rules for debates, committee procedures, and the powers of leaders.

The president and his or her administration are in charge of executing the legislation created by the Congress. The executive branch has been given extensive powers to create bureaucratic rules and interpretations. The agencies are difficult to manage or remove and have some judicial powers to judge citizens' actions under their rules and regulations.

The Supreme Court and lower federal courts are in charge of resolving disputes that arise under the federal laws. The Supreme Court has extensive powers to reject or ignore most cases brought to its attention by petition.

State governments usually reflect this system in their structure of branches, though the structures of some state legislatures differ from this model. The most notable exception is the state of Nebraska, which has a single-chamber (unicameral) legislature. Some court systems are elected by the people. Some governors have more veto powers than the president. Other governors have almost no direct control over the state executive agencies.

## EXAMPLES OF U.S. FEDERALISM: CHECKS AND BALANCES

The main purpose of the legislative branch is to create, debate, and pass the laws of the federal government. The president can veto such proposed legislation. However, Congress can override the veto with two-thirds of votes from each chamber. The president can kill legislation that is delayed until there are fewer than 10 days left in a session. This "pocket veto" is the power to consider legislation for at least 10 days. If Congress has less than 10 days left, the president does not have to veto to kill the bill.

### DUTIES OF THE SENATE

The Senate can deny presidential appointments. This action is usually acrimonious but has occurred. This is more likely to happen if the majority party of the Senate is a different party than that of the president. The president can prioritize the national agenda (State of the Union). When the public majority supports this agenda, Congress ignores it with risk. Because all members of the House and one-third of Senators are up for election within months of every other State of the Union address, this public pressure can be a powerful tool of presidential power.

The president appoints the members of the Supreme Court. Congress must approve these appointments; these events are relatively rare and very much in the news when they occur. The nation understands the importance of lifetime appointments and their impact on the entire political spectrum.

The president creates the very important priorities of the federal budget. Congress reacts to this creation, maneuvers in its own goals and biases, but still faces the veto threat. The ultimate responsibility for finalizing the budget belongs to Congress. The two mid-1990s attempts by Congress to blame President Bill Clinton for budget problems backfired, because the public and the president understood where the final responsibility rested.

Congress can impeach and remove the president or members of the Supreme Court. The House may charge (impeach), and the Senate may remove. The punishment from Congress is limited by the Constitution to stripping the person from office, blocking future government positions, and removing possible pensions. Even when the House goes to the extraordinary effort to impeach, the Senate may choose to leave the offender in office. In the famous cases of Andrew Johnson and Clinton, the House did impeach, but the Senate fell short of removal votes. Both presidents finished their terms.

The Supreme Court can interpret laws created by Congress and declare them unconstitutional. This is known as *judicial review* and was created by the court case of *Marbury v. Madison* in 1803. Judicial review was not part of the original articles of the Constitution but was included in Hamilton's arguments in the *Federalist Papers*. Some early proposals for the government included a power of "legislative" review, but the judicial version has been accepted for over two centuries. States again reflect these items in their governments, but many variations exist in how courts are chosen, how long the legislatures serve, etc.

## EXAMPLES OF U.S. FEDERALISM: FISCAL FEDERALISM

When the international economy collapsed in the 1930s, many reforms and expectations that started in the Progressive Era were expanded and made a central component of the duties of the U.S. government. The core of many programs was the distribution of monies to build dams, roads, and energy sources and to fund job programs, food supplies, and medical care. States have spotty records regarding the care of citizens in many of these areas, especially for minorities and the poor. The federal government has become a source of support in many financial areas, and with this support, the federal powers are expanded. All levels of government must cooperate to cure some of the ills of the nation, such as persistent poverty, disasters, or states in need of budget bailouts from the federal government. However, administrations and Congresses have attached controls to many of these funds. State and local governments must follow federal rules about discrimination, equality, affirmative action, and other agendas to use the federal funds.

# EXAMPLES OF NATIONAL AND STATE POWERS IN MODERN FEDERALISM

## BASIC NATIONAL POWERS

- Delegated powers: expressed, enumerated, implied, and inherent in the Constitution. These are mostly found in the Preamble, Article 1 Section 8, Article II, Article III, Article IV Section 4, and Article VI. Examples include the following:
  - Treason
  - Counterfeiting
  - Disrupting postal services
  - Issues of interstate trade

- Interpretations by the Supreme Court; for example, *Marbury v. Madison,* 1803, and *McCulloch v. Maryland,* 1819

- Rights incorporated from the 14th Amendment. *Incorporation* is the concept of federal rights being applied to state rights minimums. The key phrases used in most of such cases are the 14th Amendment requirements that states may not "deprive any person of life, liberty, or property, without due process of law; nor…the equal protection of the laws."

- Issues made federal by acts of Congress. Examples include the following:
  - Kidnapping
  - Crossing state lines with intent to commit crimes
  - Threatening or attacking federal officials
  - Violating the civil rights of citizens

## BASIC STATE POWERS

- Reserved to the states: conduct elections, select local officials, and select electors

- Rights under the 10th Amendment

- Traditional rights held by states. Examples include the following:
  - Business licenses
  - Marriage licenses
  - Legal practice licenses
  - Professional licenses
  - Civil laws not involving federal issues
  - Criminal laws not made federal
  - Education rules

# MAJOR EVENTS IN FEDERALISM

| | |
|---|---|
| 1789 to the Civil War | Dual federalism is dominant. States can define full citizenship. Specific court cases are used to define federal authority over trade, interstate commerce, and banking. |
| Civil War Amendments (1860s) | The 13th, 14th, and 15th Amendments take from the states the rights to allow slavery, define levels of citizenship, and stop black men from voting. |
| Post Reconstruction (1876 to early 1900s) | States regain authority over status of citizens in areas of voting and segregation, formalized in the case of *Plessy v. Ferguson,* 1896. |
| New Deal and World War II (1930s and 1940s) | Federal authority over commerce is expanded during the New Deal and legislation after WWII. The Employment Act of 1946 is a key example. |
| Civil Rights Era (1950s to the 1970s) | With *Brown v. Board of Education*, the Civil Rights Act of 1964, and the Great Society programs, federal authority over civil liberties and public welfare is expanded. |
| Devolution Era (New Federalism) (1980s to the present) | With the election of Ronald Reagan in 1980 and the Republican majorities in Congress in 1994, efforts have grown to limit federal controls and influence. More welfare control is given to states. More emphasis is being placed on using private companies in areas of schooling and federal assistance. |

# REVIEW QUESTIONS

## MULTIPLE-CHOICE QUESTIONS

1. Federalism contains the idea that our two major forms of government are both

   (A) sovereign.

   (B) republics.

   (C) elected.

   (D) checked and balanced.

   (E) equal.

2. In the early days of the republic, federalism was meant to

   (A) allow for strong local governments.

   (B) guarantee general equality of laws in the country.

   (C) protect the overall liberties of the nation.

   (D) encourage voting by all eligible voters.

   (E) strengthen the power of the national capital.

3. One major goal of recent Republican administrations and majorities has been to

   (A) return more control of federal monies to states.

   (B) return more control of civil rights to states.

   (C) return the administration of policies to the states.

   (D) return more tax authority to states.

   (E) All of the above

4. Major shifts in the scope of federalism were caused by

   (A) states failing to protect civil rights.

   (B) the inability of capitalist economies to avoid major collapses.

   (C) conflicts between republics and totalitarian nations.

   (D) changes in attitudes about the general rights of minorities.

   (E) All of the above

5. After the Great Depression and the Civil Rights era, interstate commerce powers of Congress came to include

   (A) the movement of goods and services across state lines.

   (B) the movement of goods but not of laborers.

   (C) the general movement of goods anywhere in the United States.

   (D) activities related to economic trade across states.

   (E) criminal acts inside states.

## FREE-RESPONSE QUESTIONS

1.  Federalism in the United States has shifted from a form known as "dual federalism" to more "cooperative federalism."

    (A)  Define the two kinds of federalism.

    (B)  Explain why this newer system of "cooperative federalism" favors the powers of the central government.

2.  Federalism was designed to protect the rights of citizens.

    (A)  Identify three ways the structure of federalism is used to protect the rights of U.S. residents.

    (B)  Explain how the three ways identified in part (A) actually work to protect citizens.

# ANSWERS AND EXPLANATIONS

## MULTIPLE-CHOICE ANSWERS

**1. A**

Federalism contains the idea that our two major forms of government are both sovereign. State governments and local governments have separate powers. Choice (B) is incorrect because republics do not need to be federal. Choice (C) and choice (D) are both incorrect because neither elections nor checks and balances are key to federalism as a system. Choice (E) is incorrect because although individually sovereign, the two major levels of government are not equal.

**2. C**

In the early days of the republic, federalism was meant to protect the overall liberties of the nation. The design of layered government was, and is, designed to meet this goal. Choice (A) is incorrect because local governments do not need to be strong or to be equal to the federal government. Choice (B) is incorrect because federalism in the early days of the republic was not meant to guarantee the general equality of laws in the country. Choices (D) and (E) are incorrect because voting levels and stronger national powers were not aims of early federalism.

**3. C**

One major goal of recent Republican administrations and majorities has been to return the administration of policies back to the states. New federalism is aimed at allowing states more control and more choice regarding the creation of policies and allowing states to maintain control of their policies, even if they use federal funding. Choice (A) is incorrect because the goal is not to cut federal control of federal funds. Choice (B) is incorrect because the goal is not to change civil rights. Choice (D) is incorrect because the goal is not to change the ability of the federal government to collect money.

**4. E**

Major shifts in the scope of federalism were caused by all of the factors listed. Choice (A) refers to the changes brought about by the Civil War, choice (B) refers to the changes that resulted from the Great Depression, choice (C) refers to the Cold War changes, and choice (D) refers to the changes that came about during the Civil Rights era.

**5. D**

After the Great Depression and the civil rights era, interstate commerce powers of Congress came to include activities related to economic trade across states. Choice (A) and choice (B) are incorrect because they represent earlier interpretations of interstate commerce powers. Choice (C) is incorrect because it is not a correct description of the interstate commerce powers of Congress. Choice (E) is incorrect because criminal acts inside states remain under state authority.

# FREE-RESPONSE ANSWERS

1. **4-point Rubric**

   ### 2 points in part (A): (define the two types)

   - Dual—state and federal governments are relatively independent, judicial rights are separate to their own jurisdictions, separate Bills of Rights, separate definitions of citizenship for states.

   - Cooperative—interstate trade in the federal realm, issues related to interstate trade (civil rights) also in the federal realm, federal funds help states but imply federal control of the rules, civil rights from the federal Bill of Rights apply to states, citizenship a national issue.

   ### 2 points in part (B): (explain how this favors the federal powers)

   - States need money and must rely on federal help; therefore, federal rules override state choices.

   - All states must follow minimum federal rights standards.

   - Interstate trade can be interpreted very widely, thus applying many federal regulations on businesses and individuals.

2. **6-point Rubric**

   ### 3 points in part (A): (identify three ways the structure is used)

   - Checks of power
   - Separations of power
   - Balances of power
   - Different jurisdictions of power
   - Reserved powers
   - Supremacy Clause

   ### 3 points in part (B): (explain how the three ways protect)

   - No branch can function fully independently without the influence of other branches.
   - Each branch has only certain powers and no others.
   - No branch should dominate (too much anyway).
   - At least three levels of powers exist, and each is often unique (local, state, national).
   - Powers are specifically protected for individuals and states, especially when not covered in the Constitution.
   - If conflicts occur, they can be resolved by national authority, especially if local and state governments abuse rights.

# CHAPTER 6: **POLITICAL BELIEFS AND BEHAVIORS**

## IF YOU ONLY LEARN SIX THINGS IN THIS CHAPTER . . . .

1.  Most political groups in the United States agree to fundamental goals of free participation, relatively limited governmental controls, and open participation.

2.  Labels of "conservative" and "liberal" have changed meaning many times. What has remained stable is the general difference between those who emphasize governmental controls and those who emphasize individual choices.

3.  Voter turnout levels in the United States are low but stable in moderate viewpoints.

4.  The political spectrum of the U.S. majority has always been relatively centrist.

5.  Influences on political beliefs in this system are still dominated by family background and a handful of other relatively stable factors.

6.  Voting access has often been restricted in the United States, but recent efforts have opened the process.

## TRADITIONS OF CITIZEN BEHAVIORS

The generally accepted goals of our political culture have revolved around some key assumptions. Communities should be active and involved in politics and government. Citizens should be free to participate in government, and governmental interference should be as minimal as possible. The government exists to give help when needed. Citizens should be informed of the decision-making process, and leaders should answer to the public and provide laws and rules. Government offices should be for public service rather than for self-aggrandizement.

A two-party system has always dominated the way the United States has reacted to such governmental goals, despite many changes in regional populations, economic developments, and party groups themselves. There are several reasons for this, but the primary causes seem to be a structure of government that allows flexible approaches by politicians and parties, long periods of growth and prosperity that kept radical groups from flourishing, electoral requirements of national support, and the relatively moderate views of most U.S. voters. The relatively open culture of the United States and the general entrepreneurial spirit that exists here have also allowed many voters to be rather neutral toward politics in general.

The two major political viewpoints, liberal and conservative, stem from the same sources. The Declaration of Independence's goals, the Article of Confederation's failures, the Constitution's simplicity, and the layered powers of federalism contribute to the beliefs of those on both sides. Political leaders across the spectrum fundamentally agree to support the system of government, the goals of individual liberty, and the general hopes of the Preamble's outline of the reasons for the government. What leads to disagreements is the possible ways that the government and citizens can most efficiently reach those goals. Should we emphasize safety and careful leadership, or should we emphasize choices and individualism? Only smaller radical groups in the United States call for significantly different forms of basic governmental powers, the reduction of private property, the large-scale mixing of church and state, or massive changes in the use of the Constitution.

## VIEWPOINT ORIGINS

The support of the goals of limited government runs deep in American culture, so as a result, governmental powers were designed to be limited. The addition of the Bill of Rights strengthened public cries for less government and politics, not more. With the exception of political "machines" in urban centers during much of the 19th century, political beliefs usually did not equate to social position or access to jobs. Radicals and fervent supporters of political causes have tended to be either regional or responses to a temporary crisis.

## EARLY REPUBLIC: CONSERVATIVES VERSUS LIBERALS

In the earliest days of the republic, American liberals and conservatives resembled their European counterparts. Conservatives wanted a more centralized system, a bit more elitism, and a focus on stable trade. Liberals were influenced by the fervor of revolution, local controls of power, expansion, and independence. Party labels came and went, but those who wanted a stronger use of the Constitution and generally more centralized government opposed those who wanted states' rights, no national banks, and private enterprise.

By the mid-1800s, the Jeffersonian views of localism had become mainstream, and early Republican calls for national guidance became almost radical. After the Civil War, support of nationalism became the mainstream, until both major parties found themselves shocked by a rising tide of calls for help for workers and farmers. The once-radical agenda of the Populists is now mainstream, with an eight-hour workday, legal unions, national transportation systems, federally controlled banks, and progressive taxes barely being debated.

The splits of the 20th century were further dominated by the Great Depression and Civil Rights Movements. Liberals became the champions of national controls of economic policies, social welfare, and civil liberties. Conservatives took over the agenda of free enterprise, states' rights, and governmental controls of many moral issues. Yet there were many periods in U.S. history in which third-party leaders continued to attack both dominant groups as being nearly identical in leadership. Extreme goals of socialists, libertarians, or even communists have never gained mass ive support.

## PARTICIPATION AND VOTING

Possibly the most critiqued issues of U.S. political behaviors are voter participation and election turnout. Although rampant fraud, "machine" coercion, and fewer eligible voters in the 19th century created higher percentage turnouts, the fact that modern voter turnout continues to drop is troubling. The greatest fear has been that citizens have grown so callous toward their leaders that they have stopped bothering to vote—the 2008 election may be an exception to this fear as voters turned out, though hardly in record numbers, to support candidate Barack Obama.

Reduced dominance of the two-parent family, greater population movement, and the general drop in church attendance have all contributed to lower political loyalty and interest. On the more positive front, reforms have started to make voter registration quicker and simpler. Statistical studies show that turnouts of those who have registered to vote have been relatively stable. This means that falling percentages are often a symbol of population growth rather than a reduction in the number of voters who care. Family influences, educational levels, age, and economic conditions continue to influence who votes, even if these factors do not influence how they vote. The Internet has also become a way for voters to learn more. With websites, viral campaign videos, and celebrity endorsements, younger voters are being educated and inspired to register and to vote.

## PARTICIPATION AND CIVIC RESPONSIBILITY

Civic participation for the good of the community is a long-standing tradition and practice in the United States. The history of frontier expansion and rapid industrial development created the expectation that U.S. residents should help build a stronger nation and a stronger political system. Civic participation is very political in nature because the groups themselves are considered independent vehicles of change, bias, and party support.

Religious groups work in civic areas for public assistance, social events, and issue lobbying. Education and youth groups exist to give children new opportunities and share in the learning of cultural and political traditions. Medical volunteer groups become advocates for many agency policies concerning public health. Business groups become powerful agents for political contacts, issue guidance, and public debates. Many groups exist just to give advocacy assistance to those with similar political goals. Environmental issue groups also play key roles influencing policy trends toward business actions. All of these groups are founded on similar principles that require individual citizens to try to make a difference in society. They are made possible by individuals making the choice to participate, the lack of large-scale governmental control of such groups, the ability of such groups to determine their own causes, and the ability of the groups to try to influence the policy makers.

One of the biggest changes in the way civic groups influence the national agenda has been the vast expansion of these groups and how they lobby the leadership. More *single-issue* groups have emerged with the expansion of the population and the expansion of legal forms of campaign influence.

In fact, numerous competing causes have emerged. The access to funds and national attention has expanded. More groups can attempt to form political action committees and hire lobbyists. The system has become more democratic and chaotic. As a result, more polls show that citizens have less faith in the power of many groups, participation in volunteering for groups is declining, and residents have lower expectations for creating changes.

# THE POLITICAL SPECTRUM

There are numerous approaches to the discussion of political beliefs and groups. This section will focus on the modern uses of the terms, how they are represented in the United States, and provide a brief description of how they have changed over time. A fundamental point to emphasize is that all political opinions in this country are influenced by the essential goals of limited government. People of the United States have agreed (in principle) to visions of less governmental involvement than occurs in almost all other countries and their political traditions. From the Declaration forward, the principles of natural rights and individual liberties have controlled the national debate of the role of parties and laws. Voters on both sides of the spectrum want limited interference, some social equality, governmental connections to the will of the people, and open "pursuit of happiness." Even with all the massive periods of immigration of non-English-speaking populations, these political biases have remained central to the vast majority of U.S. voters.

## ONE VERSION OF THE POLITICAL SPECTRUM (AS USED IN THE MODERN UNITED STATES)

**Socialism.** This is the idea that the citizens of a republic can select large parts of the economy and issues of social welfare and have them controlled and organized publicly by the government. Socialists believe that this should be done for the benefit of all. The universal public education system in the United States is an example of a socialist system. Most adults pay for the system through taxation, and then all families can access the benefits of public schooling. Even those who pay but do not have children in the schools should benefit from a better educated, trained, and skilled youth that will help carry on the creation of future wealth and freedoms of the nation. In many parts of Europe, socialist programs of this kind extend to energy production, transportation, housing, communication structures such as television, and major health care services.

**Liberalism.** Since the Progressive Era, and certainly since the Great Depression, liberals support the government taking a central role in economic development and social welfare. Since the Cold War, liberals have wanted to keep the government out of citizens' issues such as privacy, church and state relations, and free speech.

**Populism.** Modern forms include those more liberal on economic programs but generally conservative on social items. On the modern political right, leaders such as Pat Buchanan claim a form of "populism." These populists see themselves as more independent than the major parties and more concerned with U.S. issues and with U.S. cultural strengths and values. On the modern left, Ralph Nader claims a form of "populism." He and his supporters feel that the government is excessively concerned with supporting large corporations at the expense of workers, and they are opposed to governmental interference in personal choices.

**Conservatism.** Since the late 1800s, conservatives have supported the ideas of competition and free enterprise with minimal government interference. Conservatives are very supportive of capitalism. They usually believe that freedom of competitive markets will create improvements and innovations for all. They oppose socialist programs as inefficient, unfair, and controlling. Since the 1960s, conservatives in the United States have supported governmental guidance and rules concerning social issues such as school prayer, national security, and marriage.

**Libertarianism.** Libertarians in the United States occupy a curious position between liberals and conservatives. Libertarians are very supportive of the Jeffersonian ideal republic, where government provides as many freedoms as possible. Because of these historic links to purer forms of the "social contract," many Libertarian ideas about leaving the economy alone are popular with Republicans. Libertarian ideas about free choices concerning privacy and about issues such as speech strike a responsive chord with Democrats.

# OTHER MODERN TERMS AND CONCEPTS OF POLITICAL BELIEFS

**Neo-conservatives (neo-cons).** Many are the product of World War II and the Cold War. These modern, more libertarian conservatives emphasize the need for a strong defense, open competition in economic markets, and free world trade. Neo-conservatives use the example of communism to emphasize a free business climate and the understanding that other countries and cultures are often intensely hostile to our nation.

**Bible Belt conservatives (theo-cons).** A product of the forced civil rights changes in the South, these conservatives tend to be Southern Baptists and more fundamentalist Christians. They dislike central government yet support issues such as prayer in public schools. The name is a reference to the traditional stretch of support that runs across the middle of the Old South. The "Moral Majority" and "Christian Coalition" political groups represent these kinds of voters. These groups have grown rapidly in number and political power and are key to current Republican strategies. Christian voters see liberalism as attacking family structure and independence.

**Dixiecrats.** This is the traditional label given to white Southerners who remained very conservative but were very loyal to the Democratic Party from about 1880 to 1980. As the Civil Rights era and Vietnam moved the Democratic Party to more liberal stances, Dixiecrats finally forgave the Republican Party for the Civil War and joined their fellow conservatives in the Republican camp. They had always supported more conservative positions on foreign policies, states' rights, and social values, but they had worked within the Democratic Party. Between 1880 and 1980, most Southern states were run by one Democratic Party that had two major wings—conservative and progressive. When national Democratic programs headed more toward national control of civil rights, the Southern Democratic conservatives began to defect. The emergence of the Republican Party in Southern states has become a major feature of the "political realignment" that has changed the respective dominance of the two parties.

**New Deal liberals.** These groups tend to favor a central role of the government in the economy. They support unions, support Social Security as a safety net system, and generally want the government to take a leading role in economic welfare. The original coalition of New Deal liberals was built by the supporters of FDR. Key support groups were union workers in northern cities, residents of rural areas that desperately needed federal economic help, and those African Americans who were able to vote in significant numbers.

**Greens (feminist liberals, environmentalist liberals, civil rights liberals, etc.).** The civil rights struggles, the environmental movement, and reactions to Vietnam and Watergate created groups that wish to have the United States lead in the creation of social equality and environmental protections. They tend to distrust big business and the major party leaders.

**Rust Belt.** The Northeast contains many of the traditional heavy industry areas and, therefore, has more union involvement than other areas. In addition, many of the most populated urban centers contain larger minority populations and make this area more liberal.

**Sun Belt.** The South and West are the faster growing regions of the country; they contain more nonunion areas, have more of a history of supporting states' rights, and are, therefore, more conservative.

**Farm Belt.** The less populated but vast area of the middle of the country also extends to the ranching country of the West. Traditions of independence, both personal and economical, make this a conservative area today.

**West Coast**. Rapid immigration, pressing concerns over the environment, and more liberal lifestyle traditions make the area along the Pacific more liberal.

**Southern strategy.** Made popular by the Nixon campaigns, Republican strategies aimed to build a powerful and loyal conservative base in the Old South, denying Democrats one of their traditional core support areas.

## MAJOR SHIFTS IN POLITICAL LABELS IN THE UNITED STATES

The terms *liberal* and *conservative* have long histories. Liberal has been associated with the "left" at least since the French Revolution. The same is true with conservatives and "right." What has changed, often dramatically, is the goals of party groups and their association with these labels. Groups that were once liberal are no longer considered as such. Compare the table of historical changes on the next page with the tables on U.S. political party changes in chapter 8.

When the Constitution was adopted, national concerns focused on rescuing the economy, strengthening central powers, organizing better national controls, and building trade with a more conservative England. As a result, those who led the government tended to want conservative dominance, meaning a strong central government and less reliance on weak states. Hamilton's calls for fiscal controls of states were key. Liberals then became the outsiders, calling for more emphasis on individual liberties. By the mid-1800s, the liberals had become the political status quo, with conservatives mostly concentrated in the cities of the Northeast.

When the party systems were breaking down before the sectional chaos of the 1860s, liberals were again the ones calling for changes. The long dominance of states' rights and local laws was falling apart, and liberals now wanted to go to more central controls in the name of justice and order. During Reconstruction and the Gilded Age, business independence arose, leaving the dominant political conservatives re-emphasizing local and individual freedoms. Liberals now wanted direct government guidance of workers' rights, property rights, and voter rights. This Populism and Progressivism would be absorbed by both major parties around 1900, with Teddy Roosevelt standing as the major progressive/liberal voice from within the dominant Republican Party.

The early 20th century saw the development of international powers for the United States, both militarily and industrially. After 1912, conservatives rejected Progressivism as a mild version of communism, and liberals took it in as a form of workers' rights. The modern splits between liberal views of the government's role in the economy and conservative views of independence were solidified by the politics of FDR, the outbreak of World War II, and tensions between capitalism and communism.

## LIBERALISM AND CONSERVATISM

Civil rights reforms caused shifts in U.S. liberalism, as minority rights campaigns created the basis of women's rights issues and then environmental concerns. Because many environmental problems were seen as industry and corporation problems, these liberals oppose lenient controls over the powerful business sector. Conservatives chafe at national orders over cultural issues, business decisions, and forced economic assistance to some. The late 1900s saw the rebirth of conservative dominance, when it appeared that the federal government had successfully put into place the legal structure of civil rights and should stop expanding so many powers. The 1980s and 1990s were times of massive economic expansion that strengthened the calls for less interference in the economy.

## LABELS OVER TIME

| Time Period | Groups Called "Liberal" or Even "Radical" for Change | Groups Called "Conservative" or "Status Quo" |
| --- | --- | --- |
| Early 1800s | Jeffersonian Democratic-Republicans Democratic Republicans | Federalists Whigs |
| Civil War Era (1850s to 1870s) | Republicans | States' Rights Democrats |
| Late 1800s | Populists/Grange/Peoples Party | Republicans Democrats |
| Early 1900s | Progressive Teddy Roosevelt Republicans Wilson Democrats | Taft Republicans |
| Mid-1900s | New Deal Democrats Civil Rights Democrats | Republicans Dixiecrats States' Rights Democrats Goldwater Republicans |
| Late 1900s | Democrats Greens | Reagan Republicans Christian Republicans |

# POLITICAL EFFICACY AND CHANGES IN THE UNITED STATES

*Political efficacy* is the study of how citizens view their own political beliefs; how they understand the political system; and whether they believe that the system can change, help, or improve their lives. Generally, the willingness of Americans to participate in political events and systems has remained relatively constant over the decades. This is known as *internal efficacy*. What has changed is *external efficacy*, which represents the general belief that the government can be helpful and responsive to the needs of the country. The levels of positive external efficacy have dropped sharply, especially since the Civil Rights era of the early 1960s, the Vietnam era of the early 1970s, and the events of Watergate (1972–74). U.S. citizens do not trust the government as much as they used to, and they do not believe that the government will work in the general interest of the public.

## INFLUENCES ON POLITICAL BELIEFS

| | |
|---|---|
| **Family Background** | This remains the most influential reason for political beliefs. Voting patterns show that the level of political interest, voting habits, and biases toward liberal or conservative views are formed by family traditions and behaviors. |
| **Religious Affiliation** | Growing numbers of voters use religious tenets as guides for their political interests. Traditional beliefs of religions, interests in political activities, and levels of concerns are key. Those religions that emphasize stricter doctrines often see liberal or conservative goals as personal or moral threats. |
| **Gender** | With the traditional dominance of men in the business community, the trend still holds that men are more conservative in economic politics. Women have created strong majorities for social liberalism, although this varies from region to region. |
| **Education** | Traditional studies reported that those with higher levels of schooling tend to be more liberal. Two pieces of information now contradict that view. Those who have higher degrees often also have more wealth than those who don't, which often equates to modern conservatism. Conservatives have also led large-scale attacks on university programs that have radical and liberal biases. More university youth groups emphasize conservative policies. Education clearly makes a difference in voting turnout patterns. Higher-educated voters cast ballots in much higher percentages than less-educated voters. |
| **Ethnicity** | The history of immigration is a history of calls for social reforms, worker rights, and civil equality. Minorities support liberal programs. This is very true for African Americans. Hispanic Americans have generally supported the same goals, but recent inroads by conservative groups have focused on social and religious points that conservative Hispanic American and African American families tend to favor. |
| **Economic Status** | The rich vote, and the poor don't. It is an ancient tradition that those who benefit the most from the political structure will go to great lengths to keep that control. Those who could benefit the most from government help usually do not believe that the system that created the society in which they live will change. Therefore, the poor tend to vote in much lower percentages. |

# VOTER BIASES

The strongest factor in determining voter biases is party identification and support for major party issues. How the party appears to parallel an individual's beliefs about taxes, jobs, moral codes, family issues, and political freedoms paramount to party identification for the individual. This has been shown to be the main reason for votes, with almost no absolute consideration given to the actual person running. As long as the voter believes that the candidate will follow the same beliefs, support is likely. The exception to this trend occurs when several candidates of the same party are running in preliminary elections. Then personality factors are primary.

The weakest factors in determining voter biases are running mates, platform statements, media ads, and presidential debates. Even though a vast amount of attention is given to ads and debates, voters who care for political issues stand by their parties. They often complain that the party's candidate is the "lesser of two evils" but will stick with the party beliefs. Those voters who don't care much about party issues will find the candidate's personality or image more important.

# U.S. VOTER TURNOUT

Voter turnout in the United States is relatively low (especially in nonpresidential elections) if one counts all potential voters. Comparisons between U.S. voter turnout and that of other republics usually show that U.S. levels are much lower. Some factors may include the vast and diverse nature of the U.S. population, the relatively centrist politics of our major parties, and the general comfort level we have with any of our leaders. When only counting the people who have registered to vote, the turnout percentages are stronger and stable. The system has undergone tremendous changes in recent history to create more voting opportunities. Elections are also common, relatively fair, and closely monitored.

## NEGATIVE ASPECTS OF LOW U.S. VOTER TURNOUTS

Who is in charge? Are we giving power to radical minority groups that get out votes? If the rest of the population sits back in comfort, less centrist governments can be created, bringing about more radical programs that make the public less secure or confident. Do voters lack the belief that voting makes any difference? More frustration with the massive bureaucracy, vast problems, and images of an isolated and controlled central government have lowered belief in reforms. Many voters feel that the media and party insiders have too much control, so why bother? They feel that if Congress and the president can only listen to limited numbers of groups, and these groups are controlled by the superwealthy and corporations, why bother? Many reason that if the media biases are effective enough to create masses of biased voters, then individual votes will make little difference.

## POSITIVE ASPECTS OF U.S. VOTER TURNOUTS

When the United States is in a comfort zone with its government and the economy, voters tend to be complacent. We trust the freedoms provided and understand the limits of governmental actions. We see that vast areas of personal life and daily business are not affected in major ways that keep us from creating wealth and security.

Elections do not create radical changes in our system. Parties are stable and fairly centrist, and that is good. Even those with radical agendas could not change this system unless major changes in the powers under the Constitution were effected.

## FACTORS IN U.S. VOTER TURNOUT

| | |
|---|---|
| **Crisis/War** | Levels of patriotism, reactions to national threats, and panicked calls for help will bring out votes. |
| **Age** | Senior citizens vote more often, have time to vote, and tend to believe in the political system. |
| **Religion** | Evangelical Christians are registering more voters and help with vote drives. |
| **Income** | Poor residents have never voted in high numbers. |
| **Region** | Rural vote turnouts tend to be high and conservative, yet they are less important at the national level. Southern states are key to politicians with national ambitions due to extreme pockets of conservatism and trends of higher growth. |
| **Urban/Suburbs** | More votes are now found in suburbs and city centers. Suburbs tend to be more white and are, therefore, more balanced between conservative and liberal than the minority-dominated city centers. |
| **Electoral Power** | More populated states completely dominate most presidential elections. Turnout in local races can be impacted tremendously if national elections are either very close or one-sided. |
| **Apathy** | When party platforms are similar, races are one-sided, or candidates are bland, turnouts are reduced. |

## BLOCKS TO VOTING IN THE UNITED STATES (INSTITUTIONAL RESTRICTIONS)

- State registration rules have time limits that cut some voters out. Some rules are very lengthy and require paperwork months ahead of the election.

- Residency laws might require lengthy stays in the district or state in order to vote.

- So many offices are usually up for votes that ballots can be very lengthy. Some voters do not have the patience for it and ignore "down ballot" races. Voters also tend to know less about the candidates or issues for these "down ballot" offices, thus ignoring them.

- Many countries raise voting percentages by fining those who don't vote. This has not been seriously considered in the United States; U.S. residents are free not to vote and often make that choice.

*(continued on next page)*

- Primary systems across the states are often closed to many. They limit those who do not register with parties or allow only one party vote.

- The lack of any holiday status for Election Day cuts votes. Some efforts have been made to create a national vote holiday to create more votes; others object to this as a waste of money and as excessive governmental interference.

- The Electoral College system leaves many less-populated states with little influence over the presidential selection. The winner-take-all system also discourages voting by those who feel that their opposition vote will count for nothing in their state.

## BLOCKS THAT ARE INFORMAL

- The centrist views of the major parties leave many with the feeling that little will change.

- Poorer citizens believe that votes make little difference.

- In this vast republic, many believe their individual votes don't matter.

- Voter fatigue is blamed when numerous elections and campaigns occur year-round.

### RECENT EFFORTS TO INCREASE TURNOUTS (MOTOR VOTER)

Allowing voters to appear on Election Day (drive up) and vote or register on the spot is seen as a way to improve vote percentages. However, issues of fairness and honesty lead many to object to this effort. How will controls stop some from roaming around and voting more than once during the same election?

Also, why penalize those who properly take responsibility and register early? Many states have successfully extended the amount of time voters have in which to cast their ballots with weeks of early voting; easier, more convenient absentee voting; and the use of computers.

## VOTER TURNOUT TRENDS (EARLY 2000S, APPROXIMATE PERCENTAGES)

| Category: | Highest Turnout Group | Lowest Turnout Group |
|---|---|---|
| **Age** | Age 65 + (70%) | 18 to 20 (30%) |
| **Education Level** | College Degree (72%) | No HS Diploma (30%) |
| **Ethnicity** | European (55%) | Asian (43%) |
| **Gender** | Women (56%) | Men (53%) |
| **Marriage Status** | Married (61%) | Single (45%) |
| **Union Membership** | Member (65%) | Not Member (53%) |

Source: Edwards, Wattenberg, Lineberry: Government in America, 2002

# REVIEW QUESTIONS

## MULTIPLE-CHOICE QUESTIONS

1. U.S. ideas of liberalism and conservatism are grounded in

   (A) beliefs in limited government creating a better society.

   (B) combinations of needs for liberty and safety.

   (C) traditional roles of central and local authorities.

   (D) support of the Constitutional framework.

   (E) All are true for liberalism and conservatism.

2. Civic participation in the United States may be declining for all of the following reasons **EXCEPT**

   (A) growing control of a few powerful groups that dominate Washington.

   (B) lack of belief in civic participation by minority groups.

   (C) the rapid expansion of the number of groups.

   (D) declining belief that helping will make a difference.

   (E) the opening of access to campaigns to more groups.

3. The greatest change in U.S. liberalism has been

   (A) a shift from localism to nationalism.

   (B) a shift to the northeastern part of the country.

   (C) the rise of the Populist Party.

   (D) the rejection of Teddy Roosevelt by the Republicans.

   (E) the rise of women's issues.

4. The greatest change in U.S. conservatism has been

   (A) the move of Dixiecrats to the Republican party.

   (B) the rejection of Progressivism in the 1920s.

   (C) the change from emphasizing national leadership to local leadership.

   (D) the emergence of religious leadership.

   (E) the rising control of rural and western states.

5. The greatest change in political efficacy of citizens has been

   (A) the willingness of citizens to participate in the system.

   (B) the support citizens give to leaders and their hopes for reform.

   (C) the lack of reforms in the areas of civil rights.

   (D) the increasing voter turnouts.

   (E) the efforts to amend the Constitution to allow for more voter access.

## FREE-RESPONSE QUESTIONS

1. The labels *liberal* and *conservative* have changed dramatically in how they have been applied in U.S. politics.

   (A)  Identify three such changes in U.S. political history.

   (B)  Explain why these changes occurred.

2. Voter participation can be viewed as a negative for the country but also as a positive piece of evidence about our political system.

   (A)  Identify two negatives of low U.S. voter turnout patterns.

   (B)  Identify two ways the low turnout is possibly a form of positive evidence about our political system.

# ANSWERS AND EXPLANATIONS

## MULTIPLE-CHOICE ANSWERS

**1. E**

The ideas of liberalism and conservatism are grounded in beliefs in limited government creating a better society, combinations of the need for liberty and safety, traditional roles of central and local authorities, and the support for the Constitutional framework. These forces in the U.S. system have supported Constitutional limited government.

**2. B**

Civic participation in the United States is not declining due to lack of belief in civic participation by minority groups. Minority groups participate like all other groups. All of the other choices are true.

**3. A**

The greatest change in U.S. liberalism has been a shift from localism to nationalism. The other choices are also true but not as central to change as the shift from localism to nationalism.

**4. C**

The greatest change in U.S. conservatism has been the change from emphasizing national leadership to emphasizing local leadership. Again, this is the greatest change from this list; the other events listed occurred but were not as central.

**5. B**

The greatest change in the political efficacy of citizens has been the support that citizens give to leaders and their hopes for reform. Many citizens have lost hope of reforms being enacted. Choice (A) is incorrect because citizens still participate in the system. Choices (C), (D), and (E) are not true.

## FREE-RESPONSE ANSWERS

1. **6-point Rubric**

   **3 points in part (A): (identify three changes)**

   - Early Republic: Liberal meant local controls; conservative meant nationalist.

   - Jeffersonian liberal versus Hamiltonian conservative

   - Civil War: Liberal meant nationalist; conservative meant states' rights.

   - Progressive Era: liberal meant nationalist, conservative meant laissez-faire.

   - Great Depression/Civil Rights: Liberal meant national support for workers; conservative meant pro business and less government.

   **3 points in part (B): (explain)**

   - Federalists won under Washington, built a stronger government, became the status quo; localists under Jefferson were radicals.

   - Slavery and states' rights became the status quo; liberals wanted national control of citizenship.

   - Populism and Progressivism became liberal and radical, calling for national controls of unions, property.

   - Great Depression liberals further aims of national economic control and safety nets; conservatives want local controls and less national government.

2. **4-point Rubric**

   **2 points in part (A): (identify two negatives)**

   - Less political unity

   - Less support for parties and leaders

   - Less optimism about government

   - Less belief that things can change

   - Less belief in the overall republic (apathy)

   - Less belief that one vote makes a difference

   **2 points in part (B): (two ways possibly form of positive evidence)**

   - Trust in the current system

   - Trust in the two parties

   - Trust that things won't get too radical

   - Trust in economic stability

# CHAPTER 7: **PUBLIC OPINION AND POLLING**

## IF YOU ONLY LEARN FOUR THINGS IN THIS CHAPTER . . . .

1. U.S. citizens are only moderately interested in politics and often focus on job and money concerns.

2. Collecting data about public opinions and moods is important to executive and legislative leaders when they pursue agendas.

3. The public's values opinion polls, but leaders are often suspicious of public moods and the public's mastery of the facts.

4. Polls are based on statistical samples and carefully crafted questioning techniques.

## INTRODUCTION

Political scientists have defined the concept of "public opinion" as the ways that citizens of a republic evaluate leaders, candidates, issues, or institutions that control the laws and the government. Public opinion is critical to the ability of the leadership to have supporters and voters willing to follow the laws.

The general political viewpoints of voters have remained stable and relatively moderate over the past decades, because U.S. citizens are comfortable knowing that the government is stable and centrist. When compared with citizens of other republics, Americans have fewer issues of control; a large portion of the public even claims little interest in government as a whole.

In the same way, campaigns and parties tend to focus on "pocketbook" issues, sensing that the public raises its level of concern only when money and jobs are involved. Presidential elections certainly turn on such truths. For the entire 20th century, about two-thirds of all elections could be predicted on the rise and fall of election-year economic conditions. When unemployment and inflation were improving in the year of the election, the incumbent party mostly won. When unemployment or inflation were worsening, the incumbent party and candidate were in trouble.

This was proven true most recently in the 2008 election with Democratic candidate Barack Obama defeating incumbent Republican party candidate John McCain in a time when the U.S. was in an ever-worsening recession.

## THE DEVELOPMENT OF OPINIONS

Political loyalties are created by way of *political socialization*. Surveys consistently show that the biggest factor remains family training; that is, families most significantly affect a person's values, concerns, level of party loyalty, or sense of trust in government. Media presentations, on the other hand, are usually significant for short periods of time and in extremely close elections.

Another important feature of socialization is a person's level of education. Those who have higher degrees are more likely to be involved than those with less advanced degrees. Job status is important as well; for those who may have lost economic standing due to a job change or loss, participation is high. Those who live closer to the poverty level have very low levels of involvement or voting habits.

## OPINION DATA

Modern communications have made the gathering of opinion data instantaneous. Political groups use this data to determine voting patterns, economic projections, and money gathering. Political leaders use it to test support levels, check issue priorities, and watch for potential conflicts, among other things. Television and the Internet, in addition to the continued use of the radio, have dramatically changed the nature of political analysis.

Many elements of government use opinion data. Presidential staff constantly monitor the popularity of the president, the influence of the president (*bully pulpit*), and the impact of presidential speeches. Members of Congress monitor the popularity of programs, potential legislation, and their image versus that of the president. Business markets monitor the confidence of the typical consumer and use that data for economic planning.

## THE NATURE OF PRESIDENTIAL POPULARITY

Presidents face consistent trends in popularity. Right after a president is elected, the public always grants him or her a *honeymoon* period. The president enjoys a great deal of popularity at that time and is expected to take the policy initiative. Congress is aware of the public's need for change and so often goes along. After about three months, the public begins to lose some patience and interest, and Congress becomes more independent.

The middle years of second terms are notorious times of low ratings for the executive. "Lame duck status" sets in, and support for presidential initiatives is low. Voters also begin blaming the president for problems that have not yet been resolved.

## POLLS AND POLLING

The business of monitoring the views of the public was developed after coast-to-coast forms of communication were invented. The process makes careful use of statistics and bias control. *Polling*, as it is now known, is a massive, lucrative, and controversial business used by all parties.

Monitoring the views of the public dates back to the Great Depression, with the work of George Gallup. The sciences of demography and statistics expanded greatly during World War II, as did access to computerized data. Radio and television access made the data easy to sell and analyze.

With the famous exception of the 1948 election of Harry Truman over predicted winner Thomas Dewey, polling organizations have been overwhelmingly correct in predicting turnouts and election patterns. Their levels of accuracy have given them power. Parties pay careful attention to what voters want. Candidates change images and even platforms to bend to popular issues. Leaders adjust priorities based on what is on voters' minds.

There are two negative consequences to such accurate polling. First, campaign funds, and the lobby groups who control them, flow only to known leaders or to statistically even races. Polls tell us which candidates have a good chance at winning, and because few people want to venture a risk on someone with little chance for victory, unknown candidates end up with little or no access to key funds. Second, many leaders hesitate to take on unique (and often, unpopular) issues and only follow what might be popular. This means that a significant issue in need of solving might not be addressed.

Both major political parties hire polling companies, each carefully trying to select results that will help its own party image. Party leaders manage which poll information is released to the media, when it is given, and how it is analyzed. In addition, poll data is used to convince supporters to step up levels of support and build party morale.

Independent media analysts spend much time debating these political messages and their impact. Those in the public who are aware of the biases worry about parties taking over the control of data presentation. Others ignore the data when it doesn't fit their impressions of the party they support.

## FEATURES OF PUBLIC OPINION AND POLLS

| | |
|---|---|
| There is a "public" in our system. | Individuals are considered politically important, their opinions have merit, and they form groups through common interests and regions. |
| There are values to "opinions." | In our political culture, the public is allowed to express its views in speech, letters, and polls, and these views should be heard by the leaders. |
| Polls are valid tools for policy. | The aggregate of opinions collected in statistical ways reflects the overall views of the nation. |
| Most people are ambivalent about polls. | The vast majority of people value individual ideals and are suspicious when a majority will is announced. |
| Leaders distrust the public will. | Leaders have never completely trusted public opinion polls. Polls consistently show that the public knows very little about the leadership of the country and that people change opinion quickly due to emotional shifts. |
| Leaders who follow polls too much are criticized as being weak. | Leaders are expected to take charge and make decisions without always having to worry about popularity numbers. At the same time, they may face criticism for not bending to the public will. |

## ISSUES OF OPINIONS

| | |
|---|---|
| **Distribution** | How big a piece of the electorate is concerned about an issue? If a large or critical part of the entire electorate is strongly in favor of a particular issue, then consensus is reached, and that issue tends to be solved by all parts of government. If the electorate is evenly split, the issue will be addressed at a regional level or left alone. If the electorate is very fragmented or deeply divided, the nation is polarized. Polarized issues are often at the heart of party platforms in order to draw core supporters, but in reality, politicians and courts are reluctant to tackle them. That is because they only create strong reactions by the emotional opposition. |
| **Intensity** | Gun control, gay marriage, public school prayer, and abortion are but a few issues that have uncompromising supporters of opinion. These issues are often called *litmus test* issues. Core party supporters use them to determine which members are trusted to be "pure" to the cause. Litmus test issues are frequently raised in the news when a Supreme Court appointee is being questioned by Senate leaders. True to form, the 2009 nomination of Sonia Sotomayor, a Latina judge, led to seroius questions about race and reverse racism. |

*(continued on next page)*

| Latency | Leaders constantly search to understand what will move the public in the future, how they will react to possible changes, and how angry they will be if no change or resolution is attempted. Can the issue fade on its own, or will it develop into a crisis? |
| --- | --- |
| Salience | Some issues change in importance over time. Union rights caused massive conflicts and violence in the past, but they are no longer critical in most parts of the country. |

## MAJOR INDEPENDENT POLLING COMPANIES/GROUPS

| | |
| --- | --- |
| Gallup | FOX News |
| Harris | CNN/USA/Gallup |
| CBS/NY Times | ABC/Washington Post |
| Reuters/Zogby | Pew Research |

Polling should be used to determine the validity of data and to evaluate the data. The basic usefulness and accuracy of the data presented is therefore established.

## ISSUES IN POLLING

| How many people are being sampled? | Everyone can't be questioned. Therefore, all polls are restricted to specific populations. The time and expense limits the size of polls and can cut the level of accuracy. |
| --- | --- |
| How was the sample population selected? | Random polling depends on knowing all of the potential population involved. Access must be easy. Care must be taken that even seemingly random choices are actually that. The famous case of "random" telephone calls in 1948 failed to take into account that more wealthy families had personal phones at the time so the sample was biased toward the upper classes. |
| If samples are taken by request, will a random result occur? | Many news outlets and businesses invite responses that might be tainted by those who only listen to that outlet or are strongly opinionated. |
| How biased are the questions? | No form of poll question is completely neutral to all respondents. Polling groups have demonstrated this many times by getting opposite responses when a few key words of questions are changed. |
| How close to the election is the poll taken? | More mistakes can be made when polls are rushed, more participants will fake answers to confuse the messages or hurt the other side, and data processing is more rushed and prone to errors. |

# REVIEW QUESTIONS

## MULTIPLE-CHOICE QUESTIONS

1. In polling, the use of a random sample could best be described as

   (A) using complex math models in computer programs to determine calls.

   (B) ensuring any person in the population has an equal chance at being called.

   (C) containing no predetermined criteria for calls.

   (D) picking all of the potential political groups to possibly call.

   (E) using only computers to select who is called.

2. Last-minute polls often have results that are different from earlier polls. This is probably due to

   (A) the use of large numbers of questions.

   (B) the use of different questions.

   (C) an increase in sampling errors.

   (D) the lack of proper questions.

   (E) the lack of random controls.

3. The political opinions of the majority of the country have been stable about all of the following **EXCEPT**

   (A) support for the two major parties.

   (B) a generally low interest in politics.

   (C) a general emphasis on personal liberties.

   (D) a general level of concern about jobs.

   (E) a general level of mistrust in overall government.

4. National polling organizations tend to be

   (A) polarized toward parties.

   (B) accurate.

   (C) inaccurate about presidential results.

   (D) governmental agencies.

   (E) All of the above

5. Which issue can be assumed to be the least controversial among regions of the United States?

   (A) Abortion rights

   (B) Gay marriage rules

   (C) Defense spending levels

   (D) Social Security payment increases

   (E) Public school prayer

## FREE-RESPONSE QUESTIONS

1.  The U.S. public tends to view political polls in a positive light, while leaders tend to have negative opinions of polls.

    (A)  Explain two ways the public views the use and results of polls.

    (B)  Explain two ways leaders see the same polls in a negative light.

2.  Political socialization is the way voters tend to create their beliefs and actions about government.

    (A)  Identify three forms of political socialization.

    (B)  Explain the three forms.

    (C)  Identify the most important form of political socialization.

# ANSWERS AND EXPLANATIONS

## MULTIPLE-CHOICE ANSWERS

### 1. B

Randomness assumes that the polling group knows all of the potential population, how many people there are, and where they are. These conditions must all be met in order for the sample to be truly random. In fact, this is the most difficult part of good polling.

### 2. C

Polls closer to a deadline tend to have problems such as rushed data or skewed responses. Issues around questions or controls are usually not at stake, despite the last-minute factor.

### 3. A

Support for the two current majority parties has shifted considerably. The other issues have largely remained consistent among the population.

### 4. B

Major polls use very consistent methods that have proven right far more often than not.

### 5. D

Because personal economic issues tend to be consistently supported by the public, a Social Security payment issue would see the least opposition.

## FREE-RESPONSE ANSWERS

1. **4-point Rubric**

   **2 points in part (A): (two ways the public sees polls positively)**

   - The leaders are listening.
   - The media is paying attention.
   - The public has an influence.
   - The agenda will be formed by the public.
   - Parties will know who is supportive.

   **2 points in part (B): (two ways leaders see polls negatively)**

   - The public may not tell the truth.
   - The public is fickle.
   - The public intentionally misleads.
   - The public has little real knowledge or information.

2. **7-point Rubric**

   **3 points in part (A): (identify three forms)**

   - Family influence
   - Media
   - Education
   - Age
   - Wealth
   - Job
   - Religion

   **4 points in parts (B) and (C): (explain; identify the most important)**

   - Home training and patterns of parents dominate as the most important.
   - Media is important in close elections but usually short-lived in influence.
   - More education leads to more voting and interest in politics.
   - Less education equals less voting and less interest.
   - Younger people don't care or vote; older people do care and vote.
   - Wealthier residents vote more and are more conservative.
   - Whether one is union or nonunion influences voting and liberalism.
   - More religious citizens tend to be more involved and conservative.

# CHAPTER 8: POLITICAL PARTIES

## IF YOU ONLY LEARN SIX THINGS IN THIS CHAPTER . . . .

1. The two-party system has dominated the U.S. system, with major parties adopting new goals over the years.

2. The Democratic Party started as a party supporting local controls and is now a party supporting more central leadership. The Republican Party started as a party supporting national leadership and is now a party emphasizing local controls.

3. The parties have also switched areas of dominance geographically. The Democrats used to control the South and rural areas; the Republicans used to control the Northeast and the West Coast. They have flipped in these areas.

4. In areas of urban and job controls, party influence has decreased dramatically. Voting for only one party has also diminished as a pattern.

5. Financial and grassroots supports for parties have increased.

6. The current parties are diverging more and becoming more polarized in terms of issues and support groups.

## INTRODUCTION

Political scientists consider political parties as essential to a republic. Even though the general public has historically been wary about party groups and holds negative views about how they work, elections without parties are impossible. Countries that have numerous weak parties consistently have trouble making decisions.

## FUNCTIONS OF PARTIES

The fundamental goal of political parties is to win elections, control the political system, and therefore push the party's agenda.

| | |
|---|---|
| Create Candidates & "Label" Leaders | Parties search for leaders, nominate them, fund elections, and support their viewpoints. |
| Influence Voters | Parties try to build coalitions of like-minded citizens. |
| Gather Funds | Parties raise hundreds of millions of dollars for their campaigns. The leaders create policies based on information they receive from their supporters. |
| Support Leaders | Visits, calls, mailings, and other forms of group awareness can attempt to guide the agenda. |
| Oppose | No party is in control of all levels of government all the time. Parties are the "loyal opposition," trying to force compromises. |
| Build for the Future | Parties must maintain loyal support by building policies that attract large groups for extended periods of time. Otherwise, influence would be fleeting and removed easily by later parties. |

# DOMINANCE OF TWO PARTIES

The Democratic and Republican parties have controlled the main political landscape in the United States since the 1860s. Their core supporters focus on basic interpretations of the Constitution, goals of government, and issues of personal beliefs. Third parties have occasionally gained pockets of protest support but have not been able to replace either major party or create a large national following. In part, this is because the Democrats and Republicans have been able to build coalitions that address the issues brought forth by growing minorities.

Another major feature of two-party dominance is the structure of national elections. Most states have rules allowing the established parties an automatic place on the ballot. New parties must raise large numbers of petition signatures to gain access, and even then, access is not maintained for future elections. The Electoral College system requires parties to win the plurality of a state vote to get any college votes, thus making that occurrence rare for third parties.

The costs of a national election now approach multiple hundreds of millions of dollars, thus limiting new parties chances. When newer parties are able to win local and state elections, the structure of legislative committees often limits their access to positions of power. Out of frustration, no doubt, some third-party leaders have gone on to join the major parties so as to attempt changes internally. In that position, they have had a greater chance of winning some sort of national support.

One of the true strengths of the major parties is their ability to adapt, absorb, and expand. When the Republican Party was created, for instance, it was seen as radical and progressive. Democratic support of states' rights and local freedoms had become the mainstream. But with industrialization and Republican control of politics for most of the late 19th century, republicanism became the mainstream. Both parties seemed "conservative" when confronted with the Populist and Progressive agendas. Yet the parties soon changed to meet the needs of the citizens.

## CHANGES IN PARTY GOALS

> After the administration of Theodore Roosevelt, Republicans focused on business people, reaching out to a nation exploding with wealth and industry. Democrats turned to the farmers and workers, standing in opposition until the Great Depression ripped apart business leadership.

The Civil Rights Movement fit immediately with the New Deal goals, making Democrats the modern liberals who tended to side with unions, minorities, and other social liberals. The threats of communism, the unprecedented explosion of wealth in the late 1900s, and the growing religious conservatism in the Southern states were absorbed by Republicans.

The parties had, in fact, traded liberal and conservative positions from the prior century, something neatly reflected by national election patterns. In the 1800s, Republicans could count on the northeastern and West Coast states, while Democrats had the support of the South and rural areas. Today, both positions have flipped completely. Within the philosophical framework of the Constitution, Republicans are now more focused on states' rights, and the Democrats more on the national level.

## SIGNIFICANT PARTY CHANGES

Outside of the two dominant labels, party support is a much-debated point in political science. Voter loyalty has suffered for several reasons:

- The demise of powerful party machines in cities
- Smaller families
- The rapid movement of populations
- Decreasing reliance on public services in cities

Parties still hold certain key powers (finding candidates, pushing issues, and gathering funds), yet voter independence grew significantly in the late 20th century. Fewer ballots than before were cast for each major party. Republicans lost support in many urban zones and in the rapidly growing West. Democrats lost the farmers and the South. Millions would occasionally vote for protest candidates such as Strom Thurmond, George Wallace, and Ross Perot. In each case, however, the parties adjusted and drew back voters. Democrats took over almost all urban votes and the West Coast, while Republicans found new strength in the South. Voters today continue to show signs of loyalty by flooding the parties with campaign donations.

Future party alignments will probably hinge on continuing immigration. Hispanic American voters continue to grow in number, especially in the key electoral states of California, Texas, Florida, and New York. Will immigrants' traditional alignment with Democrat support for civil rights be broken up by religious concerns over abortion rights? Will the eventual rise of Hispanic workers into higher wage jobs create a more conservative business orientation? Can Democrats become the majority by forming stronger coalitions of minority groups and liberal European Americans? Will the Republican Party continue to benefit from strong support in the fast-growing states?

## BRIEF HISTORY OF THE DEMOCRATIC PARTY

Democrats claim a heritage stemming from the Jeffersonian coalition of the early 1800s. This coalition overwhelmed Federalists and dominated the country for decades. When regional interest split the Democratic-Republican majority in the late 1820s, westerners emerged as Democrats under the dynamic leadership of Andrew Jackson. The donkey symbol, in use since the mid-1800s, was originally a cartoon insult for a stubborn set of leaders, but it soon became a source of pride.

### DEMOCRATIC PARTY

| Era | Issues/Beliefs/Support Areas |
| --- | --- |
| Jacksonian Era 1830–1860 | Individual freedoms, frontier independence/states' rights, and agricultural interests were the basis of Democratic coalitions. Support was mostly in the South and West (frontier areas). This gave Democrats an advantage, because the population was growing rapidly in these regions. There was also mistrust of wealthy elites in the coastal business areas, where class distinctions seemed counter to the new spirit of democracy. |
| Post–Civil War 1870–1900 | When Federal troops left the South in the late 1870s, Democratic policies returned to states' rights and rural issues. Segregation gave power to whites and their socially conservative views. Some "liberal" support in the Northeast (e.g., Grover Cleveland) did exist, especially in urban centers where political machines manipulated numerous ethnic voting blocks. |
| Progressive Era 1900–1920 | States' rights remained powerful in the South, while support for populist and worker interests were growing in the North (e.g., William J. Bryan). Democrats built on this progressive/Southern agricultural combination to win the elections of 1912 and 1916. |
| Great Depression 1930–1945 | New Deal coalitions and economic liberalism flourished. Growing support came from Northern African Americans, Northeastern liberals, and Southern farmers (e.g., for FDR). The public programs of World War II solidified the economic changes, and their Democratic supporters flourished with large majorities. |

| Civil Rights Era 1945–1970 | Civil rights liberalism, Great Society programs, antiwar sentiments, and the Women's Movement were dominant forces for the party. Southern conservatives became frustrated and protested with separate candidates in elections. Informally called "Dixiecrats," these voters would still vote Democratic in other elections for decades (e.g., for Strom Thurmond in 1948 and George Wallace in 1968). |
| 1970 on | Growing issues of the environment, more civil liberty issues, more women's issues, and opposition to the rise of Reagan conservatism defined recent Democratic groups. Support in the Northeast and the West Coast has focused on minority groups, unions, and environmentalists. However, African-American groups are often in political conflict with Hispanic and Jewish groups. Unions are in decline and are often led by more conservative "blue collar" workers. |

The following are modern support groups for the Democratic Party:

- The New Deal coalition:
  - African Americans and their support for civil rights issues
  - Union "blue-collar" workers and labor progressives
  - Upper-class progressives or "reform" Democrats (e.g., Woodrow Wilson, FDR, and JFK)
  - Dixiecrats/Southern farmers (joined the Republicans after 1980, leading to realignment)
- The "New Left": Environmental issues, antiwar, and anti–big business
- Feminist movement: Social issues are central.
- Hispanic Americans: Generally pro-Democrat on civil rights issues, but that is changing, based on conservative religious and family issues.

As of the early 2000s, major areas of support for Democrats were urban areas, the Northeast, and the West Coast. The following news outlets and personalities are largely identified as Democratic leaning: *Washington Post*, *The Nation*, *New Republic*, CNN, and Air America Radio.

## BRIEF HISTORY OF THE REPUBLICAN PARTY

In the 1850s, Republicans were centrist and liberal reformers who emerged from the collapse of the Whigs and moderate Democrats. Party dominance can be classified in three major eras: the Gilded Age, the Roaring 20s, and post-1980.

The label *Grand Old Party* (*GOP*) was originally a reference to traditional values and English references to stability, but it was a label that stuck. And while the elephant symbol was originally a satirical reference to a large, uncontrollable, and rampaging beast, it too became a tradition and has been a symbol of the party since the late 1800s.

# REPUBLICAN PARTY

| Era | Issues/Beliefs/Support Areas |
|---|---|
| Lincoln Era 1854–1876 | National leadership, emancipation, unionism, and reconstruction dominated the agenda. Support in the industrial North and the West Coast was sufficient for many election victories because the South was still in political chaos. |
| Gilded Age 1876–1900 | Growing interest in expanding capitalism and support of the gold standard and "safe" money were dominant points of interest. Support in the North and West was massive, especially with rapid business expansion and exploding amounts of wealth available to leaders of industry. |
| T. Roosevelt Era 1901–1912 | Corrections for trusts and monopolies, along with the adoption of many progressive ideas, were goals of Roosevelt. Wide support outside the South was won due to Roosevelt's personal appeal, actions of international powers, and historically high levels of national patriotism. |
| Business Era 1912–1932 | Pro-business forces removed T. Roosevelt's influence after 1912. Industry and wealth development became core issues in the face of isolationist reaction to World War I and growing concerns with communism. Strengths lay in the heavily populated Northeast. Leadership under Warren G. Harding and Calvin Coolidge flourished, with calls for less governmental interference in the good times. |
| Anti–New Deal 1932–1945 | Hatred of FDR and his programs was the beginning of a more libertarian approach toward federal authority. Republicans distrusted the increasing federal powers, especially as a reaction against socialism and communism. |
| WW II, Cold War Era 1945–1980 | Patriotism and intense anticommunist programs helped raise support. Issues about states' rights surfaced, as did growing civil rights debates. The Southern strategy was used to capture electoral votes in traditionally Democratic areas (for Barry Goldwater in 1964 and Richard Nixon in 1968 and 1972). The process was dramatically increased with the landslide elections of Reagan in 1980 and 1984. |
| Reagan Era 1980 on | Economic libertarians joined with social conservatives. Core support areas became the South, farm regions, and mountain states. Business elites continued their support in key races. |

The following are modern support groups for the Republican Party:

- Neo-conservatives: Goldwater conservatives, Reagan conservatives, and pro-business interests

- East Coast upper-class (boardroom) conservatives: Wall Street and free trade interests

- Supply-side conservatives: Anti–big government, especially in economics

- Christian Coalition/Moral Majority conservatives: Reverend Pat Robertson, Ralph Reed
- Southern conservatives (Dixiecrats): Anti–New Deal programs, pro–states' rights
- Western Grange conservatives: Mountain states' conservatives (more libertarian)

As of the early 2000s, major areas of support for Republicans were the suburbs, Great Plains, Rocky Mountains, and the South.

The following news outlets and personalities are largely identified as Republican leaning: *Washington Times*, *National Review*, *Wall Street Journal*, Fox Network, Rush Limbaugh, and Michael Reagan.

## PARTIES IN DECLINE?

One of the original strongholds of the political party was the rapidly growing urban center. Political "machines" took advantage of immigrants to dole out jobs and support for voter loyalty. Often openly and proudly corrupt, these machines built large party coalitions for decades.

Today, the corruption has been reduced, voting privacy now protects the voters, and bosses have been eliminated. Some people believe that the formal parties are now in decline. Party loyalty is no longer critical for economic advancement, and easy movement across the country has fragmented loyalties, families, and connections. An increasing number of voters are claiming independence from parties. Polls show at least one-third of all voters today claim no strong ties to a party. Other pieces of evidence include low levels of voter turnout and the constant declarations by voters that they distrust parties and their leaders. The sudden popularity of candidates such as John Anderson, Ross Perot, and Ralph Nader is seen as evidence of a weak party structure.

There is, however, other evidence that parties are still strong and flourishing. If money is meaningful to citizens, then the vast sums given to parties indicate loyalty. Thousands of people readily give at every opportunity. Participation in meetings, demonstrations, message campaigns, and other party activities remains strong. Voter turnout among those who are registered is stable.

A possible myth may have been created about party decline after the dominance of relatively liberal policies between 1930 and 1980. With conservative options relatively weak in certain elections (e.g., 1964), voters may have felt little point in participating in the overall struggle. When distrust in government exploded after Vietnam and Watergate, more options were presented. When conservatives resurfaced in the 1980s and 1990s, more party involvement occurred. With the parties diverging more and more, party loyalty may be resurfacing.

## RECENT VOTING PATTERNS (ELECTIONS OF 2000 AND 2004)

| | |
|---|---|
| **Northeast states** | Democratic (union, blue-collar, Rust Belt) |
| **Southern states** | Republican (Sun Belt, Bible Belt) |
| **Midwest states** | Split |
| **Great Plains states** | Republican |
| **Mountain states** | Republican |
| **West Coast** | Democratic (California, Oregon, Washington) |
| **Men** | Republican, especially "NASCAR dads" of the South, farmers, and business leaders (white-collar) |
| **Women** | Democratic, except "soccer moms" who are not employed outside of the home |
| **European ancestry** | Republican |
| **African ancestry** | Democratic (overwhelmingly) |
| **Hispanic ancestry** | Hispanic church communities, especially Roman Catholic memberships, have been traditionally Democratic. George W. Bush won substantial support from Texas Hispanic voters while governor and won record numbers of such votes in the 2004 election. Republican "pro-life" and conservative family issues helped such trends. Recent GOP moves to restrict immigration may reverse such voting trends. |
| **Protestant** | In the North: Democratic<br>In the more "evangelical" South: very Republican |
| **Roman Catholic** | In the North: Democratic<br>In the more Hispanic churches of the South: growing Republican support |
| **Jewish** | Democratic |
| **Nonreligious** | Democratic |
| **Wealthy** | Republican |
| **Middle Class** | Slightly Republican |
| **Poor** | Democratic |
| **Urban Centers** | Democratic |
| **Suburbs** | Republican |
| **Rural** | Republican |

# REVIEW QUESTIONS

## MULTIPLE-CHOICE QUESTIONS

1. Which statement about parties in the United States is most correct?

    (A) Parties have been stable since they were founded.

    (B) Broad changes in party controls have often occurred.

    (C) Two parties have dominated consistently.

    (D) Parties have grown with the increasing powers of presidents.

    (E) Parties have stable patterns, supporting either liberal or conservative viewpoints.

2. How can the two-party dominance in much of U.S. history best be explained?

    (A) Parties were able to absorb new political goals.

    (B) Parties have controlled the Electoral College.

    (C) Major parties have vast sums of campaign funds.

    (D) Urban party "machines" blocked the formation of other parties.

    (E) Citizens had general distrust for parties as a whole.

3. The future balance of Democratic and Republican support will probably hinge on

    (A) continued conservative dominance in Southern areas.

    (B) continued loyalty of minorities to liberal causes.

    (C) a return of certain populations to urban centers in the North.

    (D) the ability of Democrats to access wealthy donors.

    (E) the possible switch of Hispanic voters due to social issues.

4. Progressives' demands for major changes in workers' rights affected

    (A) Republicans first.

    (B) Democrats first.

    (C) neither party.

    (D) voter loyalty to the major parties.

    (E) mostly the members of Congress.

5. Today, _____ would likely support most of the positions of Hamilton, and _____ would likely support most of the positions of Jefferson.

    (A) conservatives, liberals

    (B) Republicans, Democrats

    (C) Libertarians, Socialists

    (D) Socialists, Libertarians

    (E) Democrats, Republicans

## FREE-RESPONSE QUESTIONS

1. (A) Identify two key roles that political parties play in the politics of the United States.

   (B) Explain how the two roles you identified influence or control the agenda of the nation.


2. The Democratic and Republican parties are broad coalitions of major voting groups.

   (A) Identify three of the major subgroups of each party's coalition.

   (B) Explain how each of the party coalitions has a form of unity in beliefs.

   (C) Explain why each coalition has major points of difference in goals.

# ANSWERS AND EXPLANATIONS

## MULTIPLE-CHOICE ANSWERS

**1. B**

Especially in the early decades, several party groups came and went. Parties have changed what they support. In the early 1800s, one party alone dominated the political landscape, and Republicans mostly controlled the 1870s and 1880s. Parties have not changed much in power, primarily because of changes in presidential power.

**2. A**

The United States has been able to maintain a two-party dominance throughout its history because the parties adjusted to absorb new political goals. The other answer choices also contributed to some degree, but they are not as central in explaining why the two parties are so dominant.

**3. E**

Hispanics, the fastest-growing minority, will likely prove to affect future political balance. They helped to vote Republican George W. Bush into office in 2004, many Hispanics trended toward the Democrats in 2008.

**4. A**

Through the leadership of Teddy Roosevelt and his administration, Republicans were the first to respond nationally to the progressives' calls for reforms.

**5. E**

Today, Democrats would likely support Hamilton's positions, while Republicans would support those of Jefferson. The first three answer choices are backward: Hamilton supported stronger national controls, especially over economic policies. Jefferson wanted more individual controls, much like the modern Republicans.

## FREE-RESPONSE ANSWERS

1. **4-point Rubric**

   **2 points in part (A): (identify two key roles)**

   - Find candidates.

   - Influence the public.

   - Gather money.

   - Support those in office.

   - Provide for opposition to the majority.

   - Build political agendas.

   **2 points in (B): (explain)**

   - Parties look for qualified candidates who can get elected, and then they support and train the candidates.

   - Parties get the message of the party platform out to the public, provide information, run ads, etc.

   - Parties raise funds that can be used for ads, flyers, etc.

   - Parties can be message leaders, and can support other party members across the country.

   - Parties can band together as the "loyal" opposition to force compromises.

   - Parties canvas members for future issues and seek solutions to problems.

2. **10-point Rubric**

   **6 points in part (A): (three groups in each party identified)**

   - Democrats: African Americans, union members, liberal progressives, the "New Left," feminists, Hispanics

   - Republicans: Neo-conservatives, upper class, supply-side conservatives, Christian Coalition, Southern conservatives, westerners

   **2 points in part (B): (points of unity)**

   - Democrats: Economic guidance by government, civil rights for minorities, pro-environmental programs, pro-worker rights

   - Republicans: Economic privacy, state's rights, pro-business, less government

   **2 points in part (C): (points of difference)**

   - Democrats: Hispanics may be less loyal due to religious beliefs, splits over civil rights agendas, splits between unions and feminists

   - Republicans: Splits over religious beliefs, emphasis on business and taxes, North versus South

# CHAPTER 9: CAMPAIGNS AND ELECTIONS

## IF YOU ONLY LEARN SIX THINGS IN THIS CHAPTER . . . .

1. Elections in the United States are fairly frequent, time consuming, and expensive.

2. Over the years, the election trends have shifted from a strong Democratic presence to a Republican-dominated government.

3. The role of money in political campaigning has become a major point of controversy and has led to many attempts for stricter reforms and restrictions; however, few restrictions have been made or followed.

4. Public opinion is heightened during election times, and often it is the only time when the divisions of support expose themselves and shifts in affiliation may be seen.

5. Because the Electoral College is based on factors concerning population, larger states with more representatives can heavily affect the outcome of the election by simply having a slight advantage for one party over another, even if 49 percent of the state opposes that candidate.

6. Finance reform efforts have not had much success in the branches of government.

## INTRODUCTION

Elections in the United States are now noted for being numerous and open for universal participation. They are also expensive, especially at the statewide and national levels. They have become a game of the wealthy, the lobby groups, and major parties. Television and Internet media dominate the reporting, campaigning, and debating. Campaigns aim at controlling media presentations, spinning information to the benefit of their cause, and avoiding any negative images. Recent elections have returned to 19th-century patterns of personal attacks, innuendo, and rumor. This appears to be increasing as campaigning through independent groups that do not answer directly to party controls grows.

Individual voters are not to be forgotten. Besides voting, they play critical roles in grassroots fundraising, lobbying leaders, and campaigning. Even with strict controls over personal donations, both parties have gained huge amounts of money through efficient contacts with one voter at a time.

## THE ROLE OF MONEY

Money gathering has also had an effect on the length of campaigns. So many funds are needed for national exposure that candidates must start years in advance in order to gather the appropriate amounts. This is a critical feature of presidential elections, where funding efforts start at least two years prior to the November vote. A tangential issue is the dominance of incumbents and early front-runners. With so much money at stake, key lobby and party groups will hesitate before venturing support for an outsider, especially if another candidate has a lot of delegate support from early primaries.

## THE UNIQUE FEATURES OF THE ELECTORAL COLLEGE

The Electoral College also plays a role in the way campaigns are created. Because states with larger populations dominate the Electoral College system, campaign ads, funds, and speeches tend to be focused in these areas. Smaller states often get ignored. Another feature of the system comes into play when states tend to heavily favor one candidate. Why spend money and time there? Local leaders and their candidacies can suffer, and turnouts can drop.

# ELECTION PATTERNS

As mentioned in previous chapters, the two major parties have completely dominated national politics in the United States. They also tend to take turns dominating the political agenda for periods of time. Often, presidential elections are seen as focal points when parties create or lose dominance. Chapter 6 summarized how liberalism and conservatism have seen periods of control; the same occurred for the Democrats and Republicans, as reflected by "key" elections. The modern starting point is usually defined as the election of 1896. Traditions of traveling and campaigning, national media coverage, coordinated campaign staffs, and carefully managed candidates began with the contest between William McKinley and William Jennings Bryan. In 1912, there was a great Republican reaction to Progressivism, 1920 saw the rise of business and international neutrality, and in 1932 there was the reaction to the Great Depression. In each election, Democrats and Republicans traded places as the dominant party.

Civil rights issues began to dominate the election cycles after World War II. The beginning of the split of conservative Southerners from the old New Deal Coalition began with the candidacy of Strom Thurmond in 1948 and grew with the candidacy of George Wallace in 1968. Reagan's victory in 1980 was the complete reversal of the great liberal landslide in 1964. The election of Barack Obama in 2008 was a return to Democratic dominance after eight years of the Republican Bush administration The elections have signaled the creation of the various party coalitions that dominate the political spectrum today.

# THE ROLE OF MONEY AND REFORM ATTEMPTS

The influence of money in U.S. elections remains controversial. In a nation of 300 million people with voter turnouts of over 100 million, campaigning is expensive, and the costs continue to rise dramatically. Television advertisements are a main component of these costs, but radio, print media, and online media of a campaign. With a large percentage of voters claiming little loyalty to the parties, images are critical to attracting "swing" or independent votes each election.

The problem of money as a way of influencing politics is connected to a voter problem and a leader problem. If voters weren't as easily influenced by superficial images and emotional responses, then ads wouldn't be as effective. If voters were more critical in their analysis of the messages being presented, then attack ads and suggestive messages wouldn't as easily sway elections. There is also a fear that campaign contributions lead to policy changes, that those laws help only rich contributors, and that officials help only those who contribute. Even if it is not outright bribery, monetary assistance is still seen by many as an unfair, biased influence on the way the government operates. Efforts to control the flow of campaign contributions have increased for decades.

Efforts to make these contributions more public have led to the creation of political action committees (PACs). This plan simply increased the money involved, however because now PACs can legally build vast sums without hiding the details. Individual contributions are severely limited, but corporations and other powerful groups can "bundle" large numbers of such monies into one larger contribution. Internet communications have also allowed parties to reach millions of smaller contributors quickly and get money to many local races that never had such a level of national attention. Most recently, the greatest end run has been developed, that of "independent" groups creating vast ad campaigns that viciously attack "beyond" the control of a party or candidate.

At every turn, issues of large versus small, rich versus poor, and influential versus ignored arise. When reforms and limits are argued, a very powerful and logical counterattack is mounted: the issue of free speech. Is giving money in and of itself an evil thing? Does a restriction on being allowed to help a campaign restrict the right of political free speech? Recent Supreme Court rulings have sided with the idea that giving money is a form of speech; therefore, all proposed legal restrictions concerning campaign funds must bear that concept in mind.

# THE ROAD TO THE PRESIDENCY
## (FOR THE MAJOR PARTY CANDIDATES)

| | |
|---|---|
| At least 18 to 24 months before the election, possibly getting earlier now | Start fundraising. Build a "war chest" of available money. Contacts need to be made with lobby leaders, industry leaders, and party groups. During the primary season, thousands of dollars will be needed per day. |
| Around 12 months before the election | Declare one's candidacy and form a national campaign committee. Build a campaign staff. Rules of campaign finance must be followed. Travel is extensive to cover various early primary and caucus states. Image and debate training is conducted with the staff. |
| February of the election year | Give speeches and "stump" in the early primaries and caucuses. Try to energize the party loyalists of states like Iowa and New Hampshire. A poor showing can doom access to funding support, as donors will put their support behind candidates who "have a chance." |
| March | Conduct a national campaign in the numerous "Super Tuesday" states. Capture needed delegate votes to obtain the nomination of the party. Attend intraparty debates as scheduled. Raise money. |
| April–June | Complete the primary by campaigning in all corners of the country. |
| July–August | Settle the party platform and the VP nominee at the party convention. Work with party leaders to build a campaign platform. |
| Fall, especially after Labor Day | This is the traditional campaign season against the other major party's candidate. The candidate makes many scheduled speeches and appearances, then takes part in national debates with the opposing candidates. |
| First Tuesday after the first Monday in November of the election year (Election Day) | Receive the most electoral votes, based on state popular votes (currently 270 out of 538 are needed to win). |
| December | The Electoral College members cast their ballots. |
| January 3 | With the start of the new session of Congress, the president of the Senate formally counts the electoral ballots. |
| January 20 | The president is sworn into office. |

# PRESIDENTIAL ELECTIONS

## SIGNIFICANT CHANGES IN PRESIDENTIAL ELECTIONS

Party meetings, caucuses, and conventions once dominated the ways candidates were selected. "Smoke-filled rooms," where insiders maneuvered to support candidates to their liking or under their influence, were the norm. The late 20th century saw drastic changes in this system. Primaries that allow for the public to select local and national finalists for office now flourish. Large conventions no longer select the presidential nominees; the nominees are usually chosen months before the conventions, during the flurry of early state primaries that commit party delegates to the public's winners.

The changes have certainly opened the process to more participants but have also created problems of money and strategy. Many states hold primaries early in the year, forcing candidates to try to gather vast campaign funds well before the elections. Lesser-known, though possibly very qualified, candidates are often eliminated quickly because they do not have the funds to conduct national campaigns in key state primaries. National summer conventions are now little more than festivals at which the candidates and party leaders make speeches but where little is decided. Another subtle, but important, feature of this primary system is that Southern states traditionally hold many of the early primaries. Because they are also the rapidly growing sections of the country, their primary and electoral votes are very influential in the kind of candidate that can be nominated.

## KEY DIFFERENCES IN THE TWO MAJOR PARTS OF THE PRESIDENTIAL CAMPAIGN

To win the *nomination* means to capture the support of party regulars and loyalists. This often requires a more conservative (Republican) or liberal (Democratic) approach to issues and advertising. Issues and party platform stances are more critical. Special attention must be given to party groups that can make or break a campaign. Republicans must build a strong Southern base with issues like school prayer and family values. Democrats must gain enthusiastic support from unions.

To win the *general election*, the candidate must appeal to the interests of the general public. This might require the candidate to have a more centrist appeal without angering party loyalists. More emphasis is placed on personality and leadership. A powerful television image must be created. Quick quotes for brief impressions in the media ("sound bites") are valued. Polished answers to media questions and debate points are important in close races.

## MAJOR CRITICAL "REALIGNMENT"
## PRESIDENTIAL ELECTIONS SINCE 1896

| Year | Candidates | Issues/Events |
|---|---|---|
| 1896 | McKinley—R<br>Bryan—D | The first major national speech trips by a candidate occur (Bryan).<br>The first major use of campaign staff and managers occurs (McKinley).<br>Both parties begin to emerge in modern forms of pro-business Republican versus pro-worker Democratic. |
| 1912 | Wilson—D<br>T. Roosevelt—Progressive<br>William H. Taft—R | Republicans split and ultimately reject TR's progressive programs. |
| 1920 | Harding—R<br>James Cox—D | The modern emergence of the Republican party as pro-business is firmly established. |
| 1932 | Franklin Roosevelt—D<br>Herbert Hoover—R | The emergence of the New Deal Democratic agenda of liberalism will dominate politics for 50 years. |
| 1948 | Truman—D<br>Dewey—R<br>Thurmond—(States' Rights; Dixiecrat) | The first signal of the split from the Democratic Party by conservative Southerners occurs with Strom Thurmond's protest candidacy against early civil rights issues. |
| 1960 | Kennedy—D<br>Nixon—R | Some Southern electors refuse to vote for Kennedy. TV campaign coverage becomes central, as debates take the center stage. The extremely close loss will haunt Nixon and influence his tactics in later campaigns. |
| 1964 | Johnson—D<br>Goldwater—R | Republicans select one of the most conservative candidates to date. The election is a landslide and ultimately the high watermark of civil rights liberalism. Goldwater becomes a hero to conservatives and influences later campaigners (such as Ronald Reagan). |
| 1968 | Nixon—R<br>Humphrey—D<br>Wallace—American | Vietnam War issues disrupt the campaign. Wallace's candidacy further splits Southern Democrats from the party. |
| 1980 | Reagan—R<br>Carter—D | The revenge of 1964 becomes the emergence of modern conservatism. This will dominate the political agenda and begin the massive shifts of Southern whites to the Republican Party. |
| 2000 | Bush—R<br>Gore—D | The Electoral College mess also signals control of the South and Plains regions by Republicans and rising support from the rapidly growing Hispanic population. |

| 2008 | Obama—D<br>McCain—R | After eight years of the Bush administration, this election not only puts a Democrat, but also puts the first African American in the White House. |

# THE ELECTORAL COLLEGE

The Electoral College was created to avoid the masses selecting "demigods" and to act as a filter against mob rule. It was one of the final decisions of the Constitutional Convention, and little guidance was given as to who should serve in the important role. The Constitution forbids elected officials from serving during election years. Today, state party groups usually select well-known and loyal workers. Each state receives the number of electoral votes equal in number to its Senators and Representatives, for a national total of 538. (There are 435 representatives and 100 Senators; per the 23rd Amendment, there must be 3 for Washington DC—the same number as the least populated state.)

To win the election, a candidate needs 270 electoral votes. The largest state, California, had 55 electoral votes in 2004 and 2008. The smallest states (like Wyoming, for example) have 3 electoral votes. California has more electoral votes than many of the lesser populated states combined. It is possible for a candidate to carry the national electoral majority with the votes of only 10 states.

The votes are "reapportioned" after each census (this will be done next in 2010, for the 2012 election). States that grow faster than other states take electors from slower growing states. New York used to be the largest electoral state but now stands third behind California and Texas.

## THE PROCESS OF THE ELECTORAL COLLEGE

> States select electors; this is now usually done by state parties at state conventions. The Constitution states, "no Senator or Representative, or Person holding an Office of Trust or Profit under the United States, shall be appointed an Elector."

The popular vote winner (plurality) in each state gets all of the electoral votes from that party of that state (except for possible vote splits in Maine and Nebraska). "Plurality" means finishing first, without needing a majority of the popular votes. Electors are expected to vote for the popular winner, are bound by tradition to do so, and in some cases are required to do so by state law. However, electors are not bound by the Constitution to follow the state popular vote results. The Constitution protects such votes and would probably override any state laws to the contrary. Many electors have ignored their state mandates in the past, but none have ever caused a candidate to lose.

Electors meet in December, usually at the state capitol, and write their choices on ballots. Each ballot is sealed and sent to Congress, where the president of the Senate (the vice president) will open and count the ballots in January. The media does ask electors how they voted in December, and they usually answer.

If the Electoral College does not have a majority winner, the vote reverts to Congress. The Senate selects from the top two vice presidential candidates, and each senator gets one vote. The majority vote winner (51) can then be sworn in as vice president. This way, a fallback leader is set if needed. The House selects from the top three presidential candidates, and each state gets one vote. (Washington, D.C., does not get a vote.) The winner is the candidate who receives 26 state votes. If no candidate gets 26 votes, the House keeps revoting until someone wins.

This event has almost occurred in close elections, such as in 2000. State congres-sional delegations may have a majority opposite of the public vote. Would the congressional party leaders vote for the opposition party candidate? This would have happened in George W. Bush's home state of Texas, where one of the more conservative electorates would have been contrasted with a slightly Democratic delegation in the House.

## OBJECTIONS TO THE ELECTORAL COLLEGE SYSTEM

Many people object to the Electoral College system; it is not a system of direct, popular election, and many feel that this is needed for modern times. They reason is that voters are now informed enough and elections are honest enough to allow the people to control the votes.

The popular vote winner can lose the electoral vote. (This occurred in the presidential elections of 1824, 1876, 1888, and 2000.) This is seen by many as a miscarriage of the public's control, which is a fundamental principle of our government.

Highly populated states totally dominate the system, and less populated states are generally ignored by candidates and campaigns. States with large differences in party loyalties also cause votes for the less popular party to be meaningless, because the less popular party is unlikely to win that state's electoral votes.

## REASONS THE ELECTORAL COLLEGE SYSTEM REMAINS

There are many reasons that the Electoral College system remains, despite its problems. First, no new, better system that corrects regional votes has been proposed. Every plan offered so far has flaws that parallel the current problems.

Also, it is actually efficient and cheaper to ignore less populated areas. Making every vote equal in all parts of the nation would highlight every possible fraud or mistake. In addition, the costs of having to campaign equally across the country would raise national campaign costs beyond the already massive amounts that are now needed.

Furthermore, a change would have to come through a Constitutional amendment, and large states will not easily give up their dominance. What advantage would large states gain? They now control candidate and campaign priorities and have no incentive to go to a popular vote.

# CAMPAIGN FINANCE REFORM

National campaigns have entered the hundreds-of-millions-of-dollars range. There have been numerous debates about the need for such amounts of money, the sources of such funds, and the propriety of such collections. How fair is the system? Who controls the elections? What promises are made for contracts, jobs, votes, or influence when so much money is involved? How can the poor or middle classes compete? How much free speech is involved in the giving of money? Many of these issues came to the surface during the elections of the 1960s and 1970s, when television advertising became the central cost and feature of modern electioneering.

## MODERN CAMPAIGN FINANCE REFORM EFFORTS

| | |
|---|---|
| Hatch Act, 1939 | Federal employees and companies doing business under federal contracts were forbidden from contributing to elections. |
| Elections of 1968 and 1972, Watergate | Reactions to "slush funds," secret accounts, and money used for illegal activities gave rise to calls for federal reforms of money collections. |
| Federal Election Campaign Act, 1971, and amendments through 1979 | Controls were set on spending of funds, the Federal Election Commission (FEC) was created for oversight, disclosure rules were set, and monies for primaries were controlled. |
| *Buckley v. Valeo,* 1976 | In this Supreme Court challenge, the Court allowed Congress to control some contributions to candidates but protected other forms of funding to parties, etc. as forms of free speech. |
| McCain-Feingold-Cochran Reform Bill (Bipartisan Campaign Act, 2002) | Efforts were made by Congress to limit "soft money" contributions and the influence of PACs. |

# KEY TERMS OF CAMPAIGN FINANCE

| Term | Definition | Related Issues |
|---|---|---|
| Political Action Committees (PACs) | A group registered with the FEC and used to raise campaign funds is registered under this label. | This attempt at reform in the 1970s actually funneled more money into campaigns and raised more issues. Is the money for specific candidates or just "parties"? |
| 527s | IRS Section 527 allows nonprofit organizations to collect money and use it for political causes, such as TV ads. | Not regulated by the FEC, this loophole is not "connected" with campaigns; it therefore allows the creation of more vicious attack ads, such as those used in the election of 2004 (examples: Swift Boat Veterans or Moveon.org). |
| Hard Money | Money for specific candidates is regulated by FEC controls from individuals or PACs. | The per-election limit is $1,000 per individual for a candidate and $5,000 for PACs. |
| Soft Money | Money for parties for items such as "party building" or "voter registration efforts" is not supposed to go directly to candidate's campaigns (but there is some debate about whether it does). | How can we differentiate party issues and a specific candidate's stances? How can we limit such uses? |
| Matching Funds | Federal money is given to candidates to help level the financial playing field, based on hard money collected. | Candidates receive a dollar-for-dollar match for donations of less than $250, if at least $5,000 is gathered from at least 20 states. |
| Independent Expenditures or Independent Advertising | Money is spent by individuals or groups for their own ads. They might only suggest support for a party or candidate (or criticize a candidate) without being "part" of the party. | What is the fine line between campaign, candidate, and private spending on ads? What are the controls on attack ads? Who is responsible if the ads are misleading? |
| Candidate Spending | Money from personal wealth is often used by candidates on their own campaigns. | If a candidate accepts federal financial assistance, such as matching funds, then the limit of "candidate spending" is $50,000 of the candidate's personal wealth. |

| Bundling | Putting together "individual" contributions (hard money) into group checks is often done by companies using multiple employee contributions. | Is this legal? Do the employees know this is happening? |
| Federal Election Commission (FEC) | This six-member agency was created in 1974 to monitor election funds. | What are the powers of the Federal Election Commission? |

## SUMMARY OF CURRENT FINANCE ISSUES

The rights of individuals and groups to participate in elections are muddled by the issue of the giving of funds. The main questions revolve around the ways monies are collected, possible bribery of officials, the advantages of incumbents, the level of privacy or secrecy involved, the overall advantage of large corporations or the super-rich to sway elections, and free speech rights of candidates and parties. Are elections in the United States still fair? Should they be? Does the government have to make all campaigns equal in funds? Can the government restrict those who want to give large sums?

The controversies of campaign finance reform remain generally unresolved. Members of government who benefit the most from current advantages see little to gain by restricting the ways in which they can collect campaign funds.

## BASIC RIGHTS AND LIMITS TO CONTRIBUTIONS

**Individual contributors.** Contributions to candidates for specific elections are limited in amount and must be reported. Contributions to party organizations are completely unlimited.

**Political parties.** There are restrictions on how monies can be spent for national campaigns, when ads can occur, and whether or not they can mention federal candidates. Parties can spend unlimited amounts on "party-building" activities.

**Interest and lobby groups.** There are now limits on spending monies on ads that mention candidates or parties but few limits on "issues" that are key to the group.

**Political action committees.** PACs have limits on how much can be collected for campaigns of specific candidates and when the monies can be spent.

**527 groups.** They have discovered few limits on spending on ads that refer to the issues that candidates support or oppose or to the personal lives of candidates.

**Candidates.** There are limits on how much of a candidate's personal fortune can be used in campaigns, especially if those campaigns collect other matching federal funds.

## COMMENTS ON LOCAL AND CONGRESSIONAL ELECTIONS

Local politicians and members of the House of Representatives come up for re-election frequently. Some local races may be annual events. House members stand for votes every other year. This has created the "constant campaign." The positive side to this is that leaders must listen to their constituents, because corrections can be quickly made by the ballot. As a negative, the reliance on campaign fundraising takes a large portion of the leaders' time and energy. Incumbents in the House usually have tremendous advantages by being able to keep in constant contact with important donors and committees.

Donors are reluctant to support challengers because a loss will cost them influence. Challengers have less time to plan and campaign inside the two-year cycle. With these pressures, House incumbents spend much more time making sure their constituents are being helped and "correctly" represented by their votes. They have fewer opportunities to be independent for any length of time. Senate races, especially in larger states, resemble presidential races in terms of need for money and organizations. The Internet has also changed campaigns in both areas. The Internet enables candidates to send more information to a national audience; this way, both parties can focus on key seats and key states. The practice of funding campaigns from out of state has increased dramatically in recent years.

# REVIEW QUESTIONS

## MULTIPLE-CHOICE QUESTIONS

1. A major difference between elections of presidents and members of Congress is that

    (A) more voters cast ballots in presidential years.

    (B) congressional races are less competitive.

    (C) presidential races are easier to fund.

    (D) presidents must be more partisan.

    (E) congressional candidates must be more partisan.

2. A recent trend in presidential campaigns has been

    (A) an increase in personal attacks on candidates.

    (B) a push from party leaders to return to more state caucuses.

    (C) successful limits being imposed on the raising of funds.

    (D) the rise of successful third-party candidates.

    (E) the critical role of television debates.

3. Campaign finance reform efforts have been minimal because

    (A) political action committees have actually increased contributions.

    (B) the issue of free speech has limited restrictions.

    (C) lobby and interest groups seem to find ways around controls.

    (D) those that win under current systems see little reason to change.

    (E) All of the above

4. National party conventions are now primarily used

    (A) to give party speeches in front of television audiences.

    (B) to reward the party faithful with jobs.

    (C) to set the campaign agenda.

    (D) to support the nominee.

    (E) All of the above

5. A major dilemma of trying to get elected as president is

    (A) pleasing party loyalists enough without alienating the majority of the public.

    (B) trying to raise funds in all states.

    (C) having to raise funds after the nomination.

    (D) having to face the television debates.

    (E) having the right campaign staff that knows all the campaign strategies and tricks.

## FREE-RESPONSE QUESTIONS

1. Most efforts at restricting campaign contributions have generally failed.

   (A) Identify the difference between "hard money" contributions and "soft money" contributions.

   (B) Identify two reasons efforts at restricting contributions have failed.

   (C) Explain at least one reason some insist that campaign-funding restrictions should fail.

2. The Electoral College is clumsy and misunderstood, and it is an anachronism.

   (A) Explain two reasons the Electoral College is still in place.

   (B) Explain two reasons the Electoral College is opposed.

# ANSWERS AND EXPLANATIONS

## MULTIPLE-CHOICE ANSWERS

**1.  E**

A major difference between elections of presidents and members of Congress is that congressional candidates must be more partisan. Congressional candidates answer to smaller constituencies that are more likely to be partisan. Choice (A) is incorrect because though true, it is not a difference between the two types of elections. Choice (B) is incorrect because congressional races are very competitive at times. Choice (C) is incorrect because national races are harder to fund. Choice (D) is incorrect because presidents must be less partisan in order to reach broader electorate.

**2.  A**

An increase in personal attacks on candidates has been a recent trend in presidential campaigns. This is a return to earlier patterns and seems to reflect the growing splits between liberals and conservatives. Choices (B), (C), and (D) are false statements. Choice (E) is incorrect because many contend that debates do not really affect voters much.

**3.  E**

Campaign finance reform efforts have been mini-mal for all of the reasons listed: political action committees have increased contributions, the issue of free speech has limited restrictions, lobby and interest groups seem to find ways around controls, and those that benefit from the current campaign contribution system have little incentive to change it.

**4.  A**

National party conventions are now primarily used to give party speeches in front of television audiences. Though conventions have dwindling numbers of viewers, those with strong interest in the party still watch them. Choice (B) is a false statement. The agenda is usually set by the candidates' campaign staffs well before the convention. The nominee already has the majority support of the delegates and party.

**5.  A**

Pleasing party loyalists enough without alienating the majority of the public is a major dilemma when trying to get elected as president. Choice (B) is incorrect because candidates don't need all states to win; they only need key electoral states. Choice (C) is incorrect because candidates must raise the most funds early in the process (before they've received the nomination) in order to remain viable. Choice (D) and choice (E) are challenges that candidates must face, but they are not dilemmas.

## FREE-RESPONSE ANSWERS

1. **4-point Rubric**

   **1 point in part (A): (hard contributions versus soft contributions)**

   - Hard money contributions are regulated contributions given directly to candidates for their campaigns; soft money contributions are less-regulated monies given to parties for activities such as "party building."

   **2 points in part (B): (two reasons restrictions have failed)**

   - Too many loopholes
   - Party building can be pro or con toward a candidate
   - No limits on contributions not controlled by parties
   - Little incentive to change for those in office and benefiting from current rules

   **1 point in part (C): (one reason restrictions should fail)**

   - People should be able to spend their money.
   - Restrictions penalize the wealthy.
   - Free speech would be limited.

2. **4-point Rubric**

   **2 points in part (A): (two reasons the system remains)**

   - Large states benefit.
   - Reduces costs of campaigning everywhere.
   - Cuts potential of vote fraud in every precinct.
   - Creates greater majority than popular votes.
   - No replacement system is a real improvement.

   **2 points in part (B): (two reasons to oppose)**

   - Too biased toward large states
   - Too biased toward states dominated by one party
   - Biased against small parties
   - Blocks the public's votes

# CHAPTER 10: INTEREST GROUPS, LOBBIES, AND POLITICAL ACTION COMMITTEES

## IF YOU ONLY LEARN FOUR THINGS IN THIS CHAPTER . . . .

1. Lobbyists and special interest groups are often seen in a negative light because of the favor-for-favor manipulation that is a suspected practice. However, lobby forces have access to the decision makers and serve an important function in the relationship between the public and government.

2. Interest groups are concerned with a wide range of topics and show support for both Republican and Democratic issues, as well as independent issues.

3. Interest groups have the ability to be up close and personal with their representatives, and they have many ways of finding that access.

4. Lobby leaders are key players in the development of policies and funding campaigns.

## INTRODUCTION

James Madison and other U.S. founders had negative views of groups trying to influence policy or votes of the leaders of government. Madison referred to "factions" in the *Federalist Papers* and hoped that the federal system would protect the government from excessive influence by such groups. He was particularly afraid that elites would gain regional control of states, blocking access to government by deserving minorities. Within the new Constitutional system, protections from the central government would guarantee that no local force would shut out the freedoms provided by the republic. This key argument for the new system helped explain the need for layers of authority. It was also understood that citizens needed to be able to connect with those of similar goals, petition the various leaders, and have a voice in decision making.

## CURRENT VIEWS

Today, the public perception of interest groups continues to be relatively negative due to excessive sums spent by groups to influence elections. However, interest groups run the spectrum of political beliefs and are essentially the best avenue for all citizens to make their voices heard by the government. Interest groups such as corporations often hire professional representatives to lobby for their interests in the national and state capitols.

The flourishing of so many interest groups has become an issue. Thousands of voices compete to be heard, but no one leader has time to hear them all. Conflicts revolve around which interest groups have enough money or connections to bend the ears of key leaders. How do they hold on to such power? Is the ability to donate vast sums of money the decisive factor between groups that influence leaders and those that are ignored?

# FUNCTIONS OF INTEREST GROUPS

Interest groups exist to sway the political leadership in order to have their issues heard, changed, or put into law. Interest groups use professional lobbyists to represent their causes.

Interest groups allow citizens to network, fight for common goals, influence government, or help members. Some groups are religious in nature and want to extend the influence of religion in society and politics (the Christian Coalition). Other groups further the causes of minority citizens (the NAACP and the League of United Latin American Citizens [LULAC]). Famous organizations such as Common Cause argue for governmental accountability, and the Sierra Club furthers environmental issues.

The most powerful way interest groups try to communicate with the government is through professional influence peddlers known as *lobbyists*. Lobbyists prepare memos for Congress, meet and debate, give evidence at hearings, petition, raise campaign funds, and even draft potential legislation. Lobbies are notorious for hiring recently retired members of Congress and then using their inside experience to outmaneuver other groups. Suggestions of impropriety caused Congress to create rules requiring a waiting period before former members could begin such private consulting. Even stricter rules apply to former members of the executive branch who want to be hired for fantastic salaries to lobby their former agencies.

Because some major lobbies have vast resources, their influence over campaigns and parties remains controversial. Current examples include Republican connections to energy company lobbies and Democratic connections to union lobbies.

In addition to private organizations, local and state governments also engage in lobbying. Most states, cities, mayor associations, and governor coalitions are represented in the state and federal capitals. Foreign companies and nations also use powerful lobbyists and their money to try to influence trade pacts, military assistance, and foreign aid.

The proliferation of interest group activity also reflects a positive aspect of the American system of government. With over 4,600 political action committees registered, all kinds of groups and opinions have open access to public officials. Any group, mainstream or radical, has an opportunity to register, gather supporters and funds, and contact leaders.

## TYPES OF INTEREST GROUPS

| | |
|---|---|
| Material Goals Groups | These organizations form in order to serve the needs of the members. The group is seen as a vehicle for personal advancement, connections, and benefits. |
| Issue Groups (Purposive Groups) | When a specific political cause is seen as large scale, relatively permanent, or critical, large numbers of people may join together to help create changes or solutions. |
| Ideological Groups (Solidarity Groups) | Ideological groups are organizations comprised of voters of a given political persuasion, whether conservative, liberal, or more radical, to push that group's overall agenda. |
| Public Interest Groups | Some organizations exist to provide services to the needy. They may target children, the elderly, consumers, the poor, or others. |

## FAMOUS INTEREST GROUPS (ALSO REGISTERED AS LOBBIES)

To build their membership numbers and have more connections to governmental agencies, almost all civic and interest organizations have registered as lobbies. Most also have created political action committees properly to donate to campaigns. These groups mobilize active voters, conduct letter-writing campaigns, canvass cities, and gather substantial campaign funds. Their lobby leaders have large professional staffs that influence legislation, draft legislation, and constantly work with members of Congress and the president.

## LOBBY GROUPS

| | |
|---|---|
| American Association of Retired Persons (AARP) | The very powerful lobby force of citizens over age 55 has tremendous clout on issues such as Social Security and prescription drugs. Seniors vote in vast numbers. |
| American Bar Association (ABA) | This large and well-funded group represents the legal community. |
| American Civil Liberties Union (ACLU) | This group of legal experts focuses on court issues that might change civil rights and civil liberties. The ACLU has been criticized as being extremely liberal or libertarian in some instances, but its volunteers devote much time and money to defending those in need. |

*(continued on next page)*

## LOBBY GROUPS (CON'T.)

| | |
|---|---|
| Amnesty International | This worldwide organization focuses on human rights issues and political rights abuses. |
| Chamber of Commerce | Chamber of Commerce represents communities all across the nation, and the central lobby often represents builders, local industries, and local leaders. |
| Common Cause | This social justice support group lobbies for many liberal causes and "open, accountable" government. |
| American-Israel Public Affairs Committee | Support for Jewish communities, Israel, and minority rights are a focus. |
| American Federation of Labor-Congress of Industrial Organizations (AFL-CIO) | For decades, this group has headed the labor movement in the United States and has lobbied for worker rights. |
| Eagle Forum | This conservative group supports family values issues and laissez-faire economic policies. |
| Earth First! | This radical environmental group has been the source of controversial, violent protests, especially from splinter groups. |
| Heritage Foundation | This very conservative group started as a research center for policy and now lobbies Congress in favor of diminished bureaucracy and less government involvement in people's lives. |
| League of United Latin American Citizens (LULAC) | A group that defends the rights of Hispanic citizens, its influence is rising with the increase in the Hispanic population in the United States. |
| Mothers Against Drunk Driving (MADD) | This rapidly growing organization quickly forced major changes in many state laws concerning the penalties for driving under the influence of alcohol. |
| The National Association for the Advancement of Colored People (NAACP) | For over 100 years, this organization has been a great voice on behalf of African Americans in civil rights issues, lawsuits, and debates. |
| National Rifle Association (NRA) | Focusing on 2nd Amendment rights, this rich and powerful lobby has conservative and anti–big government roots. |
| National Right to Life Committee | This issue-oriented group seeks to make abortion illegal. |

| National Organization for Women (NOW) | Central in the failed attempt to pass the Equal Rights Amendment in the 1970s, NOW continues to support women's rights and generally takes liberal positions, such as supporting legal abortion. |
| People for the Ethical Treatment of Animals (PETA) | PETA tends to be against big business because of its use of animal testing for many products. |
| Promise Keepers | Formed in 1990, this group represents many evangelical Christians and their more conservative views. |
| Sierra Club | This long-standing environmental group focuses on conservation of wildlife, cleanliness of air and water, and the use of land in the United States. |

# LOBBY GROUP BASICS

Almost all of the major interest groups, and thousands of others, have offices in Washington, D.C., and other governmental centers. They employ professional lobbyists who spend time working with members of Congress and their staffs. The lobbyists' goal is to create legislation that helps the interests of the members of the group in question.

## LOBBYIST ACTIVITIES

| Testify | Lobbyists attend committee hearings and bring their biases and points of expertise. They have important things to say about the possible impact of bills, especially for or against the goals of their group. |
| Meet | Personal contacts are critical ways to make political arguments. Controversial versions of such meetings are *paid junkets,* where lobby organizations pay for trips and vacations for members of government. Open bias and bribery are issues. |
| Research | Lobbyists and their staffs have time and resources to gather data that can sway members of Congress when bills that the lobby supports or opposes come to a vote. |
| Lead | Lobbyists can sway the masses within the organization to call and write to the members of government. |
| Fund | Possibly the most powerful action is the raising and contributing of campaign funds. |
| Litigate | Lobby leaders can turn to the courts to attack acts, rules, and regulations that they feel are unfair to their group. |

## POLITICAL ACTION COMMITTEES (PACS)

When interest groups want to go the extra step and support specific candidates or parties, they may do so through PACs. The committees register with the Federal Election Commission and then may give financial support to candidates.

PACs may give money directly to candidates' campaigns. This is called *hard money* and is closely regulated by the Federal Election Commission. Even with these rules, millions of dollars are given in this manner.

PACs also give money to parties. This is called *soft money.* Limits to soft money donations and expenditures are a subject of constant debate.

Committees can use their money to create ads or messages for "issues," without specifically supporting a particular candidate. These kinds of expenditures are unregulated, even when it is clear that a particular candidate is being supported. (Additional details of spending rules are covered in Chapter 9.)

# REVIEW QUESTIONS

## MULTIPLE-CHOICE QUESTIONS

1. There are thousands of interest groups in the United States because

   (A) the political system is stable.

   (B) many believe they have a right to have access to leaders.

   (C) the political system is equally open to all.

   (D) the political system is rapidly changed by public input.

   (E) the parties are unable to control the political agenda.

2. Most interest groups

   (A) help the members with benefits.

   (B) support both parties.

   (C) bring out large numbers of voters.

   (D) support only one party.

   (E) hire lobbyists to work for them.

3. The political power of interest groups lies in

   (A) bringing money to campaigns.

   (B) lobbying leaders and persuading them.

   (C) gathering many members to contact the leaders.

   (D) picking key issues to protect or change.

   (E) All of the above

4. The most powerful interest groups tend to be

   (A) representatives of major industries.

   (B) representatives of issues, groups, or causes.

   (C) representatives of minorities.

   (D) only concerned with conservative issues.

   (E) the most professional.

5. Madison and other early leaders feared that "factions" would

   (A) split the country into party groups.

   (B) stop the ratification of the Constitution.

   (C) take control of regions and block minority groups.

   (D) have too much influence on national leaders.

   (E) All of the above

## FREE-RESPONSE QUESTIONS

1.  Interest and lobby groups have increased dramatically in number and influence.

    (A)  Explain two reasons for the increase in interest groups and lobby organizations.

    (B)  Explain two reasons why lobby groups have a negative image in historic and public views.

2.  Lobby leaders and lobby professionals wield many forms of power in Washington, D.C.

    (A)  Identify three ways lobby leaders wield power with Congress.

    (B)  Explain why these forms of power are effective.

# ANSWERS AND EXPLANATIONS

## MULTIPLE-CHOICE ANSWERS

**1. B**

There are thousands of interest groups in the United States because many believe they have a right to have access to leaders. Even though the access may be limited and controlled by the richest lobby groups, most believe in trying to have influence.

**2. E**

Most interest groups hire lobbyists to work for them. Some groups do some or all of the other items, but most groups do not.

**3. E**

The political power of interest groups lies in bringing money to campaigns, lobbying leaders and persuading them, gathering many members to contact the leaders, and picking key issues to protect or change. All are key ways the groups wield influence.

**4. B**

The most powerful interest groups tend to be representatives of issues, groups, or causes. Groups represent many different kinds of memberships.

**5. C**

Madison and other early leaders feared that "factions" would take control of regions and block minority groups from having any political power. Madison correctly worried that the regions and states would need a central government that could protect minorities of all kinds.

## FREE-RESPONSE ANSWERS

1. **4-point Rubric**

   **2 points in part (A): (why an increase in lobby groups)**

   - Is now legal to give campaign money.

   - Is also legal and encouraged to register and to lobby.

   - More issues and single-issue groups exist.

   - More groups exist outside of two political parties.

   - There is a more diverse population to represent.

   **2 points in part (B): (why a negative image)**

   - Too locally dominant

   - Suppress minorities

   - Too divisive

   - Too controlling of a few leaders

   - Too powerful if wealthy

   - Too likely to bribe leaders

   - Too controlled by wealth and contributions

2. **6-point Rubric**

   **3 points in part (A): (three forms of influence)**

   - Testify.

   - Contact.

   - Research.

   - Lead the group.

   - Fund campaigns.

   - Go to court.

   **3 points in part (B): (explain why powerful)**

   - Access to committees in Washington at critical debate times

   - Great control and influence one-on-one

   - Expertise and staff resources that even Congress might not have

   - Representative of large groups with many followers and lots of money

   - Tremendous influence over who gets elected or how easy it might be

   - Funds and data to go to court and sue (deep pockets)

# CHAPTER 11: MEDIA AND ITS FUNCTIONS

## IF YOU ONLY LEARN SIX THINGS IN THIS CHAPTER . . . .

1. Media coverage has shown a tendency toward biased political reporting for different candidates and parties.

2. The role the government plays in what makes the agenda for many national news outlets is under suspicion and the fodder for much controversy and speculation.

3. The media supports the government, attacks the government, and is manipulated by government officials, but the level of free speech that journalists once knew is severely diminished.

4. Most media venues are owned by multimillion-dollar corporations that often are more concerned with the profit margin than delivering quality news.

5. It is not uncommon for members of political parties or candidates to use the media to further their own causes or get their ideas out there.

6. Changes in media accessibility with the growing involvement of the Internet as a major news source are rapidly changing how facts are presented and shared.

## THE HISTORY OF MEDIA

The media's effort to present political information is as old as U.S. politics. However, the idea that the media should be neutral and unbiased is as much a 20th-century concept as radio and television. Essays, leaflets, and books dominated colonial times and were often printed to sway the opinion of the general populace. The advent of daily papers aided in the distribution of news, but early newspapers would be considered quite sensational by today's standards. Radio and television allowed for instantaneous news broadcasts, allowing a person on the West Coast to see or hear a political speech on the East Coast as it happened. But the Internet truly transformed the way in which people received their news. Instead of choosing from two different newspapers, or from among the major news networks, people could select from a seemingly infinite pool of news websites, government reports, scientific journals, and individually run blogs.

Today, the media is as much a part of American life as the three branches of government, earning it the nickname "the fourth branch." This is not to be confused with the large bureaucracy, also called a "fourth branch" by some texts and references. Political parties, through selective use of the media, present their biases, advance their propaganda, and attack media groups they see as biased against them. Media leaders must juggle the needs for profit, competition with other sources, and the difficult task of staying impartial. Added to the mix are governmental regulations requiring certain kinds of "equal time" for party ads and statements.

During the first presidential campaigns, daily newspapers did not yet exist. Writers worked for party leaders, and the goal was to present an agenda and attack opponents, often viciously. What the supporters of John Adams and Thomas Jefferson said about each other was certainly not balanced or neutral; in fact, it was often openly slanderous.

These trends continued late into the 19th century, when the telegraph and transcontinental transportation allowed early media companies to expand nationally. Essays and pamphlets were replaced by newspapers and magazines. Newspapers such as *The New York World* and *The New York Journal* used scandalous headlines and salacious stories to attract readers. With growing newspaper circulation came growing influence. Publishers like William Randolph Hearst and Joseph Pulitzer used their newspapers as a platform to propagate biases and to prevent the spread of any opposing viewpoint. When illustrator Frederic Remington requested to return home from an apparently uneventful stay in Cuba during the Spanish-American war, Hearst famously responded, "You furnish the pictures, and I'll furnish the war."

Throughout the late 19th and early 20th centuries, newspapers and their editorial staffs overwhelmingly favored Republican candidates. The invention of radio and television created a vastly different perspective on news and the media that presented it. With their faces and voices on a national stage, journalists could become national stars themselves. Men and women such as Walter Cronkite, Edward R. Murrow, and Barbara Walters became household names, translating stardom into profit and influence.

By the 1960s, the media began to be seen as more liberal. This trend, rooted in the Great Depression, was originally fostered by the liberal New Deal policies of Franklin Delano Roosevelt. After World War II, use of the G.I. Bill elevated many returning veterans to middle-class status, giving the media millions of new customers. By the time of the Civil Rights Movement, with its emphasis on progressive governmental policies, the media took a more liberal approach, especially with television news. The capstone was the media's reaction to the Vietnam War, where the violence was brought into homes across the country. Nixon's presidency and the Watergate scandals helped cement the media's role as a watchdog of a government trying to hide information and policies from the public. Every president since Nixon has been the target of thorough investigations of both his public and private lives.

# GOALS OF THE MODERN MEDIA/CONCERNS ABOUT THE MEDIA

What is the continuing power of the media? Why are biases so controversial? Can journalists balance the needs of profit, corporate demands, and personal integrity? The primary medium through which news is broadcast has changed from the newspaper to the television. Newspaper articles, which can number several thousand words, rely on thorough reporting, descriptive language, and an abundance of quotes from primary sources to create a relevant story. Televised news does not need to delve as deeply into an issue. The old adage goes, "A picture is worth a thousand words." And in the case of televised news, it is correct. Famous images, such as Neil Armstrong's first steps on the moon or the lone Tiananmen Square protestor defying a column of tanks, don't need much of an explanation; the footage provides its own.

The change in format, from news articles to news broadcasts, drastically shortened the amount of time necessary to present a news story. People were no longer relegated to reading about an event after it happened. They could now see and hear an event live, often as it was happening. Unfortunately, as the daily news became more entertaining, many important stories on government policy, which did not benefit as greatly from live television, began to be considered boring and sometimes difficult to watch.

## INFLUENCE OF THE INTERNET

The Internet is the new frontier of media presentations. Traditional media, such as magazines, newspapers, radio, and television stations, have the advantage of huge archives, time-tested credibility, and adequate funding.

However, as people demand more content in less time, the popularity of Internet-based news organizations has grown. Finding news on the Internet can be summed up in the phrase "what you want, when you want it." Vast numbers of articles, public records, even video segments are available for immediate consumption. Another benefit of the Internet is the global reach of its content. While a newspaper only can be printed a finite number of times and distributed to a limited number of locations, an online version of that same newspaper can be viewed by people anywhere there's an Internet connection. Unfortunately, the power to disseminate information can also be harnessed to disseminate disinformation. Rumors can be generated in seconds, hoaxes abound, and opinion is often confused with news. The issue of accuracy among many of the more independent news sources is a growing concern. This is especially true of blogs. Established news organizations have editors and large staffs that can verify reports and confirm accusations. What level of truthfulness is available on the thousands of individual Internet outlets?

## THE MANIPULATED MEDIA

The media has also become a tool of the president and Congress. Playing to the camera has become almost as important as a candidate's actual platform. Speeches are carefully orchestrated to meet C-SPAN coverage times, whether or not anyone else is in the chamber. Press conferences are completely controlled by using teleprompters, limiting questions, and only allowing selected persons to ask questions. Both the House and Senate have media rooms where leaders and reporters can race back for immediate coverage.

## STAGES OF MEDIA IN THE UNITED STATES

| | |
|---|---|
| Late 1700s to the mid-1800s | Almost no daily newspapers existed. Instead news was distributed via pamphlets and essays (e.g., *Common Sense*, by Thomas Paine). Organized reporting was done for political reasons and was directly controlled by supporters of different party groups. The "media" was intended to be partisan. The *Federalist Papers* were created with a partisan agenda. Political attacks were personal and extremist. |
| Late 1800s | Newspapers became national businesses (for example, the Hearst Syndicate), and profits became the motive. Selling stories was central. News organizations took pride in influencing public opinion (*yellow journalism*) or policy (*muckraking*). Newspapers were also central progressive reforms. Stories about the powers of trusts such as Standard Oil were good business and created pressure for political changes. This was an early form of the press *agenda setting*. |
| Early 1900s | Teddy Roosevelt built the bully pulpit through newspapers and the developing "press corps." His administration took the first big steps in creating media events and press conferences. Getting inside information from the White House became a status symbol. The press came to rely on the president and was often openly supportive to continue getting information (the "lapdog" function). A reporter who was overly critical would be shut out from conferences and inside information. |
| Mid-1900s | The development of radio opened new forms of communication between the leaders and the public. FDR developed the "fireside chats" as a form of agenda setting. The presidential staff knew they could reach millions with personal messages. News became war propaganda. The first major use of news as war propaganda in the United States was in pro-British, anti-German messages during WWI. Press conferences grew as media outlets, again controlled by the executive branch. |
| Late 1900s | The development of television and the computer created instant information and polling of public support. The 1960 debates brought candidate image to the center of campaigning. Media events such as the Cuban Missile Crisis came to the forefront. |

| Vietnam and Watergate | The media took on the role of protest outlet and scandal investigation (the "watchdog" function). Growing public mistrust of government led to media focusing on government flaws and mistakes. The government's reaction was to try to choreograph carefully almost any contact between the press and leaders. Presidents would be set up to answer only questions within controlled settings. Clear teleprompters gave the impression that presidents were speaking off-the-cuff, and radio transmitters would allow for messages to be sent to the president's ear. Staff members would screen the leader whenever near media in public. |
| --- | --- |
| Post-Vietnam | The creation of the Internet and explosion of talk radio led to significant fame for "attack journalism" (the "junkyard dog" function). Fame is gained by those with the most outrageous attacks and stories (Clinton scandals), and conservative and liberal groups try to outdo each other in media attacks. Blogging becomes a key of Internet news. Satellite radio is a new arena of messages and attacks occur outside of censorship rules of public broadcasts. |

# MEDIA BIAS?

Conservative groups have long held that the American media is very biased toward liberal issues and candidates. This stems from coverage of Watergate and the Vietnam protests. The main targets of such criticisms have been television reporting and lobbying done by actors who are given significant attention by the media. Polls taken by conservative groups claim who the vast majority of reporters for television and newspapers regularly vote Democratic. Polls taken by moderate, or nonpartisan, groups show that the media is relatively neutral and personal voting habits do not significantly influence coverage.

Clearly some magazines tend toward different ends of the political spectrum, but the bulk of reporting attempts general neutrality. Though the mainstream media generally tries to avoid biased coverage, there are distinct pockets of support for conservatives and liberals, such as talk-radio programs, public access programs, etc. Famous periodicals such as *The Nation*, *National Review*, *The Weekly Standard*, and *The New Republic* exist to support certain biases. Nationally syndicated columnists such as George Will and Charles Krauthammer are famous for thoughtful defenses of political sides and issues. Uncensored programs on satellite radio help to perpetuate biases.

# EFFECTS OF MEDIA ROLES IN MODERN POLITICS

Political groups focus more on image, and they attempt to control the images.

- White House staff members shield the president from many questions and control when questions are asked, how they are asked, and who asks them. Presidents universally use hidden prompts, earphones, charts, etc. so they appear more prepared and in command.

- Campaigns and debates are now events that are completely crafted down to the finest detail. The public sees only what has been thoroughly planned by the campaign staff, nothing else.

- Staff groups who try to control every image and trend also orchestrate election debates. Only certain questions are allowed, and each campaign team spends days in practice.

- Special media rooms, created by congressional leaders, afford them instantaneous access to news programs.

- Debates and speeches are timed to take advantage of news hours or C-SPAN coverage times. C-SPAN has at least two channels in most cable or satellite outlets that do constant reporting of the activities of Congress.

- Press conferences are usually held only when issues can be introduced in a positive manner.

- Presidential staffs have created a constant campaign that presents the president in favorable places and at key events in order to keep popularity polls at their highest. It is as if the election campaign never stops.

## EFFECTS OF MEDIA AND TECHNOLOGY IN CAMPAIGNS

The national reach of news reports, combined with universal access to the Internet, has had a major effect on elections and leadership roles.

- Candidates now use websites for national attention and fundraising. Elections that used to be relatively local in scope can now target a much wider audience and collect money from across the globe.

- Attacks on parties and candidates have escalated dramatically through the use of the Internet, particularly through blog sites. Any and every group can disseminate propaganda to a vast audience, without much control of facts or biases. Rapid access to data and rumors gives many such groups the advantage of speed over traditional news groups.

## THE MEDIA AND THE SHRINKING ATTENTION SPAN

The dominance of television and video images has dramatically reduced the amount of time spent presenting issues and candidates. Instead of presenting an entire speech, news organizations will use only the most relevant snippets of sentences, a technique known as *sound bite* news. Since the 1960s, the time spent by the media reporting candidate's speeches has dropped from units of about a minute to bites under 10 seconds. Media presentations are about key words, quick impressions, and flashes of faces. As a result, campaign staffs focus their efforts on only allowing quick messages, memorable lines, or quotes. Much effort is also given to trying to find memorable mistakes by the other side, thus presenting a quick, but lasting, image of the other party. Being able to sum up an agenda in 10 words or less is key to pushing that agenda on the American people.

## THE MEDIA AND THE "SETTING OF THE AGENDA"

Media outlets look for events and issues that sell well or offer controversy. These items often become the "crisis of the day" that politicians must address, or at least appear to address. The selection of such events can show a bias toward parties and leaders, change the directions of policies, or enflame public anger. Recent examples include "millions of missing children," "the Ozone Hole," "the debt crisis," and others. These are put on the front of agendas for a time and then seem to disappear if the media decides the story is no longer key or profitable.

# REVIEW QUESTIONS

## MULTIPLE-CHOICE QUESTIONS

1. Which feature of the U.S. media is most historically correct?

   (A) Free speech for all is a media goal.
   (B) Access to all is a media goal.
   (C) Fairness is a media goal.
   (D) Party bias is often a media goal.
   (E) National information is a media goal.

2. Daily news reporting became a national phenomenon because of

   (A) the invention of radio.
   (B) the invention of television.
   (C) the invention of coast-to-coast telegraph systems.
   (D) the creation of national, for-profit news companies.
   (E) All of the above

3. Media "agenda setting" is criticized for all of the following reasons EXCEPT

   (A) it gives the power of setting the priorities of problems to media leaders.
   (B) it stops political leaders from setting the political agenda.
   (C) the media is biased in most areas.
   (D) the media spends too little time on key issues.
   (E) the media spends too much time on issues of little importance.

4. The most consistent trend in media coverage in the country has been

   (A) its generally neutral stand on most party issues.
   (B) its expansion of coverage of candidates' personal issues.
   (C) its reduction of story time and coverage.
   (D) its shift toward more constant coverage of politics.
   (E) its lack of coverage of the differences between party groups.

5. The best description of the general relationship between presidents and the media would be

   (A) mutual distrust.
   (B) mutual trust.
   (C) the media forces presidents to create political priorities.
   (D) presidents hate media scrutiny.
   (E) the two groups need each other and use each other for gain.

## FREE-RESPONSE QUESTIONS

1. The media has been described as a powerful force in influencing development of the political agenda of the government.

   (A) Identify three ways in which the president or Congress attempts to control media access and influence.

   (B) Explain two ways the media appears to achieve so much influence.


2. The impact of media coverage has varied and changed over the history of U.S. politics.

   (A) Describe any two of the periods of media coverage.

   (B) Describe a goal of the media in trying to affect/bias the political agenda.

# ANSWERS AND EXPLANATIONS

## MULTIPLE-CHOICE ANSWERS

### 1. D

Throughout the history of the media in the United States, party bias has often been a media goal. Media in the United States has always been business driven and was very party driven in colonial times and in the first days of the republic. Free speech, access to all, fairness, and national information are civic goals but have not always been those of the media and its owners.

### 2. E

The invention of radio, the invention of television, the invention of coast-to-coast telegraph systems, and the creation of national news companies have all helped make daily news reporting a national phenomenon.

### 3. B

It is not true that media "agenda setting" stops political leaders from setting the political agenda. Political leaders use the media in many ways to set their agendas. Choices (A), (C), (D), and (E) are all true criticisms of media "agenda setting."

### 4. C

The most consistent trend in media coverage in the United States has been the reduction of information into sound bites. Choice (A) is incorrect because media has often been very biased. Choice (B) is incorrect because media actually reduced personal coverage during the 20th century. Choices (D) and (E) are incorrect because media outlets have reduced coverage of politics and party differences; the media used to provide much more coverage of these things.

### 5. E

The best description of the general relationship between presidents and the media would be that the two groups need each other and use each other. Choices (A) and (B) are incorrect because the level of trust between the two groups varies; some media and political leaders work closely together, while others do not. Choice (C) is incorrect because the media does not force the president to create political priorities. Choice (D) is incorrect because, in many instances, the president and his staff control media access to events and often get many benefits out of key appearances.

## FREE-RESPONSE ANSWERS

1. **5-point Rubric**

   **3 points in part (A): (ways leaders attempt to control the media)**

   - Carefully managed press conferences
   - New leaks to select members of the media at key times
   - Timed interviews, reports, access via government-run studios
   - Campaign strategies and sound bites
   - Carefully controlled debates
   - Control of questions to be answered
   - Control of who gets to ask the questions
   - Party- and partisan-controlled Internet sites (blogs)

   **2 points in part (B): (media's influence)**

   - Selecting the stories to cover
   - Selecting the bias of the coverage
   - Controlling time given to stories
   - Setting the agenda through control of issues/biases
   - Controlling reports on the public's reactions/support

2. **3-point Rubric**

   **2 points in part (A): (periods of media coverage)**

   - Political pamphlets/essays that were for or against candidates
   - Regional biases (slavery crisis)
   - National corporate news to sell issues
   - Radio/television news "from" leaders or for issues
   - Internet reports from very biased and personal viewpoints

   **1 point in part (B): (goal of media in bias)**

   - Support specific candidates or parties because the media outlet agrees with them.
   - Make money by selling crisis stories.
   - Support political agendas, such as progressivism.
   - Gain fame and wealth by exposing scandals.
   - Earn money by finding an audience.

# CHAPTER 12: THE LEGISLATIVE BRANCH

## IF YOU ONLY LEARN SIX THINGS IN THIS CHAPTER . . . .

1. The Constitution was originally a document for the branch of Congress; thus, most of the laws written concern the actions of Congress.

2. Congress has created a complex process for handling the creation of laws, making it extremely difficult to pass new laws or amendments to current ones.

3. One of the biggest duties of Congress is the creation of the massive federal budget.

4. Party leaders are very central to the control of issues, bills, and budgets.

5. Federal laws have steadily expanded the influence of the national government in public and private society throughout the 20th century.

6. Incumbent members of Congress are very difficult to remove.

## THE HOUSE AND THE SENATE

Congress was designed to be the branch of government that is most responsible for the development of the republic, and it was the only federal branch where the people directly elected members of at least one of the chambers (the House). Presidents were chosen by an aristocratic and elite set of electors, senators were chosen by state legislators, and justices were selected by the president and the Senate. Congress was also given the bulk of the duties listed in the Constitution (see Chapter 4; also refer to Article 1 of the Constitution). Even today, the House and Senate are the only parts of the federal government that are directly elected.

## DUTIES AND THE COMMITTEES

Congress exists to create laws. This critical duty is designed to be complex and deliberate, with the vast majority of potential ideas being rejected. Large-scale compromise is required and the overall process is usually messy and lengthy. The job is also overwhelming. Congress attempts to deal with thousands of pieces of legislation each session, and no single member can master, or even read, all the details. Therefore, the committee system was devised to divide the duties into smaller units. This required that sections of Congress handle areas of expertise and that all members trust some of the interpretations of other members. Leaders of the chambers and committees must have strong powers to act as filters of legislative priorities and bring the bills to more controllable numbers. The power to set the agenda and prioritize problems becomes immense. Congress is also expected to monitor other departments of government, represent the views of constituents, help with military and foreign policy, and negotiate with the president and with some foreign leaders.

## CONSTITUTIONAL DUTIES

Article 1, Section 8 lists the key duties of the federal legislature. Major duties include taxation, interstate commerce, declarations of war, and organizing the military. Interstate commerce duties have become a major area where Congress has expanded its powers, because many tangential issues such as civil rights are connected to the business of interstate trade. As mentioned previously, the last paragraph of this section (Clause 18) includes the phrase "all Laws which shall be necessary and proper." The "Elastic Clause" has allowed Congress to add to its responsibilities and controls.

## SPECIFIC CONGRESSIONAL DUTIES IN THE CONSTITUTION
### ASC = ARTICLE, SECTION, CLAUSE

| | |
|---|---|
| A1S2C5 | House: Choose a speaker and other officers; have the power to impeach. |
| A1S3C5 | Senate: Choose officers; try all impeachments. |
| A1S4C2 | Congress: Meet once a year. |
| A1S5 | Congress: Judge elections of members; compel attendance; determine rules; punish members; possibly expel members; keep a journal; list votes. |
| A1S6 | Congress: Be privileged from arrest during sessions; can't hold other offices. |
| A1S7 | Congress: Start revenue bills in the House; present laws to the president. |
| A1S8 | Congress: Lay and collect taxes; pay debts; provide for the common defense and general welfare; borrow money; regulate commerce; set rules of naturalization; make laws covering bankruptcy; coin money; fix the standards of weights and measures; set the punishment for counterfeiting; establish post roads and offices; promote the sciences and the arts; set up copyrights; create federal courts; define and set punishments for piracy; declare war; grant letters of marque and reprisal; raise and support armies, provide for a navy and call for the militia if needed; organize and discipline militias; govern the national capital's district; regulate national forts and arsenals; make laws that may be "necessary and proper". |

| | |
|---|---|
| A1S9 | Congress: Do not suspend *writs of habeas corpus* unless emergencies require it; pass no bills of attainder or *ex post facto* laws; set no taxes without a census; do not tax exports; do not give preferential laws to ports or states; do not draw money from the Treasury without laws; do not grant titles of nobility. |
| A1S10 | Congress: Monitor states' actions over imports and exports; monitor states' actions with other countries. |
| A2 | Congress: Set the times of the workings of the Electoral College. |
| A3 | Congress: Decide whether to create federal courts; set court salaries; direct where some federal trials may be heard; declare the punishment of treason but do not include the families of those accused as possible recipients of punishment. |
| A4 | Congress: Admit new states; control federal territories; protect the states from invasion and domestic violence. |
| A5 | Congress: Help propose amendments. |
| A6 | Congress: Swear to uphold the Constitution. |

## KEY DIFFERENCES BETWEEN HOUSE AND SENATE POWERS

| House of Representatives | Senate |
|---|---|
| Initiates revenue bills (both chambers must still vote on the final version). | |
| Initiates impeachments and passes impeachment bills. | Holds trial for those impeached by the House and votes on removal. |
| Possibly requests discharge petitions for bills stuck in committee. | Can filibuster bills being debated. |
| House Rules Committee controls debate limits. | Riders to unrelated bills allowed. |
| Must have a speaker as leader. | Informal leaders are party heads, with president of the Senate (VP) in a mostly ceremonial role. |
| Selects the president if the Electoral College can't. | Selects the vice president if the Electoral College can't. |
| | Approves the president's appointments to major federal posts and to the Supreme Court. |
| | Approves treaties initiated by the executive branch. |
| | Approves ambassadors as they are nominated by the executive branch. |

## CREATED PROCEDURES

To streamline the tremendous task of reviewing bills, several traditions have been created under the order to determine the rules of Congressional proceedings. The most obvious are the traditions of seniority and majority rule in committees. Members who have more years of service get more important positions. (This is based on the expectation that experience brings skills.) In addition, the majority party chooses all committee chairperson positions, therefore guaranteeing that one party can dominate and shorten debates.

Within the Congress, differences between the House and Senate are noteworthy. Representatives must stand for re-election every other year, causing a focus on campaigning and money collecting. Because there are four times as many representatives as there are senators, the amount of individual power is reduced in the House. Senators also have much larger constituencies, and those from smaller states have greater influence than their counterparts in the House because in the Senate, every state has only two votes. The tradition of open debates in the Senate gives every Senator the potential to close down business with a filibuster. Filibusters can be ended with cloture votes that were established in the early 1900s. The percentage of votes needed for cloture is currently set at 60, but recent filibuster threats have caused leaders to redebate the rules and numbers.

## CONGRESSIONAL STAFFS, SPECIALIZATION, AND CONFLICTING ROLES

Because of all their complex duties, members of Congress must rely on dedicated staffs to shoulder much of the research, strategy formulation, and other tasks.

This has often isolated members from contact with voters and limited their abilities to become policy experts. Most members try to specialize in areas of law that either affect their districts or states, or they focus where they have been able to gain significant power. This has led to sets of roles that are often openly in conflict with each other.

Members must support their constituents, their party, their leaders, their committees, and their own sense of morals. They don't have time to be experts on everything and are limited in the number of committees on which they can serve. Voting on one issue may bring them into conflict with the various groups they represent. They must maintain power, however, to keep any chance of being influential.

## THE BUDGET

No duty is arguably more important than the development of the annual federal budget. Determining funding for the trillion-dollar list of programs includes many critical debates and compromises with the president and other members of Congress. Known as the fiscal year, the federal budget starts October 1 and lasts until the end of the following September.

The executive Office of Management and Budget creates the budget outline, but Congress must prioritize the thousands of items and vote it through. Congress is also in charge of creating the tax system that will fund the budget. If Congress cannot create taxes that cover the budget, it must take responsibility for allowing the nation to borrow the necessary funds.

## ADDITIONAL DUTIES

Beyond the creation of legislation, members of Congress have other key duties. They are expected to help if constituents face problems with the bureaucracy. They are expected to help with local disasters and conflicts. They work with local and state leaders.

They are expected to meet with civic groups. They stand as an agency of oversight for national conflicts and problems. They must react to a president's demands for a national agenda and compromise on their own. Senators have further duties in approving presidential appointments.

## CURRENT STATUS

Even though its original mission was to dominate the federal system, the Congress of modern times has been superseded in the mind of most citizens by the duties of the president. Congress's slow pace often frustrates the public. Congress must struggle with every form of compromise, leaving many dissatisfied. The public has trouble keeping interest in or being informed about 535 leaders. Congress relies on the president to create issue priorities. Congress relies on the vast bureaucracy to implement and control major issues, such as the environment and transportation. In recent times, Congress is often led by a majority of the opposite party to the president or has different parties in control of the two chambers. All of these items have weakened the influence of Congress and lessened public support.

# THE BASICS OF CONGRESS

The legislative branch was designed to be the main branch of the federal government. Originally, only the House of Representatives was elected directly by the people. The Senate was selected by state legislators, the president by electors, and the Supreme Court by the president and the Senate together. Article 1, Section 5, Clause 1 states, "Each House may determine the rules of its Proceedings." This has created the committee system and rules such as filibuster, cloture, and House discharge petitions, along with many other activities.

Thousands of ideas for potential laws are generated annually. Citizens, lobby groups, state and federal agencies, executive leaders, members of Congress, and staff members all contribute ideas for potential laws. The only way for all of this to be organized is through a filtering system known as the committee system. Congress is responsible for the duties listed in the Constitution, especially the 17 clauses listed in Article 1, Section 8, plus all items "necessary and proper."

## BASIC COMMITTEES OF CONGRESS

| | |
|---|---|
| Standing Committees | These are the permanent committees that work on annual items. In the 2008 session, the House had 20 standing committees responsible for issues from agriculture and the armed services to energy, homeland security, sciences, and ways and means. The Senate had 16 such committees that year. |
| Joint Committees | Members of the House and the Senate gather basic data for Congress on many subjects, such as economics. In 2008, there were four such committees on printing, taxation, the "Economic Committee," and the committee that runs the Library of Congress. |
| Select/Special Committees | Select/special committees are temporary and set up to investigate or research issues. These committees are disbanded when the issue or conflict is resolved. There have been special committees on energy independence, Indian affairs, ethics, intelligence, and aging. |
| Conference Committees | When bills emerge from House and Senate debates, there may be significant differences between the House bill and the Senate bill in amendments, budget levels, etc. To rectify this, a Conference Committee is created, including the major sponsors of the bill from both chambers. This committee has the duty of compromising on the version differences and presenting the House and Senate with a united bill. |

## LEADERSHIP AND ORGANIZATION OF CONGRESS

**House of Representatives:** 435 members (this number was set in 1929), elected for two-year terms from state districts, with seats being distributed according to state populations

Leaders:

1. The **Speaker of the House** (required by the Constitution) is elected by majority vote of members and, in modern times, has always been a member of the majority party.

2. The **majority leader** is chosen by the majority party to represent its goals and policies.

3. The **majority whip** is the assistant to the majority leader, representing the regular membership and functioning as agenda setter, group communicator, and issue planner.

4. **Committee chairpersons** are from the majority party. Chairpersons help form the legislative calendar, committee hearings, and many bill priorities. Rules Committee members are House leaders selected to make the rules of debates and amendment options for bills. They control the final agenda of the floor.

5. The **House Rules Committee** can make or break a piece of legislation when it either restricts or loosens the time limits and scope of debates.

6. The **minority leader** is the leader of the opposition, minority party.

7. The **minority whip** is the assistant to the minority leader and liaison to the minority party members.

8. The **House Republican Conference** guides GOP bills and agendas.

9. The **House Democratic Caucus** guides Democratic bills and agendas.

**Senate:** 100 members elected for six-year terms from the entire state (rather than from a specific district, like in the House; there are two Senators per state), 33 or 34 elected every two years (staggered-term system)

Leaders:

1. The **president of the Senate** (required by the Constitution) is the vice president and can monitor debates, count electoral votes, and vote to break a tie vote of the senators.

2. The **president** *pro tempore* (*pro tem*) (required by the Constitution) serves when the vice president is not available. Generally, it is a ceremonial role given to the majority party Senator with the longest tenure (seniority).

3. A **majority leader** is elected by the majority party to lead procedures, set the agenda, etc.

4. A **majority assistant** (some texts list this as Senate whip) has the same duties as House majority whip.

5. **Committee chairpersons** are from the majority party, usually assigned through seniority. Like House committees, the chairperson can wield power over when bills are debated, how they are debated, and sometimes even whether or not they are debated.

6. A **minority leader** leads the interests of the minority party.

7. A **minority assistant** (Senate whip) has duties that parallel those of the House whips.

8. Each party has a **"Conference Caucus"** that guides policies and agendas for the parties.

## THE BASIC STEPS OF CREATING LAWS

The Constitution requires that revenue bills start in the House, but most are given simultaneous treatment by the House and Senate.

Some bills are processed by the Senate and then the House, others by the House and then the Senate. All bills must be considered by both chambers of Congress in order to become law.

Process:

1. Staff members of House and Senate leaders assign bills numbers for processing (e.g., HR 1…, S 1…).

2. Leaders get bills assigned to committees.

3. Committee chairpersons assign bills to subcommittees for study and debate.

4. Subcommittees hold public hearings, amend bills, and vote on bills. This is known as the "markup" procedure. If the bill is approved, it is then referred to the full committee.

5. The committee can hold further hearings and debates, but it often votes based on subcommittee recommendations.

6. The committee refers the bill to the full House or Senate floor.

7. Floor debates can occur, and, if passed, the bill is referred to the other chamber.

8. The powerful House Rules Committee frames House debates, times, etc.

9. Once both chambers have passed the bill, a Conference Committee is formed to join the two versions into a single bill.

*(continued on next page)*

10. Both the House and the Senate vote on the Conference Committee version of the bill.

11. The bill is then sent to the president.

12. If the president signs it, the bill becomes federal law.

13. If the president ignores the bill for 10 days (not counting Sundays), it automatically becomes law without the president's signature.

14. If the Congressional session has fewer than 10 days remaining and the president ignores a new bill, then the bill dies at the end of the session. This is the "pocket veto."

15. If the president vetoes the bill, the House and Senate can vote to override with a two-thirds majority.

## MODERN ADDITIONS AND REVISIONS TO PROCEDURES

Traditional committee procedures for debates, amendments, and votes have been modified by Congress to allow for more efficiency. Here are examples:

- **Fast tracking.** No amendments allowed; take the bill as is, or not. Because amendments are often lengthy and difficult to debate, fast tracking speeds the entire process.

- **Slow tracking.** Sequential committee hearings are required; this is usually a sign of a bill's being delayed through lengthier processing.

- **Multiple referrals.** Many bills need to be seen by different committees that cover areas of government under their control. To speed this process, bills can be sent to these committees simultaneously.

- **Outside amendments.** Some revisions can be set up by leaders to be added outside of committee meetings.

- **Unanimous consent rules.** As an efficiency measure, such rules allow for the usual procedures of votes to be suspended, as long as no single member objects. Long vote counts can be avoided.

- **King of the Hill votes.** This newer procedure has several amendment versions voted on in order. As long as amendments pass, the voting continues. When an amendment fails, the last one to win becomes the version selected for the bill. Prior amendments are then ignored.

- **Queen of the Hill votes.** This system gives the amendment with the biggest margin of approval the victory over all other amendments.

## A SAMPLE OF CONGRESSIONAL EFFICIENCY
## (DATA FROM THE 102ND CONGRESS)

| | |
|---|---|
| Total bills introduced in the two-year term: | 10,238 (100%) |
| Bills sent to committees by leaders: | 10,178 (99.4%) |
| Bills referred out of committees: | 1,205 (11.7%) |
| Bills referred from floor debates: | 1,201 (11.7%) |
| Passed by both the House and the Senate: | 667 (6.5%) |
| Finally becoming federal law: | 590 (5.7%) of all bills introduced |

## MAJOR PLACES WHERE LEGISLATION IS BLOCKED

- Leaders can assign bills to openly hostile committees or committee chairpersons.
- Chairpersons can delay the bill's consideration ("pigeonhole").
- Subcommittee and committee members can vote no. (This is done often.)
- Subcommittee and committee amendments can change the bill so much that the original sponsors withdraw their support.
- Lobby groups can create opposition and pressure to kill the bill.
- Debate rules and issues can cause changes in votes or amendments.
- Members of the Senate can filibuster or threaten to filibuster. Senators can hold the floor as long as they can stand, thus delaying any other business. This tactic of "filibuster" can force compromises when the minority cannot stop a vote in any other manner.
- Individual senators can place a "hold" on any bill and keep it from being debated on the floor.
- Floor votes in either chamber can be no.
- The Conference Committee can change the bill enough to change support in chambers.
- The president can pocket veto or veto, and Congress isn't able to override that veto.

## KEY COMMITTEES OF CONGRESS

| House Committees: | Duties: |
|---|---|
| Appropriations | Project money (pork) and other expenditures are controlled here. These are called "earmarks." |
| Budget | Oversight of government spending is watched and controlled. |
| Rules | Debate rules, bill sequence, and rules of amendments are set. |
| Ways and Means | Taxation rules, tariff issues, benefits, and Social Security are set. |
| **Senate Committees:** | **Duties:** |
| Appropriations | Federal discretionary spending programs are set. |
| Budget | Oversight of government agencies and spending is done. |
| Finance | Duties are similar to those of the HR Ways and Means committee. |
| Foreign Relations | Policy debates and treaty votes are main duties. |
| Judiciary | Judges and justices are debated and possibly confirmed. |

## WHO CREATES, CONTROLS, OR INFLUENCES THE AGENDA OF CONGRESS?

| | |
|---|---|
| Senate and House Leaders | Bills are directed to committees, priorities of bills are set, and the party agendas are formulated. |
| Committee and Subcommittee Chairpersons | Bills are prioritized, scheduled for hearings and debates, and possibly delayed or killed through pigeonholing. |
| Party Leadership Committees | Overall priorities for legislation are created, and positions of committee membership are determined. |
| Lobbyists | Their access to information, staff members, and campaign money helps influence bills and their content. |
| PACs and Interest Groups | PACs and interest groups control votes through member pressure and campaign fund access; campaign support or hostility are set. |
| Congressional Staff Members | The level of interest, expertise, and access of congressional staff members to detailed information about bills can guide Congress's votes. |
| Party Members, Party Leaders, and National Party Committees | These can be critical sources of media or campaign support. Pressure is applied for loyal votes and firm representation of the overall party goals. |
| The President and Staff | Media access, public support, leadership, and guidance of national priorities affect Congress's leanings and its work. |
| Independent Agencies and Executive Agencies | Vast bureaucracies control the way issues are monitored, the way rules are administered, and the way laws are enforced. These create more ideas and agenda items for Congress. |

# OPINIONS OF CONGRESS

Throughout recent history, citizens of the country have had a split opinion about the members of Congress. As a branch, the vast majority of citizens hold negative opinions about the leaders and about their effectiveness. We don't trust Congress; we see the members as listening only to wealthy insiders and caring only for personal power. We believe that they are disconnected from the needs of the average citizen.

Yet, when polled about the work of our local representatives, our opinions turn positive. We react favorably to pork projects that create local jobs, we enjoy contact with our representatives through various forms of communication, and we trust their leadership. As partisan splits widen in the early 21st century, we also see local leaders as important representatives of the majority beliefs of our district, often extremely different from the goals of members of Congress of the opposite party.

## SAMPLES OF MAJOR LAWS CREATED BY CONGRESS (COMMON NAMES)

| | | |
|---|---|---|
| Pendleton Civil Service Act | 1883 | Federal jobs through merit, not patronage |
| Sherman Antitrust Act | 1890 | First attempt to open trade and commerce |
| Pure Food and Drug Act | 1906 | Control over food manufacturing |
| Clayton Antitrust Act | 1914 | Monopoly and merger limits |
| Social Security Act | 1935 | New Deal safety net effort |
| Wagner Act | 1935 | Union and collective bargaining rights |
| Hatch Act | 1939 | Civil servant restrictions in campaigning |
| Smith Act | 1940 | Can't advocate the overthrow of the government |
| Employment Act | 1946 | The government must try to stabilize the economy. |
| Taft-Hartley Act | 1947 | Restrictions on union rules and powers |
| National Security Act | 1947 | Creation of Department of Defense, CIA, NSC |
| Clean Air Act | 1963 | Antismog efforts start. |
| Civil Rights Act | 1964 | Racial discrimination outlawed |
| Voting Rights Act | 1965 | Voting discrimination outlawed |
| Freedom of Information Act | 1966 | Open records and fewer secrets mandated |
| Fair Housing Act | 1968 | No housing discrimination |
| Organized Crime Control Act | 1970 | Including "RICO" (anti-mob/racketeering) |
| Occupational Safety Act | 1970 | OSHA formed to protect workplaces |
| Federal Election Campaign Act | 1971 | First "hard money" reforms, PACs |
| Title IX, Educational Amendments | 1972 | Women's athletics and funding equality |
| Endangered Species Act | 1973 | Protects threatened species |
| Budget Reform Act | 1974 | No impoundment of funds by the president |
| Toxic Waste Act | 1980 | Superfund sites and EPA funding |
| Gramm-Rudman-Hollings Act | 1985 | Effort at balancing the budget, debt limits |
| Simpson-Mazzoli Act | 1986 | Immigration reform and some amnesty |
| Americans with Disabilities Act | 1991 | Access for those with disabilities |
| Family and Medical Leave Act | 1993 | Maternity and sick leave protection |
| Patriot Act | 2001 | Department of Homeland Security created (post 9/11) |
| No Child Left Behind Act | 2001 | Federal standards, rules, money in schools |
| McCain-Feingold Act | 2002 | Efforts at "soft money" reform |
| Sarbanes-Oakley Act | 2002 | Corporate records need to be reliable |

| American Jobs Creation Act | 2004 | Restructuring of business taxes |
| Energy Independence and Security Act | 2007 | Focusing on renewable energy, improving energy efficiency, and lowering energy costs for consumers |

## CONFLICTING DUTIES OF MEMBERS OF CONGRESS

| Delegate Duties | Members should represent the wishes of their districts/states and not necessarily their own; often delegates have views that conflict with those of their constituents. |
| Trustee Duties | Members should take care of the republic and do what is best for the long-term health of the country, not just what is best for their own districts. |
| Politico Duties | Members must support party goals and party leaders and do what needs to be done to gain power; otherwise, they are seen as ineffective. |
| Partisan Duties | Often similar to duties within the party, these goals include being consistent with the ideas of liberalism or conservatism or centrism. Candidates run on such platforms and are expected to follow through with the ideals of consistent leadership and to stand for principles. |

## INCUMBENCY ADVANTAGES OF MEMBERS OF CONGRESS

House members are more difficult to defeat in re-election attempts than senators, but both groups are difficult to unseat for the following reasons:

| Name Recognition | After years of media exposure, neutral voters often select a candidate whose name is familiar to them. |
| Campaign Costs | Members of Congress have access to many groups that fund races, and senators are often privately wealthy enough to contribute to their campaigns. |
| Franking | Free communication with the home constituents throughout a term helps with name recognition. |
| Pork Projects and Claims of Credit | Local jobs and contracts help build local support, and members of Congress are not shy about reminding the public about the source of benefits. |
| Seniority Powers | As leaders get more influential positions, voters feel that they gain power in Congress as well. They hesitate to start over with a new face. |
| Party Support | Party organizations are reluctant to turn on loyal members, who are also proven winners. |
| Lobby Support | Groups that are willing to give money for future influence are reluctant to gamble on lesser-known outsiders. |

# REVIEW QUESTIONS

## MULTIPLE-CHOICE QUESTIONS

1. Each of the following was true of the founders' goals for the legislature EXCEPT

   (A) the public could not directly select members.

   (B) the legislature should have controls placed on its powers.

   (C) the legislature should defer to the executive in foreign matters.

   (D) the legislature could set its own salary level.

   (E) the legislature should be the clear leader of the national government.

2. The founders wanted to limit the legislative powers by

   (A) not letting them remove certain rights in normal times.

   (B) having only the House create tax legislation.

   (C) having the Supreme Court decide the constitutional status of laws.

   (D) giving the executive the power to increase or decrease taxes.

   (E) giving the executive the power to create independent agencies.

3. The Senate became a more democratic institution in the 20th century because

   (A) filibuster and cloture rules were clarified.

   (B) more nonwealthy citizens were elected.

   (C) more states were added to the union, thus decreasing the powers of individual senators.

   (D) the seniority system of controls was weakened.

   (E) elections were taken from states and given to the public.

4. Every 10 years, the House must

   (A) select a new speaker.

   (B) reorganize the committees.

   (C) set the national budget priorities.

   (D) redistribute the numbers of representatives the states have.

   (E) redistribute the powers of subcommittee and committee chairpersons.

5. One of the biggest problems in making decisions for members of Congress is

   (A) following the party wishes.

   (B) following the goals of the powerful leaders.

   (C) following the wishes of constituents.

   (D) balancing conflicting political goals.

   (E) keeping lobby groups happy in order to get more funds.

## FREE-RESPONSE QUESTIONS

1.  The idea of "necessary and proper" powers has been used to expand the scope of Congress's authority.

    (A) Identify the political name of the use of these powers.

    (B) Identify the power listed in Article 1 of the Constitution that Congress has most often expanded.

    (C) Identify and describe how one of the following cases was used for such expansion of powers:

    *Gibbons v. Ogden*, 1824

    *Heart of Atlanta Motel v. U.S.*, 1964

2.  Congress has created a system of lawmaking that is slow, difficult, and usually kills bills.

    (A) List and explain two ways Congress stops legislation.

    (B) Explain two reasons why this might be intentional and a positive.

# ANSWERS AND EXPLANATIONS

## MULTIPLE-CHOICE ANSWERS

**1. C**

It is not true that the legislature should defer to the executive in foreign matters. The fact that the legislature must approve treaties is an example of its involvement in foreign affairs. Choice (A) is incorrect because the public did not originally elect senators. We know that choice (B) is incorrect because the founders placed checks on the legislative branch, such as the veto power and the fact that House members are up for election every other year. Choice (D) is incorrect because Congress does set its own salaries. Choice (E) is incorrect because the founders clearly intended the legislature to be primary.

**2. A**

The founders wanted to limit legislative powers by not letting them remove certain rights in normal times. These limitations are contained in Article 1, Section 9, which states that Congress must not suspend *writs of habeas corpus* unless emergencies require it; that they may not pass bills of attainder or *ex post facto* laws; that they are prohibited from setting taxes without a census, they may not tax exports, and that they may not give preferential laws to ports or states; that they may not draw money from the Treasury without laws; and that they may not grant titles of nobility. Choice (B) is incorrect because the Senate must concur on tax bills. Choice (C) is incorrect because the power of judicial review was granted to the Supreme Court in the case of *Marbury v. Madison* in 1803; it was not listed in the Constitution. Choices (D) and (E) are false: The executive does not have the power to increase or decrease taxes or the power to create independent agencies.

**3. E**

The Senate became a more democratic institution in the 20th century because elections were taken from the states and given to the public; this was done through the 17th Amendment in 1913. Choices (A), (C), and (D) are incorrect because although they are all true statements, none of these events were as significant as the 17th Amendment. Choice (B) is not true.

**4. D**

Every 10 years, the House must redistribute the number of representatives that the states have due to the constitutionally mandated census and reapportionment of the House.

**5. D**

One of the biggest problems in making decisions for members of Congress is the balancing of conflicting political goals. The largest problem is trying to keep all of the duties balanced; they are often in conflict.

## FREE-RESPONSE ANSWERS

1. **4-point Rubric**

   **1 point in part (A): (identify)**

   - Elastic Clause

   **1 point in part (B): (identify)**

   - Commerce Clause

   - Regulate interstate commerce

   **2 points in part (C): (identify issue/describe)**

   - *Gibbons v. Ogden*, 1824—Conflicts over the control of interstate trade are in the hands of Congress. They are not in the hands of the states. Licenses across state boundaries fall within the commerce powers of Congress.

   - *Heart of Atlanta Motel v. U.S.*, 1964—Civil rights requirements from the federal government (acts of Congress) apply to private businesses if they conduct interstate trade activities or benefit substantially from interstate trade.

2. **6-point Rubric**

   **4 points in part (A): (identify and explain)**

   - Chairperson or subcommittee chairperson—pigeonhole or delay bill to death

   - Subcommittee or committee—vote bill down

   - Floor debate—vote bill down

   - Other chamber—vote bill down at some step

   - President—veto or pocket veto and bill dies

   - Congress—no override vote

   **2 points in part (B): (reasons this might be positive)**

   - Deliberation is good.

   - Majority consensus is needed.

   - Emotional responses need time to be considered.

   - Consensus from multiple branches shows need.

   - Plenty of points of access by the public, lobby forces, or other leaders is good.

# CHAPTER 13: **THE EXECUTIVE BRANCH**

## IF YOU ONLY LEARN SIX THINGS IN THIS CHAPTER . . . .

1. Executive authority over the freedoms of American citizens has expanded steadily throughout U.S. political history.

2. The image of the president is sporadic and shifts in public support daily. He may be highly criticized one day and completely back in the limelight the next, depending on what happened overnight in domestic and international affairs or how the media represented his actions.

3. Because the executive branch of government is so large and powerful, many high-level political executives have gained innumerable extraordinary powers of action.

4. Despite the negative backlash the president often takes for promoting or executing an unpopular idea or action, history has shown that Americans are usually willing to live with whatever it is after the fact.

5. It is not uncommon for normal citizens to expect members of government to behave in a certain manner and use their influence in an appropriate manner, almost to an unnatural capacity.

6. The history of the U.S. government is a history of power shifts between Congress and the president.

## THE PRESIDENT

The role of the U.S. president has greatly changed over the years. The original plan for the executive officer was for him to react to Congressional laws and monitor their implementation, to represent the nation in foreign negotiations, and to suggest a list of national priorities. The Founding Fathers did not trust a single, powerful leader and made almost all of the powers contingent on Congressional involvement. The president could command the military, but funding and rules would come from Congress. Treaties and appointments were to become official only with legislative approval. Veto actions could be overridden, and suggestions for priorities could be ignored.

Congress held Article 1 powers to deal with emergencies and was listed first in the Article 4 powers to protect the states. The first Senate demonstrated its expectations of supremacy by ignoring George Washington's request to speak to a committee and have his bills debated. He never set foot in the Capitol again, setting a precedent that stands today: Presidents are invited into the halls of Congress.

In modern times, presidents hold significantly more powerful roles than they did years ago. Crisis actions have demanded it, the public has wanted it, and Congress was unable (or unwilling) to stop it. Here are some examples:

- President Polk sent the military into conflict with Mexico, leaving Congress with the dilemma of either declaring war or calling for an unpopular retreat.

- Lincoln suspended basic civil liberties during the chaos of 1861, when Congress couldn't even gather to act.

- Teddy Roosevelt sent the fleet into Asian conflicts and dared Congress to find the funding to bring it home.

- Franklin Roosevelt's staff began economic policies without Congressional approval, and the nation demanded supportive action.

More recent presidents have sent troops into serious and violent conflicts without any declaration of war by Congress. The nation does not always have time to wait for a debate and majority vote. Sometimes, Congress is afraid of the public reaction to perceived acts of weakness. The president is able to bring his message directly to the nation, take credit quickly, and become the image of the country.

Also at the president's disposal is a huge bureaucracy. Millions of employees and hundreds of agencies must answer to executive orders and directives. The president has a large, talented, and extremely loyal staff that can conduct research, give advice, and shield their leader. Citizens can't

## THE PRESIDENT AND THE MEDIA

Not every issue goes the way the president would like. As the center of media attention, a president often takes blame for activities beyond his or her control. Congress is happy to spread that blame, even if items such as taxes and budgets are actually its responsibility. Congress helps in the attack when a president shows flaws or mistakes.

easily identify with 535 members of Congress, especially when that body is supposed to work slowly and deliberately.

Entire media groups earn their livelihood by finding flaws in the administration. Congress has also tried to legislate back some powers by attempting to limit military conflicts, force the bureaucratic spending of budget money, and stymie the approval of appointees.

The intense scrutiny of every presidential action through investigative counsels is another form of congressional counterattack. Such pressures can age a president quickly and have been shown to make the re-election process successful only 50 percent of the time.

With respect to the relationship between the presidency and Congress, there is very much a *balance of power*. Presidential authority and initiatives have expanded over time, especially since the Great Depression, World War II, and the Civil Rights era. Congress began to try to reign in the expansion of presidential power after Vietnam and Watergate, based somewhat on the mistakes of the Gulf of Tonkin Resolution and the Pentagon Papers controversies. Congress, and then the nation, were shown evidence that the White House had used fake data to gain powers during the early Vietnam mess.

Conversely, Congress increased the powers of the executive branch after the crisis of 9/11 in 2001. For example, it gave the president the right to allow the military to imprison suspected terrorists without charges or trial in U.S. courts. Federal courts upheld these powers in the summer of 2005 and again in 2009. The struggle for control, however, is bound to continue.

## QUALIFICATIONS: FORMAL AND INFORMAL

In addition to the vague descriptions of authority, the very qualifications of the office are minimal. The founders included no requirement of experience, education, or skills. The only requirements that were listed were as follows:

- A set age (35 years old)
- Citizenship (native born)
- Residency (14 years in the United States)

It was expected that the Electoral College would be careful in selecting only the most qualified individuals. Modern politics and elections make it clear that parties and citizens prefer candidates with strong party agendas, personal wealth, images of decisive leadership, good television presentation skills, and residence in important electoral states.

### CONSTITUTIONAL REQUIREMENTS FOR THE PRESIDENCY

**Must be a "natural born Citizen" (native born).** There has never been a challenge or question about a possible candidate who was born *jus soli* in a territory or *jus sanguinus* of a U.S. citizen whose parents live overseas. It is assumed that such a citizen would qualify to run for the presidency, but questions might be raised.

**Must have "attained to the Age of thirty five Years."** The youngest presidents were Teddy Roosevelt and John Kennedy, who were 43 years old at the time they took office. The oldest were Harrison and Reagan, who were in their 60s when first elected.

**Must have "been fourteen Years a Resident within the United States."** No rulings about the nature of these 14 years have occurred. Must they be consecutive years? *Jus sanguinus* citizens must reside a certain number of years after age 14, but not potential presidents.

**Must be selected by the Electoral College.** Winners need half of the electoral votes plus one. With the current number of members of the House, Senate, 50 states, and Washington, D.C., requires winning 270 electoral votes.

**Must have served no more than one previous full term or no more than six previous years as president (per the 22nd Amendment).** A president who has served a full term may run once more. If he or she has also served part of another president's term, this service may not exceed two years. No one can serve for more than 10 years.

## INFORMAL QUALIFICATIONS OF THE PRESIDENCY

Historically, citizens have chosen certain kinds of leaders for the presidency. Clearly, trends change, but to date, here are the major features of our presidents:

| | |
|---|---|
| Male | Minor parties, even as far back as the late 19th century, have nominated women candidates. The vice presidential candidacies of Geraldine Ferraro and Sarah Palin have been the highest major party female nominations. |
| European | Almost all presidents have British ancestry. Even as late as the 1980s, the nomination of a Greek American (Michael Dukakis) was considered unusual. In 2009, Barack Obama was the first African American to become president of the United States. |
| Middle-Aged | No one in his 30s has been nominated for his first run; 72-year-old John McCain was the oldest first-time nominee in 2008. |
| Wealthy | Certainly in the 20th century, presidential candidates were expected to come from financially successful families. |
| Protestant Christian | Kennedy's candidacy as a Roman Catholic was questioned enough that he decided to give a special campaign speech explaining how he would not let the Pope lead U.S. policy. |
| Graduated from College | Truman was the last president not to attend college, and many before him had graduated. Now, even the grades a candidate made in college classes have become the objects of scrutiny and debate. |
| Is in Good Health | Much scrutiny is given to possible health issues or "flaws." Certainly, any previous mental struggle would be the kiss of death for a campaign. |

| Is Relatively Attractive | Columnists, cartoonists, and television and stage comics can add a ruthless level of attacks that give a lasting impression of weakness. This may be very unfair, of course, but it is effective. |
|---|---|
| Is Married | All presidents (except Buchanan) have been married. In past times, being divorced was considered a major issue, but Reagan overcame that easily. |
| Has Leadership or Military Skills | Prior experience as a governor or member of Congress is critical. Experience as only a member of the House is probably not sufficient. Only one former Speaker of the House (Polk) has become president, but he had also served as governor of Tennessee. Being a general is considered a plus. If military service has not been completed, many explanations are needed. The Clinton presidency is a recent example of questions raised about the lack of military service, as was George W. Bush's time in the Air Force reserve, not to mention the 2004 "Swift Boat" attacks on candidate Senator Kerry. |
| Is from an Important Electoral State | U.S. presidents have come from important electoral states. Exceptions such as Bill Clinton (from Arkansas) might be overcome by being from a key region like the South, where Democrats need all the votes they can get. |
| Debates Well | Post-1960, the TV image has been emphasized. There is some disagreement over the actual importance of the debates, but both parties spend a lot of resources to make sure their candidate performs well. |

Several factors contribute to whether a president is popular. Polls show that *party identification* is the primary factor in getting elected and staying popular. How does the party in control appear to be handling the country? Do independent voters feel more positive about that party? A favorite example of this trend is the 1932 election: Even with all the problems and crises in play, 40 percent of the voters still voted for Hoover as the leader of the Republicans.

The economy is important as well. "It's the Economy, Stupid," was the catch phrase of the election of 1992, reflecting a long-held truth about voters. A century's worth of data supports this. Also important is whether we are involved in a war or crisis. Voters frequently rally around the president in a show of patriotism and solidarity.

*Personal behaviors* matter, as well. Since Watergate, political opponents—and the media—watch for every potential flaw and mistake they can find in a president. The media now gains as much fame and revenue in a colorful attack as they once did in defense. The *activities of associates*, too, can affect a president's popularity. Scandals involving relatives or friends in positions such as the Cabinet reflect back on the leader.

Finally, *timing* matters: The "honeymoon" ensures that a leader will be popular at first. Second terms tend to lower the numbers.

## STAFF INFLUENCES

Upon attaining office, a president is supported and at times controlled by powerful staff structures. The vice president can influence many decisions through Congressional contacts. The chief of staff can screen access to the president and filter information available to him. The press secretary plays the role of selecting how messages are delivered from the office to the media.

Economic and military experts guide the president in areas of policy. The Cabinet controls the daily workings of large parts of the executive bureaucracy and is in charge of suggesting candidates for most of the 5,000 jobs the president is expected to appoint.

## IMPORTANT INFORMAL DUTIES

The president fulfills a critical advisory role. He is the leader of his party, supporting candidates and the platform. He is the national focal point during times of emergency and crisis. He works face-to-face with international leaders, representing the goals of the nation.

### CONSTITUTIONAL DUTIES OF THE PRESIDENT
### (ARTICLE 2 AND ARTICLE 4, SECTION 4)

| Duties and Powers | Constraints |
|---|---|
| Serves as commander-in-chief of the military (national security leader). | Congress funds and organizes the military and makes the rules of the military. |
| Negotiates treaties with foreign governments (foreign policy leader). | The Senate must approve treaties for them to take effect. |
| Nominates top federal officials, including federal judges and justices of the Supreme Court. | The Senate must approve the nominations and, by tradition, "Senatorial courtesy" is often expected for nominations. |
| Vetoes legislation passed by Congress. | Congress can override the veto with a two-thirds vote in both chambers. |
| Can use a pocket veto. | No constraints exist if the president does not sign legislation passed with fewer than 10 days left in the session. |
| Faithfully administers federal laws (national policy leader); uses orders, proclamations, and memoranda. | Congress has set up its own agencies to counter executive priorities (Congressional Budget Office versus the White House's Office of Management and Budget) and has given many powers to independent agencies. |
| Can pardon people. | Public outrage may imperil popularity and re-election chances (e.g., Gerald Ford's pardon of Nixon). |
| Addresses Congress and the nation and sets the priorities of the legislation (State of the Union message; legislative leader). | Congress can ignore the priorities, especially if gridlock exists between the branches. |

| | |
|---|---|
| Acts as Chief of State (bully pulpit; mandate; crisis manager). | These powers are not defined in the Constitution, and low approval ratings damage the president's leadership powers. The public and the press hold very high expectations of a president's reactions in difficult times. |
| "…protect each of them (states) against Invasion… against domestic Violence." | Presidents are to act "when the Legislature cannot be convened." This is a major way that executives can expand their powers during times of emergency. |

# THE POWER OF EXECUTIVE PRIVILEGE

Presidents have used the concept of separation of powers to claim a status above the scrutiny of Congress or the courts. As leader of the executive branch, a president can claim that certain decisions, information, documents, and secrets of executive agencies are the private business of the president, the president's staff, and the military.

The most famous dispute in this area was the Watergate tapes of Richard Nixon. When Congress pressed for those tapes as part of a potential criminal investigation, Nixon refused to turn them over. He claimed that they were personal documents for his own use in creating memoirs. The Supreme Court had to step in and resolve the dispute on behalf of Congress. Presidents cannot hide behind executive privilege to put themselves above the scope of the law.

There are different types of presidential directives to the executive branch. They are as follows:

- An *executive order* has the force of law and is listed in the *Federal Register*. It affects millions of federal workers and all agencies. Such an order is a very powerful policy tool. Many environmental policies and civil rights policies, such as affirmative action, began as executive orders to the bureaucracy.
- A *proclamation* is often merely a ceremonial action and is not law.
- Memoranda are issued to specific agencies, usually for single projects, but they can affect the way that agency conducts business.

## EXECUTIVE POWERS

| Listed in the Constitution | Checked/Restricted? |
|---|---|
| Signs bills. | Only Congress creates bills. |
| Vetoes bills. | Congressional override is possible. |
| Faithfully administers executive powers. | Powers are created by Congress. Congress can impeach and remove. |
| Is the commander-in-chief. | Military rules are set by Congress. Budgets are set by Congress. Only Congress can declare war. |

# EXECUTIVE POWERS (con't)

| Listed in the Constitution | Checked/Restricted? |
| --- | --- |
| Heads the executive branch (executive departments). | Congress creates and funds the departments, can eliminate them, and can create independent agencies. |
| Grants reprieves and pardons. | These are limited to federal cases. There may be public condemnation (e.g., Ford and Nixon). |
| Makes treaties. | Senate approval needed. |
| Nominates ambassadors, public ministers and consuls, judges of the Supreme Court, and "all other Officers of the United States." | Senate approval needed. Congress can change court numbers. Congress can change judge and justice numbers. |
| Fills vacancies during recess of the Senate. | They only last until "the End of their next Session." |
| Gives Congress a "State of the Union". | Congress doesn't have to follow the priorities set by the president. |
| On "extraordinary Occasions" convenes the houses of Congress. | Not needed in modern times of year-round sessions. |
| If houses can't agree on dates, "may adjourn them". | Needed? |
| Receives ambassadors and "recognizes" governments. | Congressional restraints concerning trade and negotiations can occur. The Supreme Court can hear cases concerning "ambassadors." |
| Commissions all officers of the United States. | Congress creates the officer positions. Joint chief positions must be approved by the Senate. |

| Implied from the Constitution or Created through Time | Checked/Restricted? |
| --- | --- |
| Pocket veto | Congress can revive the legislation the next session. |
| Executive agreements with other countries | They are only "informal" agreements and not treaties. |
| Executive orders on the executive branch | They only apply to the federal agencies controlled by the executive branch. |
| Executive proclamations | They do not have the force of law and are usually only ceremonial. |
| Executive memoranda | They only apply to specific agencies or departments. |
| Crisis manager | This is informal only and restricted by the fact that Congress declares war. |
| International leader | Congress must approve treaties and can set up trade restrictions. |

| | |
|---|---|
| Party leader | This is informal only and restricted by the powers of many other party leaders. |
| "Creation" of the federal budget through the Office of Management and Budget (OMB) | Congress must approve the budget and can ignore OMB guidelines. The Congressional Budget Office (CBO) helps Congress. |

## EXPANSION OF PRESIDENTIAL POWERS

Presidential powers are not stagnant. They frequently expand. The following are major examples:

| | | |
|---|---|---|
| 1846 | Polk | As commander-in-chief, Polk ordered the army into disputed territories claimed by Mexico, thus starting battles without Congress's permission or a declaration of war. |
| 1861 | Lincoln | Lincoln declared a domestic emergency during a congressional recess, changing the way a president can act during a crisis. Lincoln took on *habeas corpus* suspension rights, even though those are listed in Article 1 (the powers of Congress). |
| Early 1900s | T. Roosevelt | Roosevelt pushed the public to demand economic reforms, used the press as his agenda vehicle, and even sent the fleet on a mission without congressional funds or approval. |
| 1930s | F. D. Roosevelt | As head of the executive branch, FDR created federal economic programs and reorganized the executive branch—without prior congressional approval. The resulting challenges put Congress in a position of reaction, not creation. When the Supreme Court started to halt New Deal programs, FDR hit it with the "packing" plan that failed, but he forced court retirements and changed the court's reaction to public pressure. |
| Late 1960s | Nixon | Nixon blocked congressional programs by "impounding" funds for programs he didn't support. Congress was forced to legislate changes in the spending of program monies. The Supreme Court supported Congress. |
| Early 1980s | Reagan | Through the Office of Management and Budget, Reagan's director, David Stockman, attacked programs by eliminating them from the budget. Congress had to go into a reaction mode again to attempt some restoration of programs. |
| Modern Times | (Several) | The power of the executive order has increased over time. By ordering the huge bureaucracy to follow specific orders about certain programs or the spending of funds, the president can effect sweeping changes in the government and economy. |

# RECENT EVENTS AND LAWS

**Gulf of Tonkin Resolution.** Presidents were given expanded powers to commit U.S. forces to combat without a declaration of war. The revelations of the Pentagon Papers caused a re-evaluation of these unilateral powers. This resolution was in force from 1964 to 1970.

**War Powers Resolution (1973).** Time limits were placed on the use of troops in combat without Congressional approval. The resolution was partly struck down by the Supreme Court, and no president has considered it constitutional.

**Curbs on the FBI and CIA.** Congress limited the ability of the FBI and CIA to conduct certain kinds of surveillance, especially on U.S. citizens while in the country. Significant changes occurred recently, however, when the Patriot Act reinstated some of these kinds of investigations.

**Congressional Budget and Impoundment Control Act (1974).** In reaction to Nixon's impoundment of funds to programs he opposed, Congress required the executive branch to spend the money legislated by Congress. The Supreme Court sided with Congress.

**Budget Reduction Act (1985).** Congress set ceilings on budget expenditures, slowing down some deficit spending. The goal with this act was to curb the power of the president to ask for money and to cut federal spending in general, thus limiting some of the power of the national government. This also led to a move to pass a *balanced budget amendment,* but as soon as Congress realized that economic recessions required significant borrowing to keep things from sliding too far, the call for such an amendment ceased.

**Iron Law of Emulation.** The idea is that organizations in conflict tend to emulate each other. As the executive has increased power through massive and growing bureaucracies, the legislature has countered with larger staffs and agencies such as the Congressional Budget Office.

**Rise of the House of 1994.** In 1994 and 1995, Newt Gingrich led a newly elected Republican majority in trying to shut down government instead of pass Clinton budgets. The president successfully turned to the public and reminded them that Congress was in charge of budget levels. As soon as services were cut and Social Security checks stopped arriving, the public blamed Congress. Pressure from powerful lobby groups forced Congress to capitulate. A second try also failed, damaging the power of Speaker Gingrich.

**Increased use of committee powers.** Senate committees, such as the Foreign Relations Committee, have increased their activities against presidential nominations. Famous examples include Senator Jesse Helms's blocks of Clinton nominees and threats of filibusters over conservative judges by Democratic senators in 2005.

**Increasing use of "independent counsels."** Investigative committees have led to growing congressional attacks on presidents. Examples include Watergate, Iran-Contra, Whitewater, the Clinton impeachment, Dick Cheney's oil policy committee, etc.

**Evidence of presidential "success" (or lack of success) as of the election of 2008.** In 18 elections, the incumbent president was successful in getting re-elected. In 19 elections, he was not. This does not include elections where former presidents were unable even to be named as their party's candidate.

## GENERAL QUALIFICATIONS FOR PRESIDENTIAL APPOINTEES

| | |
|---|---|
| White House Staff | Absolute loyalty to the president is seen as the prime qualification. |
| Heads of Cabinet Departments | Experience relating to the position is primary, as is a strong resume of party support. |
| Ambassador Positions | These are assigned for the most part as a reward for strong financial support of the campaign and party. |
| Federal Judgeships and Justices of the Supreme Court | Building a resume filled with a list of conservative or liberal decisions is the key for such appointments. (One must be careful, however, of having too many decisions on record, which might provide too much ammunition to opponents.) Recent nominees have been judges with skimpy but "correct" histories. |

# REVIEW QUESTIONS

## MULTIPLE-CHOICE QUESTIONS

1. The issue of selecting the president began as a very controversial matter. The resulting Electoral College system shows that the

   (A) founders didn't trust a strong, single executive.

   (B) founders wanted a strong executive.

   (C) founders wanted states to control the national government

   (D) founders didn't trust Congress too much.

   (E) national government was meant to be unified under one leader.

2. In being effective, a president's greatest challenge is

   (A) selecting judges and justices with similar political aims.

   (B) working with Congress.

   (C) keeping a strong and popular image through the media.

   (D) keeping fellow party members in line.

   (E) All of the above

3. One power that presidents hold without congressional checks is

   (A) selecting the leaders of the executive branch.

   (B) creating the federal budget.

   (C) guiding the year's agenda through the State of the Union message.

   (D) the ability to request that certain committees hear their priorities.

   (E) the ability to forgive the crimes of some citizens.

4. Executive orders are very powerful because

   (A) they have the same authority over the federal government as congressional laws.

   (B) they can direct millions of workers to conduct business in a certain way.

   (C) they can change the scope and direction of federal policies on issues like civil rights.

   (D) they command the entire federal bureaucracy.

   (E) All of the above

5. All of the following tend to be true about U.S. presidents **EXCEPT**

   (A) they are white.

   (B) they have some sort of military service background.

   (C) they are from an agricultural area known for strong "American" values.

   (D) they have significant personal or family wealth.

   (E) they have no revealed health issues.

## FREE-RESPONSE QUESTIONS

1. Though the founders intended Congress to be the prime federal branch, presidents now find themselves the center of more attention and power.

    (A) Identify and describe two ways this trend toward presidential power has occurred (not counting the presidential authority over the bureaucracy).

    (B) Identify and explain how presidential authority over the federal bureaucracy has increased executive powers.

2. Recent Congresses have attempted to regain authority from presidents.

    (A) Identify and describe at least two such efforts by Congress.

    (B) Identify and describe one way Congress has failed in these efforts.

# ANSWERS AND EXPLANATIONS

## MULTIPLE-CHOICE ANSWERS

### 1. A

The Electoral College system came about because the founders didn't trust a strong, single executive. They didn't think states would dominate; they thought they would be separate in powers. They did trust Congress to be the main body of the national system.

### 2. C

In being effective, a president's greatest challenge is to keep a strong and popular image in the media. The bully pulpit is actually the president's main source of strength and persuasion. Choices (A), (B), and (D) are correct but not the sources of the power to be effective.

### 3. E

One power that presidents hold without congressional checks is the power of the pardon. Choices (A) and (B) are directly checked. Congress can ignore choice (C); no president since Washington has dared to try choice (D), because the first effort was soundly ignored.

### 4. E

Executive orders command a lot of power for all of the reasons listed: because they have the same authority over the federal government as Congressional laws, because they can direct millions of workers to conduct business in a certain way, because they can change the scope and direction of federal policies on civil rights, and because they command the entire federal bureaucracy.

### 5. C

It is not true that U.S. presidents tend to be from agricultural areas with strong "American" values. Rather, presidents tend to be from important electoral states that are not rural. Although Barack Obama became the first African American president of the United States, the majority of the presidents have been white.

# FREE-RESPONSE ANSWERS

1. **6-point Rubric**

   **4 points in part (A): (identify and describe evidence of trend toward president)**

   - Military initiative; Polk's placing troops in conflict and forcing Congress to act

   - Emergency initiative; Lincoln's suspension of *writ of habeas corpus* rights during the emergency of 1861

   - Economic initiative; FDR's creation of offices and agencies to help during the Great Depression crisis

   - Deregulation initiative; Carter's starting the trend of cutting federal involvement (other examples of this nature would work)

   **2 points in part (B): (identify and explain power over the bureaucracy)**

   - Executive orders; have power of law to require actions of the agencies

   - Executive memoranda; power of actions over certain agencies

2. **6-point Rubric**

   **4 points in part (A): (identify and describe efforts by Congress)**

   - Limit military powers; take back control of troops in conflict

   - Restrict budget powers; force presidents to spend money

   - Appointments; restrict and investigate appointments more

   - Investigate; openly attack presidential behaviors

   - Budget fights; try to force policies by not passing budgets

   **2 points in part (B): (identify and describe failures by Congress)**

   - Gingrich budget fights; public ended up blaming Congress

   - Impeachment; Clinton scandals don't lead to removal

   - Crisis; powers go back to president after 9/11

   - Division; Congress continues to be split, with many supporting the president

# CHAPTER 14: THE FEDERAL BUREAUCRACY

## IF YOU ONLY LEARN SIX THINGS IN THIS CHAPTER . . . .

1. The most dramatic change in the structure of the U.S. government has been the creation and growth of the bureaucracy.

2. The bureaucracy has been given powers that are similar to those of the Congress, the president, and the federal courts.

3. The bureaucracy is both hated and loved. It is hated for its presence and the image of distance from the voters. It is loved for its creation of jobs and the solving of large, complex problems.

4. Bureaucracies are controlled by powerful and interlocking groups that benefit from the very existence of federal programs.

5. Federal agencies are present in numerous policy-making capacities, from military defense to environmental protection.

6. Although the powers of federal agencies are controversial, the bureaucracy plays a key role in the attempt to fill the needs of the public.

## THE FOURTH BRANCH

Some of the biggest changes in government structure have been the development of vast networks of agencies and departments that make up the "fourth branch." In early decades, presidents had a few key officials run small departments that handled a few embassies, created some banks and currency, worked with military leaders, and built the postal system. Other federal jobs were mostly limited to customs houses. These jobs provided excellent salary and pension opportunities, so appointments were considered highly prized payoffs for party support. Response to massive acts of corruption removed many of these patronage activities in the late 1800s, eventually leading to a civil service organization of qualified professionals.

Most of this system was dramatically changed by the Great Depression, the Cold War, and the Civil Rights era. Agencies were created to provide jobs, monitor the vast military-industrial complex, and force the acceptance of minority rights. These agencies now have an impact on business sectors, school systems, housing, the uses of the land and air, and the safety of citizens. The Cabinet has grown to include 15 departments, and Congress has added over 150 independent regulatory agencies. There are also several "governmental corporations," such as NASA and the U.S. Postal Service, which compete with businesses and charge for services.

# SCOPE OF POWERS

Perhaps the biggest controversy concerning the bureaucracy is the scope of powers given to officials not elected by public vote. Problems often stem from the technical and national scope of the issues involved. Congress and presidential staff members do not have the time, resources, or levels of expertise to monitor environmental controls, tax codes, governmental licenses, and other massive duties. Therefore, the public must deal with bureaucrats who have the advantage of working daily with complex rules and issues. Agency leaders can define how rules are applied and who must strictly follow them. Thus, agencies have an advantage when controlling business and personal licenses. How can individuals mount a legal challenge when they are being monitored by an agency and not a court system? Agencies also play a powerful role in the development of the rules themselves, because Congress often relies on these experts to formulate possible changes in the laws. Critically, agencies also control the spending of vast sums of public monies and the creation or change of local jobs and economies.

The bureaucracy typically works with two central powers: *rule making* and *rule adjudication*. When agencies are asked to create rules that will govern their actions, they are completing a form of legislative power. Agencies often announce the creation of rules and hold public hearings to allow for input, but once the rules are finalized, the public has to abide by their structure. If businesses or citizens are found to be in violation of the administrative rules, the first line of authority and control is the agency itself. This form of judicial power allows the agencies to fine or revoke licenses. Agencies such as OSHA (Occupational Safety and Health Administration) have a great deal of authority over business actions and can punish them severely for breaking codes.

## CONTROLS ON BUREAUCRACY

The bureaucracy is not without outside controls. The president and the Office of Management and Budget control agencies' budget access. If no budget resources are assigned, then the agency loses power. Courts can interpret challenges to agency actions to limit the ways agencies wield power. Congress can revise statutes that create the mission of the agencies. The Senate can change the focus of agencies by approving leaders who want to contract or expand their powers. Congress can also change budget priorities and send in the General Accounting Office to hold lengthy audits, checking the propriety of an agency's spending. The Office of Personnel Management controls the merit level of administrators and monitors their training.

# BASICS OF THE BUREAUCRACY

Bureaucracies grow during economic crises and in periods of war. Because of regulations and the numerous jobs created, bureaucracies are very difficult to remove or reduce once established. Some efforts have been created to "audit" agencies and force them to go before a commission to explain their value, but dissolving an agency has never been seriously attempted at the national level.

About 3 million people work for the federal government. This is economically very significant to many communities and states. Recent objections to the closing of many obsolete military bases is a good example—groups who have spent years objecting to wasteful defense spending suddenly object when their regions lose jobs and funds. The classic acronym NIMBY (Not In My Back Yard) applies to the creation or removal of programs. Citizens want prisons, halfway houses, housing for the poor, and other such structures, but not near their homes. National problems are so massive and complex that Congress can no longer solve, monitor, or reduce these issues. However, Congress does not have the time or expertise to run the complex government on a day-to-day basis permanent bureaucracies are able to approach reasonable solutions.

Bureaucratic leaders are experts in science and other disciplines, and that gives them high levels of influence. A large number of agencies now employ enough citizens that they are critical to the local economies of many communities. Bureaucracy rules are complex and give those in the agencies a great deal of leverage in the running of these rules.

Most bureaucracies are staffed by qualified and trained professionals. The Pendleton Act of 1883 ended patronage as the main form of civil service access, and now tests such as the Postal Service Exam and the Foreign Service Exam are used to find qualified candidates. Modern powers of agencies are controversial because of the necessary "legislative" authority to create policies and rules, "executive" authority to monitor policies, and "judicial" authority to determine rules for licenses, seizures, etc. Agencies are often supported locally due to jobs created in a community.

## THE MAJOR UNITS OF THE BUREAUCRACY

### THE EXECUTIVE BRANCH

| | |
|---|---|
| Executive Office of the President (EOP) | |
| The Vice President's Office (VP) | |
| The White House Office (WHO) | The daily staff of the president ("West Wing"), including the Chief of Staff |
| Council of Economic Advisors (CEA) | Three economic policy experts |
| The National Security Council (NSC) | VP, Secretary of Defense, Secretary of State, leaders of the Joint Chiefs, CIA Director, NSC Advisor |
| Office of Management and Budget (OMB) | Creating the federal budget |
| U.S. Trade Representative (USTR) | Policy with groups such as the World Trade Organization |
| The Cabinet: 15 Departments (as created by Congress) | Includes State Department and Homeland Security |

### THE LEGISLATIVE BRANCH

| | |
|---|---|
| Congressional Budget Office (CBO) | Congress's fiscal policy experts |
| General Accounting Office (GAO) | Congress's agency that monitors the spending of federal funds |
| The Library of Congress (LOC) | The national library and data system |

### OTHER AGENCIES

Congress has created about hundreds of agencies that are separate from the presidential Cabinet. These agencies, known as *independent agencies*, were created to work on problems not covered by the Cabinet's traditional duties or to keep powers from the Cabinet's controls.

The greatest trend in governmental employment has been a shift from national to state bureaucracies. Since the 1960s, the number of federal employees has decreased, but the number of state employees has increased significantly. This is partly due to more mandates and responsibilities being given to state and local authorities.

| Major Independent Agencies | Duty Areas |
| --- | --- |
| Consumer Product Safety Commission (CPSC) | Product warnings, recalls |
| Environmental Protection Agency (EPA) | Air, land, water |
| Equal Employment Opportunity Commission (EEOC) | Fairness in the workplace |
| The Federal Reserve (The FED) | National banking and U.S. bond markets, interest rates |
| Federal Emergency Management Agency (FEMA) | Federal assistance to disaster areas |
| National Aeronautics and Space Administration (NASA) | Federal space research |
| National Endowment for the Arts (NEA) | Funds for public arts |
| National Science Foundation (NSF) | Grants for research, especially to universities and laboratories |
| Nuclear Regulatory Commission (NRC) | Domestic power from nuclear fission sources |
| Peace Corps | International assistance |
| Securities and Exchange Commission (SEC) | Monitoring the fairness of stocks and bond markets |
| The Smithsonian Institution | National museums and their collections |

# THE POWERFUL IRON TRIANGLES OF POLICY

Agencies are a key part of political power known as "iron triangles of power." Iron triangles were first defined by the political analyst Hedrick Smith to describe why policies become locked in place and to determine whether or not they helped the public. A famous example is tobacco subsidies. They are supported by legislators from states where the crop is grown, large cigarette lobbies, and the Department of Agriculture. The department needs the funds to monitor and control, the lobbies love the profits, and the politicians love the campaign funds. Other examples are weapons programs that turned out to be so poorly designed that even the Pentagon did not want to use them. However, the billions of dollars at stake for weapons manufacturers, the local jobs involved, and the leaders of those regions caused the weapons to be built regardless.

## COMPONENTS OF IRON TRIANGLES

1. Members of Congress whose districts/states benefit financially from programs will vote to keep them in the budget. The local jobs and pork programs are central points of the support.

2. Lobby and interest groups that get help and influence from the programs will transfer that help into campaign funds, influence peddling, and massive letter drives.

3. The federal agencies that benefit from running and monitoring the programs need the programs in order to have something to control. The agency might not even need to exist if the programs ended.

## WHY IRON TRIANGLES ARE SO POWERFUL

- Government issues are now so vast and complex that smaller governmental units find themselves independent and very much in charge of local and regional policies.

- All three of the main groups that control the triangles benefit from keeping the programs in place, whether or not the public or other agencies see the need.

- Members of Congress get more campaign funds, more name recognition in the district, and more credit for jobs and money.

- Lobby and interest groups keep their supporters in power and keep their contracts, jobs, and benefits.

- Federal agencies have more reasons to exist.

# REVIEW QUESTIONS

## MULTIPLE-CHOICE QUESTIONS

1.  It has been said that many have a negative opinion of government. The bureaucracy probably contributes by

    (A)  not tackling national problems.

    (B)  not following congressional and presidential directives.

    (C)  existing far from the controls of the public.

    (D)  not providing jobs for the public.

    (E)  being comprised by political appointees.

2.  One of the more controversial aspects of the "fourth branch" is that agencies

    (A)  have quasi-legislative and quasi-judicial powers.

    (B)  can change the scope of their own powers.

    (C)  are cut, costing many their jobs.

    (D)  do not help local economies.

    (E)  are mostly staffed by minorities.

3.  The bureaucracy system is now critical to our government because

    (A)  it is so difficult to remove once created.

    (B)  problems are too vast and complex for Congress to control.

    (C)  it has no effective controls on its powers.

    (D)  the executive branch wants power.

    (E)  the Supreme Court has ruled that the system must exist to help Congress.

4.  Ineffective and unwanted programs are often difficult to remove. This is best explained by the fact that

    (A)  iron triangles of power benefit from their existence.

    (B)  federal agencies benefit from their existence.

    (C)  local communities want the jobs that go with the programs.

    (D)  powerful lobby forces support the industries and contracts behind the programs.

    (E)  leaders of agencies benefit from their continued existence.

5.  Which agency is in charge of monitoring the proper spending of federal monies?

    (A)  Office of Budget and Management

    (B)  Congressional Budget Office

    (C)  General Accounting Office

    (D)  Council of Economic Advisors

    (E)  All of the above

## FREE-RESPONSE QUESTIONS

1. The federal bureaucracy has gained power within the federal system.

   (A) Identify and explain a "legislative" power that the bureaucracy has assumed.

   (B) Identify and explain an "executive" power assumed by the bureaucracy.

   (C) Identify and explain a "judicial" power assumed by the bureaucracy.

2. Many see the bureaucracy as growing too rapidly and gaining too much power.

   (A) Identify how each of the three branches of the federal government can attempt to control the bureaucracy.

   (B) Explain at least one option the general public has in controlling bureaucratic powers.

# ANSWERS AND EXPLANATIONS

## MULTIPLE-CHOICE ANSWERS

### 1.  C

The bureaucracy probably contributes to its low public approval by existing far from the controls of the public. The workers are appointed or hired and are difficult to remove. Business-minded citizens are not happy with this practice. The bureaucracy does tackle issues, follow directives, and provide many jobs. Patronage appointments do not affect the vast majority of government workers.

### 2.  A

One of the more controversial aspects of the "fourth branch" is that agencies have quasi-legislative and quasi-judicial powers. Agencies must rely on Congress for power changes, they are seldom cut, they help local economies, and they are staffed by all ethnic groups.

### 3.  B

The system of bureaucracy is now critical to our government because problems are too vast and complex for Congress to control. Choice (A) is incorrect because the issue of removal is not a critical feature. Choice (C) is incorrect because the agencies are controlled by budgetary decisions, court ratings, and congressional actions. Choice (D) is incorrect because the executive has a lot of power, though many independent agencies exist with marginal executive controls. Choice (E) is incorrect because the Supreme Court has not ruled that the system must aid Congress.

### 4.  A

Ineffective and unwanted programs are often difficult to remove because iron triangles of power benefit from their existence.

### 5.  C

The General Accounting Office is in charge of monitoring the proper spending of federal monies. The Office of Budget and Management (A) drafts budget priorities, the Congressional Budget Office (B) helps guide Congress in keeping its priorities in the budget, and the Council of Economic Advisors (D) gives advice to the president.

## FREE-RESPONSE ANSWERS

1. **6-point Rubric**

   **2 points for each identify and explain in (A), (B), (C)**

   - Legislative: Agencies must create the rules and regulations needed to enact their duties, because Congress doesn't have the time or expertise.

   - Executive: Agencies put general rules into effect, often after they have had the duty to create the very rules they execute.

   - Judicial: Agencies rule on licenses, access, and activities allowed for businesses and individuals, with penalties and fines possible.

   - Congress does not have time.

   - Congress doesn't have the expertise.

   - The president does not have time.

   - The court system can't handle all possible agency problems.

2. **4-point Rubric**

   **3 points in part (A): (identify how branches can control the bureaucracy)**

   - Legislative: Controls the budgets, creates new rules/restrictions, and can cut agency.

   - Executive: Orders and memoranda direct agencies to follow presidential directives.

   - Judicial: If challenges are brought, the agency actions can be cut down, overturned, and eliminated.

   **1 point in part (B): (public controls)**

   - Lobby Congress.

   - Lobby the agency directly.

   - Challenge agency in court.

# CHAPTER 15: THE JUDICIAL SYSTEM AND CIVIL LIBERTIES

## IF YOU ONLY LEARN SIX THINGS IN THIS CHAPTER . . . .

1. The judicial system of the United States is clearly divided into state jurisdictions and federal jurisdiction, with state controls over most civil and criminal cases.

2. The modern interpretations of the 14th Amendment represent one of the greatest legal shifts in the history of the nation. All states must provide all citizens due process and equal protection rights, thus beginning the process of the "incorporation" of national standards into state legal codes.

3. Federal court judges and justices have strong political leanings and views. These views are expressed as liberal and conservative biases and are used by judges and justices to try to steer courts in certain political directions.

4. The Supreme Court hears a small minority of cases sent to it on appeal. Supreme Court rulings tend to be on cases of national significance with regard to the interpretation of civil rights and obligations.

5. The majority of the most famous Supreme Court decisions were brought to the court in the 1960s and 1970s, during many of the major civil rights debates.

6. Courts have very carefully structured methods of deciding cases, defining rights and defining the groups of citizens who might be affected by cases.

## INTRODUCTION

Legal issues in the United States are classified in several ways. *Civil cases* cover issues of claims, suits, contracts, and licenses. *Criminal cases* cover illegal actions or wrongful acts and can result in fines, imprisonment, and possibly even the death sentence. When courts rule, they use four kinds of law. The first is *common law*, which is derived from precedents set by courts of the past. Common law traditions can extend back to rights established in colonial, English, and some French courts (Louisiana). When legislative bodies create laws, these codes become *statutory law*. Because the public elects the representatives who create statutory law, courts consider it more compelling than common law. When agencies create rules and rulings that concern their areas of influence, these become *administrative law*. *Constitutional law* covers the broad area of interpretation under judicial review.

# TWO-COURT SYSTEMS

The court structure of the United States remains one of the best examples of the federal system. States have unique legal traditions, handle most civil and criminal cases that occur in the country, and have separate systems for appeals from lower courts. The states' jurisdictions have always been given the label *general law*.

Federal courts work within the boundaries of federal law—cases that are "*limited and exclusive jurisdiction*" go to federal courts. Only those cases arising from interstate issues, conflicts with federal authorities, issues specific to sections of the Bill of Rights, and crimes listed as federal in nature by Congress are heard in federal courts. The Supreme Court has ruled in many cases to expand federal authority, but such expansions only occur after specific legal challenges. States continue to hold rule over most legal activities in the country.

## BASICS OF THE DUAL COURT SYSTEM

The following fall under "general law and jurisdiction" of the United States:

- Most civil disputes between citizens are settled in state civil courts.

- Most criminal disputes in the United States are settled in state criminal courts.

- Appeals from state courts are sent to state appeals court systems. Such appeals may end in state supreme courts. Many of these are known as "courts of last resort."

The following fall under "limited and exclusive jurisdiction" of federal law:

- Federal civil disputes are heard in specific federal courts or federal district courts.

- Federal criminal cases are usually heard in federal district courts.

- Examples of federal "limited and exclusive jurisdiction" from the Constitution or laws passed by Congress include these:

  - Citizens of one state versus citizens of another state

  - The counterfeiting of U.S. currency

  - Kidnapping

  - Mail fraud

- Interstate trade conflicts

- National banking conflicts

- Conflicts with federal officials, agencies, and the federal government

- U.S. border issues

- Crossing state lines with the intent to commit crimes (i.e., RICO laws covering interstate crime syndicates)

- Conflicts with the civil rights of citizens

- Conflicts over patents, copyrights, and customs rulings

## LAYERS OF DUAL COURTS

Both the states and the federal court systems consist of layers of courts. At the federal level, most cases begin in *district courts* that are found in most urban centers. If appeals are granted, cases move to regional *courts of appeals* or *circuit courts*. There are 12 such courts of appeals.

If further appeals are allowed, the Supreme Court of the United States finalizes the case. A few cases listed in Article 3 of the Constitution are given *original jurisdiction*, which means they are heard first and only by the Supreme Court. Such cases involve ambassadors, public ministers, or states suing other states. In modern times, such cases are usually limited to state disputes concerning boundaries, water, or mineral rights. All cases brought to the Supreme Court on appeal from lower courts (appellate jurisdiction) can be accepted or rejected by the Supreme Court, unless a lower state or federal court has declared a law unconstitutional.

# CREATION OF "JUDICIAL REVIEW"

The single most significant change in judicial history was the creation of the power of *judicial review*. The Supreme Court used the twists and turns of the 1803 decision in *Marbury v. Madison* to establish its authority over interpreting the constitutional status of the acts of Congress. Some early leaders, such as Thomas Jefferson, would have preferred *legislative review*, but the court precedent has stood the test of the centuries.

William Marbury headed a list of Federalist appointees that claimed that Jefferson and his Secretary of State James Madison were hiding their appointment papers. Marbury demanded that the Court force the delivery of the papers by using a law that Congress had created, giving the Supreme Court the power to make the ruling. Chief Justice John Marshall ruled that the law that gave them such powers was itself unconstitutional and, therefore, they couldn't give the order to the president. Jefferson and the Congress had to accept the idea of judicial review or grant the Supreme Court power to demand any order it chose over the other branches. The court took over the power to interpret the words of the Constitution.

# THE "SECOND" CONSTITUTION

Within the dual court system, the greatest change has been the use of the 14th Amendment to apply many sections of the Bill of Rights to state laws. As previously mentioned, states have separate sets of jurisdiction. This was originally interpreted to mean that the civil rights listed in the Bill of Rights applied only to federal cases and the actions under the federal government. But when the Civil War solved the issue of states practicing slavery, the 13th, 14th, and 15th Amendments were written to redefine how states could legally deal with residents' rights of freedom, citizenship, and voting. The 14th Amendment contains language that requires all states to give all citizens *due process* and *equal protection*.

Case decisions in the 20th century caused interpretations where specific rights in the other amendments applied to states through the 14th Amendment's requirements. This development is now known as the *Incorporation Doctrine*. Now states must, in their own courts and laws, give citizens protections such as rights to counsel and rights for limited search, seizure, or arrest. Because courts must wait for specific challenges to be brought before them by litigants, some sections of the Bill of Rights have not been *incorporated* through the 14th Amendment.

## THE 14TH AMENDMENT

Prior to the 14th Amendment (1868), dual federalism dominated views of federal laws. The legal sections of the Constitution were for federal courts and claims. State constitutions covered state laws. The Bill of Rights held for federal courts, not state courts.

Key phrases in the 14th Amendment include the following:

- "All persons born…in the United States" (therefore in all states)

- "No State shall make or enforce any law which shall abridge the privileges…of citizens of the United States"

- "…nor shall any State deprive any person of life, liberty, or property, without *due process of law*; nor deny to any person…*the equal protection of the laws*." Note the key legal shift. The amendment slides into the area of matching state rules with federal rules.

- The Bill of Rights can become the foundation of limits for all states. This legal principle is known as *incorporation*. The Supreme Court has given a great deal of consideration to the amount of incorporation in different cases. As the Supreme Court has analyzed various Bill of Rights claims through the 14th Amendment, the issue of selective incorporation of the due process clause has come to the forefront. In the late 1800s, a railway and property case contained early uses of incorporation. The Gitlow case of 1925 is noted as the key and significant incorporation of free speech rights. Several major cases of the civil rights era selectively incorporated other Bill of Rights sections. As of 2005, the "equal protection" section of the 14th Amendment had not been used for incorporation cases, nor have

Bill of Rights issues of indictment by grand juries (the 5th Amendment), the right to a civil trial in civil suits (the 7th Amendment), or the need for 12 jurors and unanimous verdicts. The Supreme Court's incremental application of incorporation is the essence of selective incorporation.

## RIGHTS IN THE BILL OF RIGHTS THAT HAVE BEEN "INCORPORATED" THROUGH THE 14TH AMENDMENT VIA SUPREME COURT RULINGS

Note that not *all* of the rights listed in the Bill of Rights have been "incorporated," because some of the rights have not been challenged in cases or have not been accepted for such challenges by the Supreme Court.

- Privacy (not listed in the Bill of Rights but implied and interpreted from several amendment cases)

- Free speech (1st Amendment)

- Free press (1st Amendment)

- Freedom of religion (1st Amendment)

- Assembly and petition rights (1st Amendment)

- "Association" (1st Amendment)

- Search and seizure (4th Amendment)

- "Exclusion" of evidence (implied in cases dealing with the 4th Amendment, such as *Mapp v. Ohio*)

- Self-incrimination (6th Amendment)

- Confront witnesses (6th Amendment)

- Impartial jury (6th Amendment)

- Speedy trial (6th Amendment)

- Right to counsel (6th Amendment)

- Public trial (6th Amendment)

- Cruel and unusual punishment (8th Amendment)

# STRUCTURE OF THE FEDERAL COURT SYSTEM

**Lower Federal Courts** (trial courts where juries may be present; run by federal judges)

- U.S. District Courts (94 sitting across the country, as of 2009)
- Various military courts and tribunals
- Courts, hearings, panels of various federal agencies, including independent agencies
- Bankruptcy Courts (officially they are units of the District Courts)
- U.S. Court of Federal Claims (claims against the United States, 16 judges run this court)
- U.S. Court of International Trade
- U.S. Tax Court
- Courts of the District of Columbia
- U.S. Territorial Courts (Guam, Northern Marianas Islands, U.S. Virgin Islands)
- Foreign Intelligence Surveillance Court

**Appeals Courts** (also run by federal judges)

- Legislative Appeals Courts
- U.S. Court of Appeals for the Armed Services
- U.S. Court of Appeals for the Federal Circuit (from Federal Claims Court…)
- The U.S. Courts of Appeals (13 circuits, including DC, 6 to 28 judges in each; these 13 courts hear appeals from the Federal District Courts)

**The Supreme Court**

- **Nine federal justices** (The number is set by Congress.)
- **Original jurisdiction** cases cover foreign diplomats, United States versus a state, a state versus another state, a state versus citizens of another state, a state versus a foreign country.
- **Appellate jurisdiction** covers cases granted from U.S. courts of appeals, state supreme courts, the U.S. Court of Appeals for the Armed Services, and the Court of Appeals for the Federal Circuit.
- The vast majority of cases appealed to the Supreme Court under *writs of certiorari* are denied hearings by the Supreme Court justices. Thousands of requests are made annually, but the Supreme Court will hear only about 100 cases. Those cases not granted hearings are returned (*remanded*) to the last court, where that decision stands.

## FEDERAL JUDICIAL TERMS

Federal judges and Supreme Court justices can serve for life terms. This makes their initial selection important and very political. Members of the judiciary are expected by liberals and conservatives to express strong political viewpoints on the uses of the Constitution. The spectrum of opinions forms around the issue of the powers of government, just like the sides taken by parties. Liberals want a stronger use of the laws aimed at providing flexible protections with the goal of equality. They believe that the Constitution can be interpreted broadly and adapted easily for the changing issues of modern times. Conservatives support more limited controls by courts, emphasizing liberty and regional governments like states. When presidents are trying to fill the many court vacancies, they rely on advisors and members of Congress to suggest names of judges and lawyers whose political viewpoints are parallel to their own.

Once a nomination is sent by the president, the Senate Judiciary Committee plays the key role of supporting or opposing the judge's political slant. Those who favor a more open interpretation of the powers of the Constitution are labeled *judicial liberals*, and those who oppose that view are *judicial conservatives*.

# THE SUPREME COURT'S WORK

Justices of the Supreme Court must be nominated by the president and approved by the Senate. The work and decisions of the Supreme Court are the focus of national scrutiny. The vast majority (99 percent) of cases appealed to the court are *remanded*, making the lower court's decision final. Challenges of constitutional importance can stem from business contracts, interstate and international trade, criminal case challenges, and issues as simple as traffic stops. Appeals are submitted through *writs of certiorari*, and cases are usually supported by national organizations that want to help argue the positions with briefs and summaries. These "*Friends of the Court*" submit *amicus curiae* briefs to help the court interpret challenges and legal histories. Groups such as the American Civil Liberties Union (ACLU) are famous for their legal teams that volunteer to help with costs and court procedures to help clarify important civil rights and liberty questions.

## FUNCTIONS OF THE SUPREME COURT

The Supreme Court functions in a very egalitarian manner. The chief justice is a guide and meeting chairperson but has no special voting powers. The chief does not have to be part of the majority. Conferences and debates in the court have traditionally been relatively secret events, with only recently books and memoirs published revealing how decisions are argued or finalized. In the few times that public hearings are held in Washington, D.C., the procedures are formal. Attorneys are very limited in their presentations, and any member of the court can ask any question he or she considers important.

Once the court has a majority of five to nine justices, it can explain to the legal community what it wants the decision to mean for the law. The *majority opinion* becomes the guide to interpreting the decision's effect on the use of the Constitution. If one to four justices disagree with the ruling, the court can publish a *minority opinion* explaining those opinions. Minority opinions are often used by the legal community for future challenges. Sometimes justices who voted with the majority may not agree with the legal principals given in the majority opinion. They might publish *concurrent opinions* that signal a different approach to the way the majority ruling might be used by the legal community.

## JURISDICTION OF THE U.S. SUPREME COURT

- The Supreme Court hears original cases as listed in Article 3 of the Constitution.

- It also hears cases that are granted an appeal hearing by the Supreme Court from lower federal courts (*writ of certiorari* grants under the Rule of 4).

- If any four of the justices want to rule on a case, the entire court hears it.

- If state laws are declared unconstitutional by a lower federal court, then they move to the Supreme Court.

- If federal laws are held unconstitutional by a state court, then they move to the Supreme Court.

- Appeals granted from cases in state supreme courts can be heard by the U.S. Supreme Court.

## SUPREME COURT ACTIVISM AND RESTRAINT

A second, and equally important, form of interpretation occurs with Supreme Court decisions. *Judicial restraint* is the guiding principle that courts will not overturn previous court decisions and opinions. Courts will focus on the limits of government, the responsibilities of legislatures to correct social disputes, and the rights of states. *Judicial activism* has goals of correcting previous decisions through new cases that overturn previous rulings and correcting mistakes made by other governmental bodies. "Activism" can take on liberal or conservative agendas, and the term has been divided by some into *policy activism* versus *structural activism*. Policy activism concerns rulings that attempt to correct problems with civil liberties, such as privacy. Structural activism is aimed at correcting the ways different layers of government have attempted to change their powers.

## THE IMPORTANCE OF COURT RULINGS

Supreme Court rulings are central to understanding the development of civil rights and civil liberties in the United States. Civil rights stem from the Declaration of Independence statement that "all men are created equal," rights given by the "equal protection" section of the 14th Amendment, and laws from Congress. They cover minority group issues such as racial discrimination, voting rights, and privacy. Civil liberties cover the freedoms that citizens have from governmental interference and control. Many federal liberties were incorporated under the due process section of the 14th Amendment as it applies to the other portions of the Bill of Rights. Courts have used different legal tests (see the cases that follow) to determine which groups can claim which kinds of rights. Courts have determined that women are a minority group due to persistent historic forms of discrimination. Minority status also applies to ethnic minorities and to people with certain disabilities.

Precedent-setting court cases are the focus of much study and memorization. They have been used to create a list of law interpretations, limits on police powers, limits on citizens' rights, and limits on governmental actions. These cases, listed in the following table, summarize the various interpretations of key rights such as speech, religion, and search and seizure.

## SOME OF THE MOST FAMOUS COURT CASES

Different texts and sources list various "famous" or "key" cases. The following table attempts to present those cases likely to be mentioned in AP exams.

| | |
|---|---|
| *Marbury v. Madison*, 1803 | Judicial review established. |
| *McCulloch v. Maryland*, 1819 | Federal "implied powers" supreme; federal banks allowed. |
| *Gibbons v. Ogden*, 1824 | Commerce Clause gives Congress broad powers. |
| *Dred Scott v. Sanford*, 1857 | Slaves are not citizens but property. |
| *Munn v. Illinois*, 1876 | Feds can regulate businesses crossing state lines. |
| *Plessy v. Ferguson*, 1896 | "Separate but Equal" allowed for state laws. |
| *Schenk v. U.S.*, 1919 | "Clear and Present Danger Test" to limit speech. |
| *Gitlow v. New York*, 1925 | Limits on "anarchy," but free speech "incorporated." |
| *Near v. Minnesota*, 1931 | No "prior restraint" of the freedom of the press. |
| *Korematsu v. U.S.*, 1944 | Government can intern (detain) citizens in emergencies. |
| *Brown v. Board of Ed.*, 1954 | Overturned *Plessy* in public schools. |
| *Roth v. U.S.*, 1957 | Obscenity is not free speech. |
| *Mapp v. Ohio*, 1961 | Warrants needed for evidence to be used (exclusion). |
| *Baker v. Carr*, 1962 | State apportionment must be "one man = one vote." |
| *Engel v. Vitale*, 1962 | No school-led daily prayer in public schools. |
| *Gideon v. Wainright*, 1963 | States must provide attorneys in state courts. |
| *Heart of Atlanta v. U.S.*, 1964 | Commerce Clause applies to private business/interstate activities. |
| *Griswold v. Connecticut*, 1965 | Information about birth control is a privacy right. |

*(continued on next page)*

# SOME OF THE MOST FAMOUS COURT CASES (con't)

Different texts and sources list various "famous" or "key" cases. The following table attempts to present those cases likely to be mentioned in AP exams.

| | |
|---|---|
| *Miranda v. Arizona*, 1966 | Police must explain rights at the time of arrest. |
| *Terry v. Ohio*, 1968 | Police can search and seize with probable cause. |
| *Lemon v. Kurtzman*, 1971 | Some government aid to church schools is allowed (Lemon Test). |
| *N.Y. Times v. U.S.*, 1971 | No prior restraint of the stolen *Pentagon Papers*. |
| *Miller v. California*, 1973 | Community standards determine obscenity. |
| *Roe v. Wade*, 1973 | First trimester abortions legal as medical privacy. |
| *U.S. v. Nixon*, 1974 | Executive privilege does not extend to criminal cases. |
| *Gregg v. Georgia*, 1976 | Death penalty upheld within the 8th Amendment. |
| *Buckley v. Valeo*, 1976 | Campaign money limits, but independent and personal money allowed. |
| *Regents v. Bakke*, 1978 | No racial quotas allowed, but race can be considered. |
| *New Jersey v. TLO*, 1985 | School searches without warrants possible. |
| *Hazelwood v. Kuhlmeier*, 1988 | School newspapers can be edited by teachers, administrators. |
| *Texas v. Johnson*, 1989 | Flag burning is a form of political free speech. |
| *Planned Parenthood v. Casey*, 1992 | States can put some restrictions on *Roe* rights. |
| *Santa Fe ISD v. Doe*, 2000 | No school-led prayers at extracurricular events. |
| *Gratz v. Bollinger*, 2003 | Affirmative action at colleges okay but limited. |

## THE CHIEF'S ROLE

Courts are named after the chief justice, but the chief has no special powers over the other justices. The chief organizes meetings and guides discussions, but all other justices have equal votes. Any five justices make the majority vote in a case, whether or not the chief is one of the majority. If the chief is part of the majority, he or she assigns the writing of the majority opinion to one of the justices. This might affect how the opinion is expressed to the legal community.

There have been 17 chief justices under 44 U.S. presidents. The following four are possibly the most famous and represent significant court eras and changes:

| | | | |
|---|---|---|---|
| John Marshall | 1801–1835 | 34 years | Helped found many early court powers. |
| Roger Taney | 1836–1864 | 28 years | Dominated mid-1800s and Civil War. |
| Earl Warren | 1953–1969 | 16 years | Major civil rights changes and cases |
| William Rehnquist | 1986–2005 | 19 years | Major conservative influence |

# CIVIL LIBERTIES AND EQUAL PROTECTION

Categories of people who are considered for equal protection include the following:

- Age groups
- Racial classification groups
- Gender groups
- Economic status groups

Who is qualified for assistance and who isn't? How do the categories match needs? If people are told that they are not qualified for assistance, how may they challenge that governmental decision?

## TESTS COURTS USE TO DETERMINE CLASSIFICATION STATUS OF CITIZENS

| | |
|---|---|
| **Rational Basis Test (now replaced)** | If the state can prove that a classification scheme is rational, it might be allowed to separate citizens, as on the basis of gender. |
| **Strict Scrutiny Test** | The state must prove a "compelling state interest" in the classification scheme and must narrowly use items such as race to classify citizens. |
| **Intermediate Scrutiny Test** | This is usually used for gender classification systems and must be substantially related to the need for the scheme. |
| **Heightened Scrutiny** | This has generally replaced the rational basis test and requires that government classifications based on gender must be related to an important governmental objective that doesn't discriminate. |

# THE JUDICIARY AND THE POLITICAL SPECTRUM

Justices and judges have political interests and agendas. Federal judges try to build a legacy of political biases to improve their standing for advancement under Republican or Democratic administrations. The selection of Supreme Court justices has always been a game of maneuvering for liberal, conservative, or moderate ideals. The history of presidents and judicial appointments has been a history of selections for the "correct" biases. Recent famous examples include Eisenhower's disappointment with Earl Warren's liberalism, the Senate's rejection of Reagan's conservative nominee Robert Bork, and Antonin Scalia's rise as the conservative standard on the court.

Presidents have a long and consistent record of selecting an overwhelming number of judges and justices with political beliefs similar to their own. Members of the courts tend to follow the biases of the major parties, with the additional consideration of broad or limited interpretations of the Constitution. This is known as *judicial restraint* versus *judicial activism*.

# KINDS OF JUDICIAL BIASES/VIEWPOINTS

Judicial Liberals | They tend to support the following:

- Broad interpretations of the Elastic Clause ("necessary and proper")
- Broad interpretations of civil rights acts and laws
- Pro-choice decisions
- Strict limits on the separation of church and state (no school prayer)
- Affirmative action programs to end discrimination

Judicial Conservatives | They tend to support the following:

- Stricter limits on the use of the Commerce Clause (less power for feds)
- Limited uses of "necessary and proper" in context of Article 1, Section 8
- More local and state control of civil rights questions
- Pro-life decisions
- Community standards for speech and obscenity
- The government's role in protecting from obscenity, immorality
- Affirmative action as a form of reverse discrimination
- Community and moral limits to lifestyle choices

Judicial Restraint | Also known as *strict constructionism* or *original intent*
They tend to support the following:

- The idea of not overturning previous cases if possible
- Natural rights of citizens that government must leave alone
- Article 3 as a statement of Supreme Court powers to resolve disputes only
- Article 3 as *not* giving the Supreme Court the right to "create" policy
- The 9th and 10th Amendments, leaving rights to citizens and states
- The idea that Congress should be in charge of new policy or create amendments
- The idea that proper state authority should be emphasized
- The idea that the Founding Fathers built a government of limits and these should be followed

| Judicial Activism (Policy Activism; Structural Activism) | Also known as *broad constructionism* or *loose constructionism*<br>They tend to support the following: |
|---|---|

- Overturning previous cases more easily if those are seen as wrong
- Judicial review as a proper and well-established power
- The 14th Amendment giving the federal government power to "incorporate"
- The idea that the history of state and local courts is a history of abuses of civil rights and segregation and the feds should step in
- The idea that the Constitution is silent on rights like "privacy" and "innocent until proven guilty" so the courts can protect these broadly
- The idea that the Founding Fathers expected leaders to adapt the Constitution over time and wrote the document with this in mind
- The idea that courts might try to correct laws, institutions, or state controls over issues such as search and seizure rights, privacy rights, counsel rights. (These are often seen as pro-liberal in bias.)
- The idea that courts might try to change the ways the federal, state, or local governments try to set up rules, controls, laws that affect the federal system. (These are liberal or conservative biases.)

## STATUS OF THE JUDICIARY AND THE PUBLIC

**Ways the judiciary is insulated:**

- Once appointed, judges and justices may serve for life.
- Due to judicial review powers, the Supreme Court interprets the Constitution for the rest of the country.

**Ways the judiciary "answers" to the public:**

- Judges and justices may be impeached and removed by Congress.
- Past records of opinions and actions are used to evaluate judges for their appointments.
- Congress can react to unpopular decisions by leading the charge to amend the Constitution to reflect a more popular form.
- Future court cases may be used to reverse decisions.
- The Supreme Court can hold off on extremely controversial issues by not accepting lower court appeals that concern such issues.

# BILL OF RIGHTS AND OTHER AMENDMENTS: JUDICIAL TERMS

| Term/Phrase | Amendment | Notes |
| --- | --- | --- |
| Civil War/ Reconstruction Amendments | 13, 14, 15 | No slavery, national citizenship, votes not denied due to "race, color." |
| Clear and Present Danger Test | 1 | Government can limit speech if the speech endangers the nation or a state. |
| Community Standards | 1 | What kinds of speech/art are obscene according to the community affected? |
| Confrontation Clause | 6 | "…to be confronted with the witnesses against him…" |
| Cruel and Unusual Clause | 8 | "…nor cruel and unusual punishments inflicted" (defined by Supreme Court challenges and decisions). |
| Double Jeopardy Clause | 5 | "…nor shall any person be subject for the same offence to be twice put in jeopardy of life or limb…" |
| Due Process Clause | 5 | "…nor be deprived of life, liberty, or property, without due process of law…" |
| Eminent Domain/ Takings Clause/ Just Compensation Clause | 5 | "…nor shall private property be taken for public use, without just compensation." |
| Equal Protection Clause | 14 | "…nor shall any State…deny to any person within its jurisdiction the equal protection of the laws." |
| Establishment Clause | 1 | "Congress shall make no law respecting an establishment of religion…" |
| Exclusion/ Exclusionary Rule | 4 | If evidence is searched and seized illegally then it cannot be used in court but must be "excluded." |
| Free Exercise Clause | 1 | "Congress shall make no law…prohibiting the free exercise thereof…" (religion). |
| Freedom of the Press | 1 | "Congress shall make no law…abridging…the freedom of the press…" |
| Good Faith Exception | 4 | If some evidence is collected improperly, but the police are not to blame, it might be used in court. |
| Incorporation (of the Bill of Rights) | 14 | Which parts of due process rights under the 14th Amendment apply to state laws and procedures? |
| Libel and Slander | 1 | What penalties are possible for written or spoken words that are created to damage someone? |

| | | |
|---|---|---|
| Liberty Clause | 5 | "…nor be deprived of life, liberty, or property, without due process of law…" |
| Loyalty Clause | 14 | "No person shall be…in Congress…[if] engaged in insurrection or rebellion against…" |
| Penumbra Rights | Several | Rights not specifically listed in the Constitution but still protected (such as privacy) |
| Prior Restraint | 1 | What kinds of press freedoms are limited before publication? |
| Pure Speech | 1 | Speech that is spoken or written |
| Reserved Powers | 10 | Which powers do states control? What are the limits and range of such powers? |
| Right to Counsel | 6 | When must the state provide counsel? At every trial? At questioning? To whom must counsel be provided? |
| Search and Seizure Clause | 4 | "The right of the people to be secure in their persons, houses…against unreasonable searches and seizures…" |
| Selective Incorporation | 14 | Rights in the Bill of Rights, taken from specific cases, applied to state laws under the 14th Amendment's requirements |
| Self-Incrimination | 5 | It is not the duty of the accused to provide evidence to be used by the prosecution or be compelled to do so. |
| Symbolic Speech | 1 | Actions of political nature, or protest "statements" that are not just spoken or written |
| Trial by Jury Clause | 7 | "In Suits at common law…the right to trial by jury shall be preserved…" |
| Women's Suffrage Clause | 19 | "The right…to vote shall not be denied or abridged by the United States or by any State on account of sex." |

# REVIEW QUESTIONS

## MULTIPLE-CHOICE QUESTIONS

1. Which of the following Supreme Court decisions established the concept of judicial review?

   (A) *Plessy v. Ferguson*

   (B) *McCulloch v. Maryland*

   (C) *Griswold v. Connecticut*

   (D) *Marbury v. Madison*

   (E) *Buckley v. Valeo*

2. The Supreme Court has original jurisdiction in all of the following instances **EXCEPT**

   (A) cases covering foreign diplomats.

   (B) cases that involve the United States versus a state.

   (C) cases dealing with the armed forces.

   (D) cases where one state is opposing another state.

   (E) cases where one state is opposing a foreign country.

3. Which statement concerning the judicial system is **NOT** correct?

   (A) Civil cases cover issues of claims, suits, contracts, and licenses.

   (B) Common law is derived from precedents set in previous courts of the past.

   (C) Statutory law is derived from legislative bodies creating statutes.

   (D) Constitutional law is derived from the broad area of interpretation under judicial review.

   (E) Administrative law is derived from the traditions of the French and English.

4. Which of the following statements is **NOT** consistent with the concept of judicial conservatives?

   (A) They are basically supporters of local and state control of civil rights questions.

   (B) They are basically supporters of pro-life decisions.

   (C) They are basically supporters of expanded interpretations of the "elastic clause."

   (D) They are basically supporters of applying community standards for speech and obscenity.

   (E) They basically feel that affirmative action is a form of reverse discrimination.

5. The power of the government to seize private property for the public good is represented by which of the following terms?

   (A) *Amicus curiae*

   (B) *Writ of mandamus*

   (C) *Ex post facto*

   (D) *Writ of certiorari*

   (E) Eminent domain

## FREE-RESPONSE QUESTIONS

1.  The judicial system of the United States is still the most "federal" part of the government.

    (A)  Define how the court system is "federal" in structure.

    (B)  Identify three kinds of authority federal courts control and what this overall level of power is called.

    (C)  Identify two kinds of authority state courts control and what this overall level of power is called.

2.  Cases can reach the Supreme Court in two main ways.

    (A)  Define the two ways cases go to the Supreme Court.

    (B)  Identify two kinds of cases that go directly to the Supreme Court.

    (C)  Identify at least two steps that occur when cases are appealed and accepted by the Supreme Court.

# ANSWERS AND EXPLANATIONS

## MULTIPLE-CHOICE ANSWERS

**1. D**

The court case of *Marbury v. Madison* established the concept of judicial review—the power to interpret the meaning of laws and their Constitutional status.

**2. C**

Cases dealing with the armed forces do not fall under the area of original jurisdiction of the Supreme Court. The Supreme Court has original jurisdiction in cases covering foreign diplomats, in cases that involve the United States versus a state, in cases where one state is opposing another state, and in cases where one state is opposing a foreign country.

**3. E**

It is not correct that administrative law is derived from the traditions of the French and English. Administrative law is created by government agencies through their rules and rulings.

**4. C**

Judicial conservatives would not support expansion of the elastic clause but would rather see limited implementation of its use.

**5. E**

Eminent domain is the power of the government to seize private property for the public good.

## FREE-RESPONSE QUESTIONS

1. **8-point Rubric**

   **1 point in part (A): (define)**

   - Dual court system: Two distinct levels of jurisdiction, strong state involvement

   **4 points in part (B): (three kinds of federal, label)**

   - "Limited and exclusive jurisdiction"
   - Federal civil law
   - Federal criminal law
   - Federal appeals
   - Constitutional jurisdiction counterfeiting, interstate conflicts, state versus state
   - Crimes made federal, kidnapping, civil rights abuses, attacking federal officials

   **3 points in part (C): (two kinds of state authority, label)**

   - "General law/general jurisdiction"
   - State civil laws
   - State criminal codes
   - State appeals
   - Common law of state courts
   - State statutory laws

2. **6-point Rubric**

   **2 points in part (A): (two ways to the Supreme Court)**

   - Appeal from lower federal courts
   - Appeal from the highest state courts
   - Original jurisdiction cases

   **2 points in part (B): (two cases that go directly to the Supreme Court)**

   - State versus state
   - Ambassadors and public ministers

   **2 points in part (C): (two steps to acceptance)**

   - Submission of *writ of certiorari*
   - Rule of Four vote

# CHAPTER 16: THE FEDERAL BUDGET AND ECONOMIC POLICIES

## IF YOU ONLY LEARN SIX THINGS IN THIS CHAPTER . . . .

1. The creation of the federal budget is one of the central tasks of national government.

2. The Office of Management and Budget creates the basic budget and uses this duty as a way to control the priorities of agency support. Congress battles this power with its own budget agency, the Congressional Budget Office.

3. One of the biggest budget problems facing the nation is the growing amount of annual "mandatory" spending, which limits "discretionary" spending.

4. There are two central, opposing theories, open competition versus governmental guidance, of governmental policy toward the economy.

5. The 20th century saw the rise of national expectations that the federal government would cure business ills, moderate business cycles, and stabilize competition.

6. Rules created by Congress without funds available for enforcement is a major controversy of economic policy. These "unfunded mandates" are a source of conflict between national and local governments.

## THE BUDGET

Tax collections and budget expenditures now approach trillions of dollars annually. Every area of society, business, and government is affected by the control of funding—bureaucracies, legislatures, courts, and citizens are involved in the massive process of creating and spending the federal budget. The federal budget process prioritizes where funds go and what can be done with them. Controlling economic growth has become the measure of how effective the government is at creating a stable infrastructure and atmosphere for improvement.

The federal budget year, called the *fiscal year*, goes from October 1 through September 30. The Office of Management and Budget (OMB), under the executive branch, is responsible for drafting the budget. The Congressional Budget Office (CBO) is the professional staff group responsible for giving Congress budget projections and priorities and balancing the OMB's priorities with Congress's policy interests.

The Senate Appropriations Committee and the House Appropriations Committee are in charge of final budget numbers. Chairpersons of these committees are considered some of the most powerful leaders of Congress. Each committee has 12 subcommittees that deal with budget issues concerning the different parts of government (defense, energy, security, etc.). The chairpersons of the 24 subcommittees are known as the "Budget Cardinals" and have vast influence over program priorities. They dispense pork benefits, cut some area funds, and generally have control over the federal money trough.

The main focus of the budget is on "discretionary" programs, which Congress can choose to fund. Mandatory programs are already set for funding. Congress might have to decide to authorize borrowing to cover all these forms of funding.

## RECENT BUDGET EXAMPLE OF REVENUES AND EXPENDITURES (EARLY 2000s)

| **Revenues** and Sources = $1.946 Trillion | Approximate % |
| --- | --- |
| Individual Income Tax Receipts | 50% |
| Social Security Taxes and Contributions | 32% |
| Corporate Income Tax Receipts | 10% |
| Federal Excise Taxes | 3% |
| Deposit on Federal Earnings | 2% |
| Estate, Gift Tax Receipts | 1% |
| Federal Customs, Duties, Tariff Receipts | 1% |

| **Expenditures** and Sources = $2.052 Trillion | |
| --- | --- |
| Social Security Payments | 22% |
| Defense | 16% |
| Income Security | 14% |
| Net Interest Payments on the Public Debt | 12% |
| Medicare Payments | 11% |
| Health Payments | 8% |
| Veterans' Benefits | 3% |
| Federal Education Funding | 3% |
| All Other Spending on Programs (running the government agencies, transportation funds, energy funds, court funds, etc.) | 11% |

# CREATING THE BUDGET—NEEDS AND PRIORITIES

Creating the budget takes three major policy steps: *agenda building, policy formation,* and *policy adoption.* At the center is the money needed to run any program or agency that will execute laws. Once programs are in place, further *evaluation* occurs to determine if programs work as intended or if they need modification.

The Constitution requires that Congress, and specifically the House, initiate the collecting and spending of revenues annually. The federal government cannot raise revenues without legislative action and votes.

The OMB gathers the data needed to create a budget. Directors of the OMB have come to understand that this is a powerful way to add or subtract monies to programs they and the president may favor or oppose. The quantity of data, the thousands of pages of text, and the complexity of the information make budget creation a massive and political undertaking. Congress becomes a reactionary group, trying to figure out how the OMB has created priorities, dealing with biases, and then attempting to support or change them. Congressional leaders and committees must also try to add all of their pork projects as amendments or separate pieces of legislation. To help with this monumental task and to attempt to balance some of the control of data by the OMB, Congress created the CBO, whose staff helps guide the leaders of the legislature with their priorities.

Congressional committees are central in the development of the budget. Membership on the Senate and House Appropriations Committees is seen as a key position of power over projects and party priorities. Subcommittee and committee chairpersons are some of the most powerful influence peddlers in Washington.

# TYPES OF SPENDING

Three major issues now dominate all discussions of budget and policy. The first is the growing obligation of *mandatory spending* programs, such as Social Security. Mandatory spending programs require that the federal government pay back the contributions previously taxed from citizens. As the lifespan of the average person increases, fewer children are born, and benefit expectations grow, the government faces rising obligations to give citizens back the money that has been collected for retirement costs. This has caused a percentage drop in the amount of money available for *discretionary spending* on all programs from defense, to roads, to running the government itself. Added to set discretionary programs are the exploding number of *pork projects* that members of both parties use as rewards for their constituencies and to garner promises of future voting support.

## GOVERNMENT DEBT

> The second issue is the massive government *debt* that has accumulated in record amounts since the 1980s. Hundreds of billions of dollars are now needed annually just to keep up with the interest payments on the various government bond promises.

In recent years, the debate has become even more political as foreign governments, such as South Korea and the People's Republic of China, have purchased substantial sums of the bonds. Will future taxpayers be willing to see vast fortunes pass on to governments hostile to the United States? As more *annual deficits* add to the total debt, more interest payments are needed, thus further decreasing the amount available for future discretionary needs.

The third controversy stems from key disagreements about the government's role in economic policies. Federal statutes require that the government must try to keep the economy stable and growing, but there is no consensus on how this is best done or even if the government should try. Interest rate policies, reactions to inflation, reactions to tax systems, and subsidy programs are expensive and may only be beneficial to some portions of the country.

# ECONOMIC POLICY TERMS AND THEORIES

## Laissez-Faire, Classical Capitalism, and Supply-Side Policies

A more conservative and libertarian approach to government's role is to allow for private competition to run the economy as much as possible. Taxes should be minimal, profit motives should be rewarded, and helping the rich conduct more business will help the middle class and poor find more jobs. Government should make fair competition the goal and limit blocks to competition such as monopolies, unions, and tariffs. Many conservative groups strongly support these views.

## Keynesian Policies

Named after the British economist John M. Keynes (pronounced to rhyme with "canes"), this system greatly influenced New Deal policies. It argues that when the economy stalls and falls into recessions/depressions, Congress should lower taxes and create jobs. When the economy overheats and suffers from inflation, Congress should raise taxes and cut jobs. The key assumption is that *laissez-faire* policies will generally underperform and leave the nation vulnerable to drastic business cycle swings. Safety nets and safe banks that are closely regulated are key policies. Many liberals support these arguments and programs.

## MONETARY POLICY

Also based on some ideas of Keynes, monetary policy is central bank policy, which is conducted in the United States by the Federal Reserve Board. It states that when the economy is in recession, government should force lower interest rates and buy bonds from the public. When there is too much inflation, the Federal Reserve should force higher interest rates and sell bonds to the public, thus lowering the supply of money. Conservatives who disagree with Congress running the economy often concur that the central bank system works to regulate business cycles.

## MONETARIST POLICY

Based on antisocialist theories, monetarism is also conservative and more *laissez-faire*. The main role of government should be to support free competition and control the amounts of money in the economy. This aims to provide stable growth and control inflation. Many of these ideas were presented by the famous economist Milton Friedman and supported by the political writings of Friedrich Hayek.

## "TRICKLE-DOWN" POLICIES

This term gained popularity in the 1980s when it described the effort to cut government control of business and emphasized the need to help businesses create more wealth. This wealth would trickle through all of the economy. Opponents of this policy used the term "voodoo economics," as during primary campaigning by candidate George H.W. Bush while he was still running against Ronald Reagan.

# PRESIDENTIAL ECONOMIC PROGRAMS

| Program | President | Description |
|---|---|---|
| Trust Busting/Progressivism | T. Roosevelt | Early 1900s<br>These efforts were results of the late 1800s Populist votes and growing demands for industrial reforms. |
| New Deal | F. Roosevelt | 1930s<br>Massive help from government programs was needed and became key social efforts. |
| Fair Deal | H. Truman | Late 1940s<br>Early efforts at civil rights equality began in federal programs such as the military. |
| New Frontier | J. Kennedy | Early 1960s<br>Civil rights laws get passed. Early forms of affirmative action and environmental programs begin. |

*(continued on next page)*

| Program | President | Description |
|---|---|---|
| Great Society | L. Johnson | Mid-1960s<br>Vast attempts were made to rebuild inner cities, give jobs, and provide assistance. |
| Price Controls<br>New Federalism | R. Nixon | Early 1970s<br>Rapid inflation was met with attempts to stop price increases through mandates. |
| Whip Inflation Now (WIN) | G. Ford | Mid-1970s<br>More federal attempts at stopping rapid price increases were required, but efforts did not help. |
| Reaganomics/Trickle-Down<br>Supply-Side/Devolution<br>New Federalism | R. Reagan | Early 1980s<br>The goals were to cut federal programs and business regulations. Tax cuts in the name of expansion were central. |

## FEDERAL MANDATES AND THE BUDGET

Many recent forms of federal assistance have come with "strings attached"—mandated rules that must be followed by states that use the money. Highway funds of the past were controlled by speed limit and driving age rules. Education funds have recently been connected to testing requirements.

When the federal government passes rules without supporting funds, known as *unfunded mandates*, states can balk at the regulations. Recent suits by local governments over unfunded gun control rules were won by states, and the rules did not have to be followed. When states need the money for important social programs, however, they must follow national guidelines.

# REVIEW QUESTIONS

## MULTIPLE-CHOICE QUESTIONS

1. The Congressional Budget Office performs which of the following responsibilities?

   (A) It consists of a professional staff responsible for giving Congress budget projections and priorities and balancing the Office of Management and Budget priorities.

   (B) It consists of senators and representatives who keep watch over committee spending.

   (C) It consists of members of the executive and legislative branches who oversee congressional spending.

   (D) It is made up of congressional assistants who manage the spending of their superiors.

   (E) It consists of members of the state department who are responsible for overseeing congressional spending.

2. The Fair Deal economic program was named and developed by which of the following presidents?

   (A) Lyndon Johnson

   (B) John Kennedy

   (C) Franklin Roosevelt

   (D) Ronald Reagan

   (E) Harry Truman

3. Which of the following statements concerning economic policies is **NOT** correct?

   (A) The term *inflation* refers to overall rising price levels in the economy due to excessive consumer demand or spikes in the costs of producing goods.

   (B) Discretionary spending deals with programs that Congress can choose whether or not to fund.

   (C) A flat tax is tax rate that escalates the more income one earns.

   (D) The term *fiscal year* for the federal government refers to the period from October 1 to September 30.

   (E) Mandatory spending refers to budget items Congress is required to fund.

4. The term *New Federalism* refers to which of the following?

   (A) The growing influence of iron triangles on the federal budget

   (B) The growing power of the federal government over local and municipal governments

   (C) Increased government spending in the area of education

   (D) The conservative movement's desire to return more power and control of money to the states

   (E) The economic policy of eliminating the graduated income tax and replacing it with other forms of governmental income

5. Legislation used by members of Congress to gain favors for home constituents and to pad a Congressman's voting support from his local constituents is called

(A) *ex post facto* legislation.

(B) discretionary legislation.

(C) *de jure* legislation.

(D) *de facto* legislation.

(E) pork barrel legislation.

## FREE-RESPONSE QUESTIONS

1.  The executive branch has taken over the initiative in the overall process of federal spending.

    (A)   Identify and explain a way the executive branch has done this.

    (B)   Identify and explain a way Congress has attempted to block this power of the executive.


2.  Discretionary spending programs have become MORE difficult for the federal government.

    (A)   Identify three reasons for this trend.

    (B)   Explain how the identified reasons have contributed to the difficulties.

# ANSWERS AND EXPLANATIONS

## MULTIPLE-CHOICE ANSWERS

**1. A**

The Congressional Budget Office is made up of professionals responsible for giving Congress budget projections, among other things.

**2. E**

President Harry Truman called his economic program the "Fair Deal." Choice (A) is incorrect because President Lyndon Johnson called his economic program the "Great Society." Choice (B) is incorrect because John Kennedy's program was called the "New Frontier." Choice (C) is incorrect because Franklin Roosevelt's economic program was called the "New Deal," and choice (D) is incorrect because Ronald Reagan's program was called "Reaganomics."

**3. C**

With the flat tax, the tax rate does not escalate the more one earns. Rather, the flat tax applies the same tax rate, regardless of the amount of income earned. Under a graduated tax, the rate increases as income increases.

**4. D**

The term *New Federalism* refers to the conservative movement desiring to return more power and control of money to the states.

**5. E**

Pork barrel legislation is used by Congress to gain favors for home constituents. It is one of many reasons that defeating an incumbent is so difficult.

## FREE-RESPONSE ANSWERS

1. **4-point Rubric**

   **2 points in part (A): (identify and explain executive)**

   - Bully pulpit/State of the Union; setting the overall agenda and getting public support for priorities

   - OMB; creating the massive budget, raising or lowering amounts for programs supported or opposed by the executive

   - Veto; threats are often sufficient to guide Congress's votes

   **2 points in part (B): (identify and explain Congress's attempts to block)**

   - CBO to counter the information and expertise of the OMB

   - Potential to override veto

   - National attention/leaders trying to mobilize the public to their goals

   - Laws stopping presidents from ignoring funding mandates

2. **6-point Rubric**

   **3 points in part (A): (identify three reasons)**

   - Mandatory spending increases

   - Debt service

   - Population growth

   - Politics/pork

   - Economic demands

   **3 points in part (B): (explain)**

   - Aging population and Social Security/Medicare/Medicaid

   - Continuing deficits adding to interest payments

   - More services needed for more people, infrastructure

   - More programs from Congress and local districts

   - More needs due to recessions, demand for stability

# CHAPTER 17: DOMESTIC POLICY DEVELOPMENT

## IF YOU ONLY LEARN SIX THINGS IN THIS CHAPTER . . . .

1. The public has come to demand large-scale domestic policies that address problems such as retirement needs, bank stability, stock stability, and the needs of the poor.

2. Federal policies assist businesses and individuals directly, create rules that encourage certain behaviors, and help those who are unable to help themselves.

3. Many federal priorities are set through financial assistance to states and local governments in the form of grants.

4. The federal government often sets policy priorities based on a comparison between the potential expenses and the potential rewards of programs being considered.

5. Domestic policy changes were often brought about by new industrial developments, monopoly abuses, economic crisis events, and civil rights needs.

6. Federal grants are basic ways that the national government can guide assistance to states and to the general population.

## INTRODUCTION

National priorities have become more elaborate, and the scope of federal involvement in public policy has grown in recent times. As mentioned in several other contexts, the Great Depression was a key event that changed the way people perceived the role of government. Recent conservative movements have advocated for certain social reforms and a reversal of some of the powers granted to the government during the Depression, but overall public opinion is favorable toward government programs such as Social Security, affirmative action, urban renewal, and public transportation. Debates will certainly continue about the effectiveness of government in trying to solve social problems or economic ills, but some reforms, such as the Securities and Exchange Commission (SEC), which regulates the stock market, and the Food and Drug Administration (FDA), which ensures that harmful foods and medicines are not released into the population, are supported by most citizens.

## KINDS OF POLICIES

Policies of the U.S. government fall into three basic categories. The first category encompasses *distributive* policies. Distributive policies are aimed at specific groups and are very selective in nature. Farm and industrial *subsidies* provide billions to companies that grow critical food supplies or build important products. Prescription drug companies, energy providers, and the airline industry all benefit from government subsidy programs. These programs are also popular with political leaders, as they tend to create healthy voter support among the employees of such companies, while also garnering generous campaign contributions from the corporations themselves.

*Regulatory* policies are aimed at changing behaviors, such as criminal activities or alcohol and tobacco use. Clean water and air policies might also be used to force industries to change how they produce pollutants. The Environmental Protection Agency (EPA) regulates the amount of pollutants that can be released into the air and water. The SEC is a regulatory commission that oversees the stock market as well as other financial exchanges. The SEC was initially created to prevent another depression; however, its modern role also includes investigating corporate corruption, such as the Enron scandal, and fraud, such as Bernie Madoff's Ponzi scheme in 2008.

*Redistributive* policies are aimed at giving assistance to those who are seen as needing financial assistance. Welfare programs originated during the Great Depression and have become a source of controversy in recent years. Public opinion remains divided on whether or not welfare should continue in its present form or if it should be substantially reduced.

## GRANT PROGRAMS

The system of federal grants continues to be a source of controversy with regard to policy and funding. Congress can grant states money for programs that the states control but require certain federal rules be followed. States often chafe under federal rules but are stuck with following them or losing the key support. One example of this practice is how the federal government regulated highway speed limits, although that power was officially left up to the states. A 1973 law prohibited federal highway grants for states with interstate speed limits set higher than 55 mph. The law was repealed in 1995, but for more than 20 years, the federal government was able to regulate the speed limit on a national level. A more modern example of the federal grant regulation can be seen in our public education system. One federal education plan emphasizes the accountability of schools in many state-run public education systems. However, the program has been accused of being an *unfunded mandate*. This means that the government has created stricter federal requirements but has not allotted any federal funding to help the schools adhere to the new requirements. The Americans with Disabilities Act, which requires nearly all private businesses to be accessible to disabled members of the population but does not assist business owners with the cost of conforming to the act, is another example of an unfunded mandate.

# THE BASICS OF POLICY DEVELOPMENT

- **Agenda setting.** What are the priorities? What is important to the voting population? Congress often listens to public opinion as a cue to what issues should be addressed. Polls and media reports often influence perceptions of what issues appear to be most important.

- **Policy formulation.** How can government attack the problem? Proposed actions require studies of potential costs, logistical requirements, long- and short-term effects on the affected parties, as well as other complexities. To create a clearer picture of the effects of a proposed policy, reviewers look at *cost-benefit analysis* data to compare the probable costs with the projected rewards. If a prohibitively expensive problem exists and the proposed policy would only help a very few, then the issue might be dropped as too costly.

- **Policy adoption.** This is the part of the process that receives the most media attention. A policy is submitted as a bill to Congress. It is debated and revised until it either dies or passes through Congress to the executive branch.

- **Policy implementation.** Someone must apply the new rules of the policy. Depending on the scope of the policy, an agency within the executive branch may be selected. In response to the terrorist attacks of September 11, 2001, a new cabinet position was created to oversee homeland security policies. Independent government agencies, such as the SEC or the EPA, are more specialized and don't generally implement policies outside of their specific focus.

- **Policy evaluation.** The public and the members of government react to the new laws and decide whether or not changes are needed. In theory, if the problem is solved, the government reduces controls, but history shows that agencies rarely go away. They just evolve to perform new forms of monitoring or new kinds of duties.

## MAJOR DEVELOPMENTS IN DOMESTIC POLICY

| Late 1800s: Gilded Age and Populism | The beginnings of policies for workers developed. Major battles occurred over the issue of union rights. European reforms on child labor influenced the United States. The People's (Populist) Party platform of 1892 brought "radical" calls for policy changes. Examples included legal unions, public transportation, civil service reform, a national currency, graduated income taxes, and new national bank controls. |
| --- | --- |

## MAJOR DEVELOPMENTS IN DOMESTIC POLICY (con't)

| | |
|---|---|
| Early 1900s: Progressive Era | The breakup of Standard Oil signaled moves to control excessive business practices, monopolies, and trusts. The Panic of 1907 brought calls for banking reforms and led to the eventual creation of the Federal Reserve system. The collapse of the stock market in 1929 led to calls for controls on insider trading, now monitored by the SEC. |
| Mid-1930s: The Great Depression, New Deal | The executive branch moved to the forefront of economic development and job programs. Social Security was adopted as a major public safety net. WWII military spending created a long-term reliance on military jobs, contracts, bases, and industries. |
| Late 1900s: Cold War Era, Great Society | Government led the attempts to reduce poverty, support agricultural production through subsidies, control inflation with interest rates, and spur economic growth with reduced taxes. Medicare and Medicaid programs were expanded, and discussions were held concerning changes in medical care. Environmental programs were expanded, protections were added for those with disabilities, and the government moved to increase support of public schools. |
| Early 2000s | Although the environment has remained a major issue, renewable energy and less reliance on foreign oil have come to the forefront. Universal healthcare and whether this is possible in the United States has also been an issue, especially since President Obama took office in January 2009. |

## MAJOR FORMS OF FEDERAL ASSISTANCE TO STATES AND LOCAL GOVERNMENTS

| | |
|---|---|
| Grants-in-Aid (Categorical Grants) | Grants can be given for specific policy programs. |
| Block Grants | Community development, law enforcement, and education programs are examples of purposes for specific blocks of money. |
| Formula Grants | Federal rules indicate who gets the grants and how they apply. If states want to use the money, they must abide by the rules. |
| Project Grants | Competitive bids are required, and often some matching monies are be committed required from state and local governments. |
| Matching Funds/ Grants | Rules are put into place requiring a specific percentage of local money be committed before federal monies are given. |

# REVIEW QUESTIONS

## MULTIPLE-CHOICE QUESTIONS

1. Which type of grants require competitive bids and often also require some matching money?

   (A) Grants-in-aid
   (B) Project grants
   (C) Formula grants
   (D) Block grants
   (E) None of the above

2. During which domestic policy period was the concept of Social Security adopted as a major public safety net?

   (A) Gilded Age
   (B) Cold War
   (C) Great Society
   (D) Progressive Era
   (E) Great Depression/New Deal

3. When programs for assistance require recipients to show the government proof of need, usually based on low income levels, they are using which of the following?

   (A) Block grants
   (B) Cost-benefits analysis
   (C) Means testing
   (D) Earned income tax credits
   (E) Workfare policies

4. Which of the following describes the process of "unfunded mandates"?

   (A) The federal government passes laws and governmental requirements without allocating specific funds to implement the changes.
   (B) The federal government passes a law that requires no spending on a state's part.
   (C) The federal government only suggests that states follow certain policies.
   (D) The state government passes laws that require certain actions on the federal government's part.
   (E) None of the above descriptions fit the process of "unfunded mandates."

## FREE-RESPONSE QUESTIONS

1. When large-scale problems are facing the nation, solutions are attempted. The government works in predictable patterns in order to put solutions in place.

   (A) Identify and explain any three steps the government uses to address problems.

   (B) Describe how cost-benefit analysis can affect this process.

2. The government enacts different kinds of policies.

   (A) Identify three types of policies the government enacts.

   (B) Describe the political goals of the three types of policies.

# ANSWERS AND EXPLANATIONS

## MULTIPLE-CHOICE ANSWERS

**1. B**

Project grants require competitive bids, and they also often require some matching funds.

**2. E**

Social Security was adopted as a public safety net during the Great Depression/New Deal period. It began as a program to aid the elderly and to help spur economic activity during the Great Depression. It was a part of the New Deal under Franklin Roosevelt.

**3. C**

When programs for assistance require recipients to show proof of need (usually a low income level), they are using means testing.

**4. A**

Unfunded mandates occur when the federal government attempts to pass on laws and governmental requirements without allocating specific funds that local and state governments can use to implement the changes.

## FREE-RESPONSE ANSWERS

1. **7-point Rubric**

   **6 points in part (A): (identify and explain three steps)**

   - Agenda setting; decide the priorities based on needs, public opinions, national concerns.

   - Policy formulation; study possible solutions, analyze approaches, and debate solutions, laws, rules, funding, possible benefits.

   - Policy adoption; put legislation together, create rules, set funds.

   - Policy implementation; agencies begin to regulate, solve.

   - Evaluation; feedback creates information for more revisions, better solutions, reduction of regulations, etc.

   **1 point in part (B): (cost-benefit analysis)**

   - The financial costs of programs are compared to the possible financial rewards. If rewards are not financial, how are they valued? This analysis can determine if the program should be attempted.

2. **6-point Rubric**

   **3 points in part (A): (identify)**

   - Distributive

   - Regulatory

   - Redistributive

   **3 points in part (B): (describe the goals)**

   - Give assistance to individuals, groups, or companies for social help, financial help, or competitive market help.

   - Create or limit behaviors of the public and businesses, stop certain activities, or encourage some activities.

   - Help those who need assistance or have been denied access and assistance.

# CHAPTER 18: FOREIGN POLICY: MILITARY AND ECONOMIC

## IF YOU ONLY LEARN FOUR THINGS IN THIS CHAPTER . . . .

1. The vast majority of military conflicts involving the United States were conducted without congressional declarations of war. This shows the primacy of the executive in the development of foreign policy.

2. Treaties have often been replaced by executive agreements that do not require Senate approval.

3. The president is able to rely on a large staff and support network when considering foreign policy decisions. Congress does not have this network at its disposal.

4. Not without controversy, the United States remains a leader of key international organizations such as the United Nations and the World Trade Organization.

## INTRODUCTION

Foreign policy decisions have always been a special power of the executive branch. The need for single and forceful leadership, speedy decisions, and direct negotiations gives presidents control over most interactions with foreign powers. Congress has authority to ratify, but the president's roles as negotiator, receiver of diplomats, and commander-in-chief are paramount.

The history of power changes in the government often also details the history of presidents pushing foreign and military initiatives. The vast majority of past military conflicts have occurred because the president ordered troops into dangerous situations that often lasted years. In only five instances in the past did Congress itself actually declare war.

## WARS DECLARED BY CONGRESS

- 1812: Against the United Kingdom

- 1846: Against Mexico

- 1898: Against Spain

- 1917: Against Germany, Austro-Hungary, Turkey

- 1941: Against Japan (Germany and Italy declared war on the United States after December 8, 1941.)

## MILITARY CONFLICTS WITHOUT DECLARATIONS OF WAR

- 1801: Barbary Coast

- 1817: Florida, Spain

- 1845: Mexico: Border fight

- 1861: Civil War

- 1899: Philippines

- 1899: Cuban insurgents

- 1900: China (Boxer Rebellion)

- 1917: Mexico (Pancho Villa)

- 1918: Russian Revolution

- 1950: Korea (until 1953)

- 1954: Guatemala

- 1958: Lebanon

- 1961: Cuba (Bay of Pigs)

- 1962: Vietnam (until 1972)

- 1965: Dominican Republic

- 1970: Cambodia

- 1980: Iran (hostage crisis)

- 1983: Grenada

- 1983: Lebanon

- 1987: Persian Gulf

- 1989: Panama (Noriega)

- 1991: Iraq/Kuwait

- 1992: Somalia

- 1999: Bosnia/Kosovo
- 2001: Afghanistan
- 2003: Iraq

## THE RISE OF "AGREEMENTS" OVER TREATIES

In addition to military conflicts, the executive branch has direct diplomatic contacts that the legislature does not control. Presidents make executive agreements with foreign leaders that do not require senatorial approval. These agreements are so common in modern times that "treaties" are rarely proposed anymore. In recent examples, treaties aimed at the reduction of nuclear weapons have been met with considerable congressional opposition. Administrations find it much simpler to cut deals at the agreement level and then wait to see if they work. If formal treaties are then needed, they can be negotiated. International organizations, such as the United Nations and the World Trade Organization, have run recent treatylike events. Moves to reduce tariffs across the globe have reduced the need for many economic treaties. The collapse of the Soviet Union has also reduced the need for military alliances through treaty agreements.

## HELPING THE PRESIDENT

A large bureaucratic system backs the president's agenda. The State Department runs hundreds of embassies with legions of highly trained foreign service workers. The U.S. "intelligence committee" includes the CIA (Central Intelligence Agency), the NSA (National Security Agency), and lesser-known agencies that provide the president with detailed and secret sets of data. The Defense Department also has many resources at its disposal, including many companies that affect policies through governmental contracts.

## THE IMPORTANCE OF POLICY DECISIONS

Foreign policy decisions are critical and long lasting. They usually do not involve military attacks. Most policies concern programs of financial assistance through grants, loans, or building projects. The United States also works with the major international organizations—it is the major funding country of the United Nations (UN), hosts its headquarters, and is a permanent member of the governing Security Council. The United States was central in the development of the World Trade Organization (WTO), which takes a leading role in the negotiations covering trade and tariff concerns. The United States also remains a leading member of the North Atlantic Treaty Organization (NATO), the North American Free Trade Agreement (NAFTA), and other international associations. In August 2005, President Bush signed the legislation for the Central America-Dominican Republic-United States Free Trade Agreement (CAFTA-DR). On January 1, 2009, the agreement expanded to include Costa Rica, making the agreement complete among all seven participating countries. In the summer of 2005, the Congress debated and voted on U.S.

involvement and influence concerning the creation of the Central America Free Trade Agreement/
Association (CAFTA).

## U.S. AND INTERNATIONAL TRADE

The United States will probably face a world of increasing international trade and interlocking political connections. There are serious domestic debates between the parties about the value of the role of the UN and the WTO, with many pointing to the lack of independence and efficiency and ultimate effectiveness of such organizations.

Conservatives dislike the idea that the United States must bend to the will of foreign governments. Liberals dislike the abuses that international corporations heap on workers and the environment under free trade agreements. This conflict will be difficult to solve, but the arguments will not stop the continued internationalization of world governments and markets.

## MAJOR LEADERS IN FOREIGN POLICY

- **President**—the role of "chief diplomat"

- **White House staff and vice president**—assist, filter news, and help with decisions

- **Joint chiefs of staff of the U.S. military services**—provide military options and data

- **Leadership of the Central Intelligence Agency**—in charge of key information, options, and strategies

- **Ambassadors and staff of the Department of State**—keep the leaders informed of the situation overseas and often act as negotiation intermediaries.

- **National Security Council (president, VP, Secretary of Defense, Secretary of State)**—the formal group that meets to declare policy and actions

- **Appropriate committee chairpersons of Congress**—kept informed of foreign negotiations, can help with those negotiations, push through any needed funds and rules.

- **Foreign Intelligence Advisory Board**—section of the executive office that guides the gathering of information from various agencies concerned with other countries

- **Assistant to the President for National Security Affairs**—the head of many executive teams that specialize in such issues

- **Secretary for Homeland Security**—works with other agencies in developing strategies for handling threats to the United States.

- **Council of Economic Advisors (three appointed members)**—give advice on tax and other money programs that affect domestic and international trade.

- **National Economic Council**—in charge of gathering information and advice about foreign economies and trade

# INTERNATIONAL ORGANIZATIONS AFFECTING FOREIGN POLICY

- **CAFTA.** The Central American Free Trade Agreement, enacted in 2005, forms a trade zone for this region.

- **European Economic Union (EEU, EU).** Although not a member, the United States is greatly affected by the formation of Europe as a large free-trade zone. The currency of the EU, the euro, competes with the dollar for international investments and exchanges. Most members of the EU use the euro, but some (like the United Kingdom) have kept their old currencies. In the summer of 2005, moves to further consolidate the union politically were rejected by France and Denmark. The EU will continue to evolve. As of 2009, Croatia, the former Yugoslav Republic of Macedonia, and Turkey are all candidates to join the EU.

- **G-8 "summits."** These are meetings that are held by leaders of the United States, Great Britain, Russia, China, Germany, France, Japan, and Canada. The meetings are set to further international cooperation and development through the Group of 8.

- **International Monetary Fund (IMF).** The United States is a leading member of this organization, which attempts to promote monetary cooperation.

- **Multinational corporations.** Foreign policy is being changed rapidly by increasingly multinational ownership of property, financial instruments, and companies.

- **NAFTA.** The North American Free Trade Agreement was approved during the Clinton administration and gives the United States, Canada, and Mexico free trade among the three nations.

- **North Atlantic Treaty Organization (NATO).** Originally organized to protect Western Europe from communist aggression, NATO has changed and expanded greatly since the end of the Soviet Union. NATO now includes former communist countries of Central and Eastern Europe.

- **United Nations (UN).** The UN attempts to build world security, rights, and stability. It contains 192 country members and is headquartered in New York City.

- **World Bank.** This international organization gives loans and subsidies to many countries, especially developing nations.

- **World Trade Organization (WTO).** Created in the late 1990s, the WTO is an international effort to control tariffs, expand free trade, and protect international laws concerning copyright and intellectual property.

# REVIEW QUESTIONS

## MULTIPLE-CHOICE QUESTIONS

1. Which of the following is the international organization that gives loans and subsidies to many countries, especially developing nations?

   (A) EEU

   (B) UNICEF

   (C) World Health Organization

   (D) World Bank

   (E) World Trade Organization

2. Which definition describes the concept of bilateral agreements?

   (A) This type of agreement deals only with the issue of military bases in the Pacific basin.

   (B) This type of agreement is between two nations with the purpose of creating joint policies.

   (C) This type of agreement deals with offensive-type weapons only.

   (D) This type of agreement deals only with missile deployment.

   (E) None of the above definitions describe the concept of bilateral agreements.

3. Which of the following dealing with the European Economic Union is true?

   (A) The United Kingdom decided to keep its old currency, even though it is a member of the EEU.

   (B) Even though the United States is not a member of the EEU, it is greatly affected by the formation of the EEU.

   (C) Croatia and Turkey are candidates to join the EU.

   (D) The official currency of the EEU is called the *euro*.

   (E) All of the above statements are true concerning the EEU.

4. Which of the following statements is NOT true concerning foreign policy dealing with military and economic policies?

   (A) Most military conflicts in which the United States has been involved have not resulted in a declaration of war by Congress.

   (B) Presidents make "executive agreements" with foreign leaders that do not require senatorial approval.

   (C) Foreign policy decisions are critical and long lasting and usually do not involve military attacks.

   (D) The Defense Department runs hundreds of embassies with legions of highly trained foreign service workers.

   (E) There is a large bureaucratic system backing the president's foreign policy agenda.

## FREE-RESPONSE QUESTIONS

1.  NAFTA is a significant and well known example of foreign policy of the
    United States.

    (A)  Identify and describe the goals of NAFTA or any other important
         international organization of which the United States is a member.

    (B)  Identify and explain one reason why different U.S. political groups
         might oppose an organization such as NAFTA or the organization
         you identified.

2.  Executive decisions concerning foreign policy are checked by the legislative
    branch.

    (A)  Describe two ways such policies are checked.

    (B)  Identify and describe the major way such checks are informally
         avoided by the executive branch.

    (C)  Explain why the president has a clear advantage in foreign policy
         decisions.

# ANSWERS AND EXPLANATIONS

## MULTIPLE-CHOICE ANSWERS

**1. D**

The World Bank specializes in giving loans and subsidies to many countries, especially developing nations.

**2. B**

Bilateral agreements are agreements between two nations for the purpose of determining joint policies. This is in contrast to unilateral policies, when a single country announces changes in policies or relations with other countries.

**3. E**

All of the statements listed are true concerning the European Economic Union: The United Kingdom decided to keep its old currency although it is a member of the EEU; although the United States is not a member of the EEU, it is greatly affected by formation of the EEU; Croatia and Turkey are candidates to join the EU; and the official currency of the EEU is the euro.

**4. D**

It is not the Defense Department that runs the hundreds of United States embassies around the world. That responsibility falls under the direction of the State Department.

## FREE-RESPONSE ANSWERS

1. **4-point Rubric**

   **2 points in part (A): (identify and describe goals)**

   - North American Free Trade Agreement; cut tariffs and increased trade
   - United Nations; create global cooperation and restrict warfare
   - World Trade Organization; more free trade and protections worldwide

   **2 points in part (B): (identify and explain opposition)**

   - No protections for U.S. workers/unions
   - No protections for foreign workers
   - No protections for the environment
   - Fewer protections for children
   - Too much control to international businesses/military governments
   - Too little independence for the United States
   - Too much interference from other countries
   - Too much support for hostile nations
   - Bulky bureaucracies/costly organizations

2. **5-point Rubric**

   **2 points in part (A): (describe two ways policies checked)**

   - Confirmation hearings for ambassadors
   - Budget and rules for the State Department
   - Treaty confirmation votes
   - Budget controls over programs to other nations

   **2 points in part (B): (identify and describe way to avoid)**

   - Executive agreements/deals between leaders
   - No Congressional approval needed
   - Easier/powerful

   **1 point in part (C): (explain presidential advantage)**

   - One-on-one possibilities
   - Information, contacts via State Department/embassies
   - Information from agencies such as CIA
   - Speed and decisive action needed.
   - Public turns to executive and demands action.

# Part Four

# PRACTICE TESTS

# HOW TO TAKE THE PRACTICE TESTS

This section of this book contains two full-length practice tests. Taking a practice test gives you an idea of what it's like to sit through a full AP U.S. Government & Politics exam. You'll find out in which areas you're strong and where additional review may be required. Any mistakes you make now are ones you won't make on the actual exam, as long as you take the time to learn where you went wrong.

The two tests here each include 60 multiple-choice questions and 4 free-response questions. You will have 45 minutes for the multiple-choice questions and 100 minutes to answer the free-response questions.

Before taking a test, find a quiet place where you can work uninterrupted for three hours. Time yourself according to the time limit at the beginning of each section. It's okay to take a short break between sections, but for the most accurate results, you should approximate real test conditions as much as possible.

Remember to pace yourself. Train yourself to be aware of the time you are spending on each problem. Take note of the general types of questions you encounter, as well as what strategies work best for them.

When you are done, read the detailed answer explanations that follow. These will help you identify areas that could use additional review. But don't focus only on the questions you got wrong. For those you got right, you also can benefit from reading the answer explanations. You might learn something you didn't already know.

For the *free-response questions*, consider the following points:

1. Use your time carefully. Read all of the questions and answer the one you know best first.

2. Answer the parts of the question in the order they are asked. Each part is worth points, and real people are scoring these. Give them the opportunity to see the points clearly.

3. Provide examples to help explain your points but don't get lost in examples.

4. Answer in full sentences. Don't get caught up trying to answer the questions with bullets. AP does not allow incomplete sentences to score points.

5. Finally, and most obviously, ANSWER ALL PARTS OF THE QUESTION!

6. The sample free-response answers that follow the exam are intended to help you understand how a reader will look for the correct information.

Good luck!

# HOW TO COMPUTE YOUR SCORE

## SCORING THE MULTIPLE-CHOICE QUESTIONS

To compute your score on the multiple-choice portion of each test, calculate the number of questions you got right. If you got six questions wrong, your score would be a 54 for the multiple-choice portion of the exam. Then divide that number by 60 to get your percentage correct.

## SCORING THE FREE-RESPONSE QUESTIONS

The readers will have specific points that they will be looking for in each essay (called a rubric). Readers use the rubric as the guide for assigning points. Each free-response question is worth a certain number of points, and each point is awarded based on the answers that you provide. Each piece of information that they are able to check off in your essay is a point toward a better score.

To figure out your approximate score for the free-response questions, look at the key points found in the sample response for each question. For each key point you include, add a point. Figure out the number of key points there are in each question. Add up the total number of key points earned, and divide that by the total number of possible points.

## CALCULATING YOUR COMPOSITE SCORE

Your score on the AP U.S. Government & Politics exam is a combination of your score on the multiple-choice portion of the exam and the free-response section. The free-response section and the multiple-choice section are each worth 50 percent of the exam score.

To determine your score, obtain the percentage of points you earned in your free-response and multiple-choice sections. Multiply each of these scores by 0.5 and then add those amounts together. Multiply this number by 100 to get your final score.

Many students and teachers ask what kind of raw score will create the appropriate final score. Each year's scores differ based on the relative difficulty of the questions. Usually, a raw score of over 70 percent will place you near the top of the list with the 5s. A composite score above 60 percent is within the usual range of 4s. The test is challenging but manageable. If you can manage 45 correct answers on the 60 multiple-choice questions and achieve 45 points on the free-response, you can achieve a high final score.

# Practice Test 1 Answer Grid

1. Ⓐ Ⓑ Ⓒ Ⓓ Ⓔ
2. Ⓐ Ⓑ Ⓒ Ⓓ Ⓔ
3. Ⓐ Ⓑ Ⓒ Ⓓ Ⓔ
4. Ⓐ Ⓑ Ⓒ Ⓓ Ⓔ
5. Ⓐ Ⓑ Ⓒ Ⓓ Ⓔ
6. Ⓐ Ⓑ Ⓒ Ⓓ Ⓔ
7. Ⓐ Ⓑ Ⓒ Ⓓ Ⓔ
8. Ⓐ Ⓑ Ⓒ Ⓓ Ⓔ
9. Ⓐ Ⓑ Ⓒ Ⓓ Ⓔ
10. Ⓐ Ⓑ Ⓒ Ⓓ Ⓔ

11. Ⓐ Ⓑ Ⓒ Ⓓ Ⓔ
12. Ⓐ Ⓑ Ⓒ Ⓓ Ⓔ
13. Ⓐ Ⓑ Ⓒ Ⓓ Ⓔ
14. Ⓐ Ⓑ Ⓒ Ⓓ Ⓔ
15. Ⓐ Ⓑ Ⓒ Ⓓ Ⓔ
16. Ⓐ Ⓑ Ⓒ Ⓓ Ⓔ
17. Ⓐ Ⓑ Ⓒ Ⓓ Ⓔ
18. Ⓐ Ⓑ Ⓒ Ⓓ Ⓔ
19. Ⓐ Ⓑ Ⓒ Ⓓ Ⓔ
20. Ⓐ Ⓑ Ⓒ Ⓓ Ⓔ

21. Ⓐ Ⓑ Ⓒ Ⓓ Ⓔ
22. Ⓐ Ⓑ Ⓒ Ⓓ Ⓔ
23. Ⓐ Ⓑ Ⓒ Ⓓ Ⓔ
24. Ⓐ Ⓑ Ⓒ Ⓓ Ⓔ
25. Ⓐ Ⓑ Ⓒ Ⓓ Ⓔ
26. Ⓐ Ⓑ Ⓒ Ⓓ Ⓔ
27. Ⓐ Ⓑ Ⓒ Ⓓ Ⓔ
28. Ⓐ Ⓑ Ⓒ Ⓓ Ⓔ
29. Ⓐ Ⓑ Ⓒ Ⓓ Ⓔ
30. Ⓐ Ⓑ Ⓒ Ⓓ Ⓔ

31. Ⓐ Ⓑ Ⓒ Ⓓ Ⓔ
32. Ⓐ Ⓑ Ⓒ Ⓓ Ⓔ
33. Ⓐ Ⓑ Ⓒ Ⓓ Ⓔ
34. Ⓐ Ⓑ Ⓒ Ⓓ Ⓔ
35. Ⓐ Ⓑ Ⓒ Ⓓ Ⓔ
36. Ⓐ Ⓑ Ⓒ Ⓓ Ⓔ
37. Ⓐ Ⓑ Ⓒ Ⓓ Ⓔ
38. Ⓐ Ⓑ Ⓒ Ⓓ Ⓔ
39. Ⓐ Ⓑ Ⓒ Ⓓ Ⓔ
40. Ⓐ Ⓑ Ⓒ Ⓓ Ⓔ

41. Ⓐ Ⓑ Ⓒ Ⓓ Ⓔ
42. Ⓐ Ⓑ Ⓒ Ⓓ Ⓔ
43. Ⓐ Ⓑ Ⓒ Ⓓ Ⓔ
44. Ⓐ Ⓑ Ⓒ Ⓓ Ⓔ
45. Ⓐ Ⓑ Ⓒ Ⓓ Ⓔ
46. Ⓐ Ⓑ Ⓒ Ⓓ Ⓔ
47. Ⓐ Ⓑ Ⓒ Ⓓ Ⓔ
48. Ⓐ Ⓑ Ⓒ Ⓓ Ⓔ
49. Ⓐ Ⓑ Ⓒ Ⓓ Ⓔ
50. Ⓐ Ⓑ Ⓒ Ⓓ Ⓔ

51. Ⓐ Ⓑ Ⓒ Ⓓ Ⓔ
52. Ⓐ Ⓑ Ⓒ Ⓓ Ⓔ
53. Ⓐ Ⓑ Ⓒ Ⓓ Ⓔ
54. Ⓐ Ⓑ Ⓒ Ⓓ Ⓔ
55. Ⓐ Ⓑ Ⓒ Ⓓ Ⓔ
56. Ⓐ Ⓑ Ⓒ Ⓓ Ⓔ
57. Ⓐ Ⓑ Ⓒ Ⓓ Ⓔ
58. Ⓐ Ⓑ Ⓒ Ⓓ Ⓔ
59. Ⓐ Ⓑ Ⓒ Ⓓ Ⓔ
60. Ⓐ Ⓑ Ⓒ Ⓓ Ⓔ

# PRACTICE TEST 1

## Section I: Multiple-Choice Questions

**Time: 45 Minutes**
**60 Questions**

**Directions:** Select the answer choice that best answers the question or completes the statement.

1. The most common form of political activity by citizens of the United States is

   (A) participating in campaigns.
   (B) donating money to candidates.
   (C) voting in presidential elections.
   (D) placing yard signs for statewide elections.
   (E) voting in local and state elections.

2. Which of the following factors is the most important for predicting the outcome of congressional elections?

   (A) The amount of money spent by the candidate
   (B) The size of the voter turnout
   (C) The success of the parties' presidential candidate within the particular congressional district
   (D) Whether or not the candidate is an incumbent
   (E) Whether or not there are some hot-button issues during the campaign

3. Which of the following statements is true concerning committee chairs in the House of Representatives?

   (A) They are always members of the majority party of the House.
   (B) They are chosen by the party whip.
   (C) They are always endorsed by the president.
   (D) They are selected by the Supreme Court and ratified by the full House membership.
   (E) They are always the people with the most seniority in the House.

4. The most common determining factor when people vote for a presidential candidate is

   (A) a candidate's stance on specific issues.
   (B) a candidate's position on fiscal policies.
   (C) the effectiveness of a candidate's mass media campaign.
   (D) the amount of time a presidential candidate has spent in a voter's local area.
   (E) the candidate's political party identification.

GO ON TO THE NEXT PAGE

5. Who authored the *Federalist Papers*?

    I. James Madison
    II. Benjamin Franklin
    III. Alexander Hamilton
    IV. John Jay

    (A) II only
    (B) III only
    (C) I, II, and III
    (D) II and III
    (E) I, III, and IV

6. A closed primary is a

    (A) primary election that allows eligible voters to vote only within their district.
    (B) primary open to all voters, who may vote for candidates from any party for each office.
    (C) primary that is for local offices only, not statewide offices.
    (D) primary in which a voter is required to identify a party preference before voting and cannot split the ticket.
    (E) primary in which only presidential preferences are determined and lower offices are not decided.

*Use the following table to answer questions 7 and 8.*

### VIEWS ON GAY MARRIAGE

| | Favor % | Oppose % | DK % |
|---|---|---|---|
| East | 42 | 50 | 8 |
| South | 23 | 67 | 10 |
| Midwest | 33 | 56 | 11 |
| West | 36 | 58 | 6 |
| Urban | 36 | 52 | 12 |
| Suburban | 38 | 54 | 8 |
| Rural | 22 | 69 | 9 |
| White | 32 | 60 | 8 |
| Black | 28 | 60 | 12 |
| Hispanic | 36 | 51 | 13 |

Source: Pew Research; Center for People and the Press

7. Which of the following statements is **NOT** true about attitudes toward gay marriage?

    (A) Opposition to gay marriages is equal between blacks and whites.
    (B) Opposition to gay marriages is strongest in rural areas.
    (C) The highest percentage of respondents who replied "don't know" were Hispanics.
    (D) People in the South are the most accepting of gay marriages.
    (E) People in the East are the most accepting of gay marriage.

8. The widest gap between those favoring and those opposing gay marriage occurs in

    (A) respondents from the West.
    (B) respondents who are white.
    (C) respondents from rural areas.
    (D) respondents of Hispanic origin.
    (E) respondents from the East.

GO ON TO THE NEXT PAGE

9. The formal writ used to bring a case before the Supreme Court is called the

(A) *writ of mandamus.*

(B) *writ of certiorari.*

(C) *writ of habeas corpus.*

(D) *writ of theocracy.*

(E) *writ of court consent.*

10. Which of the following statements concerning the Virginia Plan at the convention is **NOT** correct?

(A) It basically favored the larger states with its proposals.

(B) It called for a national legislature that would have supreme powers on all matters that the separate states were not competent to act upon.

(C) It called for one legislative chamber to be elected by the people and a second to be chosen by that popularly elected chamber from people nominated by state legislatures.

(D) It called for a strong national union with three branches of government—legislative, executive, and judicial.

(E) It prohibited a state's population from being a factor in any issue considering representation.

11. The officials directly elected by registered voters are

(A) justices of the Supreme Court.

(B) president and vice president.

(C) Cabinet secretaries in the presidential Cabinet.

(D) House and Senate members.

(E) members of the Electoral College.

12. Which of the following sources contributes most to the workload of the Supreme Court?

(A) Cases referred by Congress

(B) Cases from its appellate jurisdiction

(C) Cases referred by regulatory commissions

(D) Cases from its original jurisdiction

(E) Cases referred from the executive branch

13. The ruling in the Supreme Court decision of *McCulloch v. Maryland*

(A) established the important constitutional concept of eminent domain.

(B) denied the federal government jurisdiction in disputes between states.

(C) established the supremacy of the national government over state governments.

(D) established that only the federal government controls international trade agreements.

(E) established the need for the popular election of U.S. senators.

14. Which of the following statements best describes the importance of Shay's Rebellion?

(A) It reinforced the fact that the institution of slavery was too controversial to deal with at the time the Constitution was written.

(B) It proved that the Indian uprisings were only temporary and would soon come to an end.

(C) It illustrated the need for a strong national government that could protect property and maintain order.

(D) It illustrated a need for a national currency free from local inflation.

(E) It proved that the federalism system of government would work in the colonies.

GO ON TO THE NEXT PAGE

15. The individual rights promised to citizens in the Bill of Rights were later extended to apply to the states, due in part to the Supreme Court interpretation of Constitutional Amendment

   (A) 12
   (B) 14
   (C) 16
   (D) 10
   (E) 18

16. Which of the following powers is **NOT** given to the president by the U.S. Constitution?

   (A) The president has the power to grant pardons for federal crimes.
   (B) The president can create new Cabinet-level departments as he or she feels necessary.
   (C) The president has the power to veto bills sent to him or her by Congress.
   (D) The president commissions officers in the various branches of the military.
   (E) The president has the power to appoint ambassadors with the advice and consent of the U.S. Senate.

17. Due process protects a U.S. citizen from

   (A) having his or her private property seized without just reimbursement.
   (B) having untrue things written about him or her.
   (C) being imprisoned without a proper trial.
   (D) being forced to house soldiers in his or her home.
   (E) being required to register for military service.

18. When the House of Representatives debates a bill under a "closed rule," which of the following conditions exists?

   (A) No amendments to the bill can be offered.
   (B) The debate will not be of public record.
   (C) The vote on the particular bill will be kept confidential.
   (D) The amount of debate on the particular bill is predetermined at 10 minutes for each representative.
   (E) The debate will be limited to only the bill's sponsor and one opponent to the bill.

19. Which of the following best describes the view expressed in the *Federalist Papers* concerning the development of political parties and interest groups?

   (A) They were viewed as necessary and beneficial to the expression of citizens' views and healthy for the country.
   (B) They were viewed as an integral part of the constitutional process.
   (C) They were endorsed numerous times in various parts of the Constitution as beneficial.
   (D) The writers of the *Federalist Papers* considered them basically evil.
   (E) They were basically discussed as favorable, but they were to be carefully monitored.

GO ON TO THE NEXT PAGE

**20.** The best definition for the term *interest group* is

(A) a formal organization of people with common interests who run candidates who believe in those same interests.

(B) an organization of people with shared policy goals who enter the policy process at numerous places in an attempt to advance those goals.

(C) a group of individuals who are hoping to accomplish nonspecific goals for the general improvement of society.

(D) a formal organization that sponsors activities that are narrow in scope and focus; it pursues essentially single issues.

(E) a group of people who share common ideas but have no formal membership and exert very little political influence.

**21.** Which of the following Supreme Court decisions dealt with the concept of the exclusionary rule and evidence being obtained by illegal means?

(A) *Mapp v. Ohio*

(B) *Korematsu v. United States*

(C) *Bakke v. Board of Regents*

(D) *Plessy v. Ferguson*

(E) *Munn v. Illinois*

**22.** Which of the following statements is true of most bills introduced in the House of Representatives and Senate?

(A) Most bills are passed by committees but die from lack of support in the respective chamber.

(B) Almost every bill in Congress dies from lack of support in the House Rules Committee.

(C) Most bills are passed by one chamber of Congress but die from lack of support in the opposite chamber.

(D) Most bills are withdrawn by the bill's sponsor before even being considered.

(E) Most bills are referred to appropriate committees but are never sent to the full Congress; they simply die in committee.

**23.** Which of the following definitions best describes the term *iron triangle*?

(A) The close working relationship among the three levels of the judicial branch

(B) The cooperation among federal, state, and local governments

(C) The relationship among diplomats, the president, and the Senate in treaty negotiations

(D) The close relationship between an agency, a congressional committee, and an interest group that often becomes a mutually advantageous alliance

(E) The cooperation of the military, executive branch, and the legislative branch when planning and financing a military action

GO ON TO THE NEXT PAGE

24. Important industries experiencing extreme problems might expect government help in all of the following ways **EXCEPT**

   (A) the government might intervene with subsidies.

   (B) the government might pass tax break legislation.

   (C) the government might fund product research and development.

   (D) the government might fix prices within a particular area.

   (E) the government might guarantee loans to assist the industry through the difficult period.

25. According to the framers of the Constitution, one of the primary functions of government is to

   (A) expand the number of democracies in the world as years go by.

   (B) increase the population of the United States by establishing liberal immigration policies.

   (C) protect individual property rights in the United States.

   (D) develop an equitable system of individual income tax in the United States.

   (E) develop an educational system that reaches all U.S. citizens.

26. Based on numerous studies, which of the following statements concerning the news media is considered to be true?

   (A) A slight Democratic bias was discovered.

   (B) A strong liberal bias was discovered.

   (C) No bias was detected, and the news was generally determined to be neutral.

   (D) A slight conservative bias was discovered.

   (E) A strong Republican bias was discovered.

*Use the following table to answer questions 27 and 28.*

## OVERALL PRESIDENTIAL APPROVAL RATINGS 1953–2001

|              | Average % | High % | Low % |
| ------------ | --------- | ------ | ----- |
| Kennedy      | 70        | 83     | 56    |
| Eisenhower   | 65        | 79     | 48    |
| G.H.W. Bush  | 61        | 89     | 29    |
| Clinton      | 55        | 73     | 37    |
| Johnson      | 55        | 79     | 35    |
| Reagan       | 53        | 65     | 35    |
| Nixon        | 49        | 67     | 24    |
| Ford         | 47        | 71     | 37    |
| Carter       | 45        | 74     | 28    |

Source: Gallup Organization

27. Which of the following presidents had the biggest difference between their highest and lowest approval ratings?

   (A) G. H. W. Bush

   (B) Clinton

   (C) Kennedy

   (D) Ford

   (E) Johnson

28. Which of the following presidents had the most consistent approval ratings?

   (A) Eisenhower

   (B) Reagan

   (C) Clinton

   (D) Nixon

   (E) Kennedy

GO ON TO THE NEXT PAGE ▷

29. The overwhelming majority of criminal cases in the United States are tried in

(A) federal district courts.

(B) appellate courts only.

(C) state and local courts.

(D) federal appellate courts.

(E) federal judiciary courts.

30. Which of the following concepts are mentioned in the Preamble to the Constitution?

I. Establish justice.

II. Provide for the common defense.

III. Secure the blessings of education.

IV. Promote the general welfare.

(A) III and IV only

(B) I, III, and IV

(C) I, II, and IV

(D) I and IV only

(E) All of the above are mentioned in the Preamble.

31. Which of the following was the most immediate reaction to the Supreme Court decision in *Brown v. Board of Education* (1954)?

(A) Surprisingly, an almost immediate end to segregated education took place.

(B) A constitutional amendment was passed to strengthen the ruling.

(C) Bussing of inner-city students to suburban schools was established voluntarily.

(D) There was a rapid growth in private white schools in the South.

(E) There was a national show of support for a long-overdue Supreme Court decision.

32. Most of the delegates to the Republican and Democratic national conventions at the present time are chosen by

(A) precinct caucuses.

(B) regional caucuses.

(C) state party conventions.

(D) local party caucuses.

(E) presidential primaries.

33. Which of the following conditions would most benefit retired persons on fixed incomes?

(A) A period of low inflation

(B) A period of high unemployment

(C) A period of high inflation

(D) A period of low unemployment

(E) A period of stagnant employment

34. The largest single source of health care dollars in the United States is

(A) charities.

(B) private insurance companies.

(C) doctor-owned HMOs.

(D) private citizens through out-of-pocket spending.

(E) government.

35. Which of the following statements is **MOST** true concerning political parties over the past 40 years?

(A) Party loyalty has remained relatively the same.

(B) Party loyalty has decreased.

(C) Party loyalty has increased significantly.

(D) Party loyalty has grown only in urban areas.

(E) Party loyalty has grown significantly in suburban areas.

GO ON TO THE NEXT PAGE

**36.** Which of the following is an action Congress can take if the Supreme Court declares a federal law unconstitutional?

(A) Congress can override Supreme Court decisions with a two-thirds vote.

(B) Congress can request that the executive branch veto the court decision with a simple majority vote.

(C) Congress can attempt to amend the Constitution.

(D) Congress can vote to have the federal appeals court start the case back through the system for reconsideration.

(E) Congress can vote to have the Supreme Court issue a *writ of certiorari*.

**37.** Which of the following definitions **BEST** describes *inalienable rights*?

(A) Rights based upon the common consensus

(B) Rights established through political justice

(C) Rights based upon a military code of fairness

(D) Rights based on nature and Providence

(E) Rights established through political compromise

*Use the following table to answer questions 38 and 39.*

### Public Opposed to Overturning
*Completely overturn* Roe v. Wade?

| | Yes % | No % | Don't know % |
|---|---|---|---|
| **Total** | 30 | 63 | 7 |
| Men | 31 | 62 | 7 |
| Women | 29 | 64 | 7 |
| White | 31 | 63 | 6 |
| Black | 28 | 60 | 12 |
| Hispanic | 31 | 62 | 7 |
| Ages 18–29 | 29 | 66 | 5 |
| Ages 30–49 | 28 | 65 | 7 |
| Ages 50–64 | 32 | 62 | 6 |
| Ages 65+ | 34 | 57 | 9 |
| College graduate | 20 | 75 | 5 |
| Some college | 32 | 63 | 5 |
| High school or less | 35 | 57 | 8 |
| Republican | 48 | 47 | 5 |
| Democrat | 19 | 75 | 6 |
| Independent | 25 | 69 | 6 |
| Conservative Republican | 62 | 33 | 5 |
| Moderate/Liberal Republican | 25 | 71 | 4 |
| Conservative/ Moderate Democrat | 23 | 72 | 5 |
| Liberal Democrat | 13 | 82 | 5 |
| White Protestant | 37 | 56 | 7 |
| Evangelical | 52 | 41 | 7 |
| Mainline | 21 | 71 | 8 |
| White Catholic | 31 | 65 | 4 |
| Secular | 12 | 82 | 6 |

### Attend Church

| | | | |
|---|---|---|---|
| Weekly or more | 46 | 48 | 6 |
| Sometimes | 22 | 70 | 8 |
| Seldom or never | 17 | 77 | 6 |

Source: Pew Research; Center for Religion and Public Life

GO ON TO THE NEXT PAGE ⟹

38. According to the table, which age group shows the most support for the *Roe v. Wade* decision?

    (A) 18–29

    (B) 30–49

    (C) 50–64

    (D) 65+

    (E) None of the above

39. According to the chart, which of the following statements is **NOT** correct?

    (A) The strongest support for overturning *Roe v. Wade* comes from the conservative Republican category.

    (B) The largest group responding "don't know" comes from the category of black.

    (C) The most evenly divided group is the group labeled Republican.

    (D) The percentage of Hispanics not wanting to overturn *Roe v. Wade* is double that of the Hispanics wanting to overturn it.

    (E) Women support overturning *Roe v. Wade* more than men.

40. Which of the following statements concerning the Speaker of the House of Representatives is true?

    (A) The Speaker is chosen by the president and confirmed by the Senate.

    (B) The Speaker only votes whenever the House vote has ended in a tie.

    (C) The Speaker is elected by the majority party in the House of Representatives.

    (D) The Speaker must be at least 35 years of age.

    (E) The Speaker must be endorsed by the Supreme Court because of the importance of the position.

41. Historically, bureaucracies in the United States have grown significantly during which of the following events?

    (A) Periods of economic stability

    (B) Periods of prosperity

    (C) Periods of depression

    (D) Periods of war

    (E) Periods of recession

42. Which of the following determines the number of delegates to a national party convention and the rules under which they are chosen?

    (A) State party conventions

    (B) The national committee of the particular party

    (C) State legislatures

    (D) The state party leadership

    (E) Local party caucuses

43. Which of the following Supreme Court decisions reversed the earlier decision of *Plessy v. Ferguson?*

    (A) *Korematsu v. U.S.*

    (B) *Mapp v. Ohio*

    (C) *Marbury v. Madison*

    (D) *Brown v. Board of Education*

    (E) *Gideon v. Wainwright*

44. The person who serves as the president's chief civilian advisor on the military is the

    (A) chairperson of the Joint Chiefs of Staff.

    (B) Secretary of State.

    (C) director of the Federal Bureau of Investigation.

    (D) Secretary of Defense.

    (E) National Security Advisor.

GO ON TO THE NEXT PAGE

45. Which of the following theories encourages the government to create jobs for people during times of high unemployment so that more money can get back into the hands of consumers and stimulate economic growth?

   (A) Supply-side economics
   (B) Military-industrial economics
   (C) Keynesian economics
   (D) Reaganomics
   (E) Wilsonian economics

46. Which of the following best describes the concept of presidential coattails in recent elections?

   (A) This effect is stronger for Republicans than for Democrats.
   (B) This effect has been increasing over the last half of the 20th century.
   (C) This has rarely affected recent elections due to more ticket splitting.
   (D) This effect is seen more in House rather than Senate races.
   (E) This effect is stronger for Democrats than for Republicans.

47. *Franking privilege* is the

   (A) right of members of Congress to be exempt from income taxes.
   (B) right of the government to subpoena individuals and compel them to testify before Congress.
   (C) legal term for the right of people to not testify against themselves.
   (D) right of members of the Supreme Court to be exempt from testifying in legal proceedings.
   (E) right of members of Congress to send mail to their constituents free of charge.

48. Which of the following statements is **NOT** true of the Electoral College?

   (A) Each state has as many electoral votes as it has U.S. Senators and Representatives.
   (B) Except for Maine and Nebraska, every state has a winner-take-all system.
   (C) If no candidate receives an Electoral College majority, then the election goes to the House of Representatives.
   (D) The state parties select slates of electors; these are often assigned as a reward for faithful service to the party.
   (E) Electors are bound by the Constitution to vote the way their state voted, and they cannot vote their conscience.

49. Which of the following powers is designated only to the national government?

   (A) The power to levy taxes
   (B) The power to take private land for public use
   (C) The power to make and enforce laws
   (D) The power to regulate commerce with foreign nations
   (E) The power to create and maintain a judicial system

50. The 22nd Amendment to the U.S. Constitution did which of the following?

   (A) It repealed the policy of prohibition established earlier.
   (B) It limited U.S. presidents to two terms.
   (C) It established a system for presidential succession and presidential disability.
   (D) It lowered the voting age in the United States to 18 years of age.
   (E) It changed the method by which Congress can raise its salaries.

GO ON TO THE NEXT PAGE ⟩

**51.** Which of the following is the Latin term for "let the decision stand," the principle of precedent in the judicial system?

(A) *Stare decisis*

(B) *En loco parentis*

(C) *Habeas corpus*

(D) *Writ of certiorari*

(E) *Pluribus principalus*

**52.** Which of the following statements is **NOT** true about the U.S. Senate?

(A) There is no rules committee to limit debate in the Senate.

(B) The vice president presides over the Senate and only votes in the event of a tie.

(C) Until the 17th Amendment, senators were elected by state legislatures.

(D) The membership of the Senate has always been made up of more common individuals rather than the rich elite.

(E) It shares the ability to declare war with the House of Representatives.

*Using the following graph, answer question 53.*

Children in poverty
by race/ethnicity and residence, 2000

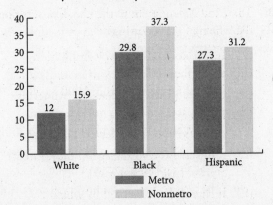

Source: Calculated by ERS from March 2001
Current Population Survey.

**53.** Which of the following statements concerning children in poverty is correct according to the graph?

(A) Poverty for metro white children and metro Hispanic children is essentially equal.

(B) Poverty for nonmetro black children is lower than poverty for nonmetro Hispanic children.

(C) Poverty for metro white children is about equal to poverty for metro black children.

(D) Poverty for metro Hispanic children is higher than poverty for metro black children.

(E) Poverty for metro black children is lower than poverty for nonmetro Hispanic children.

"A well regulated Militia, being necessary to the security of a free State, the right of the people to keep and bear Arms, shall not be infringed."

**54.** The above text is from which amendment to the U.S. Constitution?

(A) 5th Amendment

(B) 4th Amendment

(C) 10th Amendment

(D) 2nd Amendment

(E) 6th Amendment

**55.** A progressive income tax can best be described as a(n)

(A) innovative form of taxation that incorporates sales taxes and tariffs.

(B) system of taxation that is considered more fair because it taxes all citizens at the same rate.

(C) equitable tax, because only those who are high-rate consumers are taxed.

(D) tax where those with more income pay a higher rate of tax on their income.

(E) innovative tax, because as a person's salary increases annually, his or her tax rate decreases, encouraging investment.

GO ON TO THE NEXT PAGE

**56.** News coverage by the print and broadcast media is **BEST** described by which of the following?

(A) It is extensive and in depth.

(B) It is very ideological in its presentation.

(C) It is presented at a relatively high educational level.

(D) It is very superficial.

(E) It is mostly sensationalized.

**57.** The term *critical election* can best be described as a

(A) term used for elections where serious economic differences exist between the candidates.

(B) term used to describe elections when the nation is in a state of war.

(C) term used for elections where party realignment takes place.

(D) term for an election where Supreme Court vacancies are anticipated.

(E) term for any election where one party has won the previous three elections and this election is critical to the minority party.

**58.** Which of the following terms describes a president's ability to hold onto a bill if Congress is in the last 10 days of a session and let it die by not signing or vetoing it?

(A) *En loco parentis*

(B) Hidden veto

(C) *Writ of certiorari*

(D) *Writ of mandamus*

(E) Pocket veto

*Using the following graph, answer the questions 59 and 60.*

Distribution of Households by Size:
1900 and 1940 to 2000

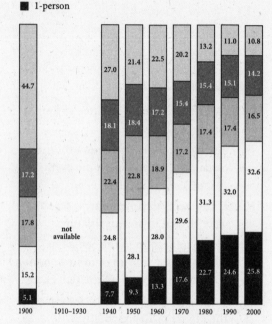

Source: U.S. Census Bureau, decennial census of population, 1900, and decennial census of housing, 1940 to 2000.

**59.** According to the graph, which of the following statements is correct?

(A) The graph shows growth in households with three persons from 1900 to 2000.

(B) The graph shows that growth in two-person housing tripled from 1900 to 2000.

(C) The smallest decline in housing is shown to be that of four-person housing.

(D) The largest increase in housing type from 1900 to 2000 is in single-person housing.

(E) The graph shows an increase in four-person housing from 1980 to 2000.

GO ON TO THE NEXT PAGE

60. Beginning in 1950, which decade shows the largest decline in five-or-more-person housing?

(A) 1950 to 1960
(B) 1960 to 1970
(C) 1970 to 1980
(D) 1980 to 1990
(E) 1990 to 2000

**STOP**

# Section II: Free-Response Questions

**Time: 100 Minutes**
**4 Questions**

**Directions:** You have 100 minutes to answer all four of the following questions. Unless the directions indicate otherwise, respond to all parts of all four questions. It is suggested that you take a few minutes to plan and outline each answer.

Spend 25 minutes to complete each question. In your response, use substantive examples where appropriate. Make certain to number/letter each of your answers as the question is numbered/lettered below.

1. A recent problem for our government has been the issue of gridlock. This can occur within Congress or between Congress and the president.

   (A) Describe the condition of gridlock.

   (B) Give an example of how gridlock might exist between the House and Senate.

   (C) Give an example of how gridlock might exist between Congress and the president.

   (D) Explain why gridlock has been more of a problem in recent years.

2. One of the most important issues has been the selection process for Supreme Court justices.

   (A) Describe the process for selection and appointment to the Supreme Court.

   (B) Discuss why that process has been more difficult recently by citing two reasons for this increased difficulty.

   (C) Discuss one reason why Supreme Court appointments are very important.

GO ON TO THE NEXT PAGE ⟩

Source: Cox and Forkum

3. Using the cartoon provided and your knowledge of limited state government and politics, answer the following questions:

   (A) What point concerning the 2004 election is the cartoonist making?

   (B) Define *independent expenditure*.

   (C) Explain one positive and two negatives provided by independent expenditures and 527 groups.

4. The Electoral College is one of the most misunderstood entities in the U.S. political system. Discuss the following concerning the Electoral College:

   (A) One rationale for establishing the Electoral College

   (B) Two major flaws that have been exposed in the Electoral College process over the years

   (C) Two proposals for altering or replacing the Electoral College concept

GO ON TO THE NEXT PAGE

**STOP**

# ANSWERS AND EXPLANATIONS

## SECTION I: MULTIPLE-CHOICE QUESTIONS

**1. C**
Statistics show that the most common form of political participation by U.S. citizens is voting during presidential elections.

**2. D**
Incumbency has proven to be an extreme advantage in congressional elections. Connections to political action committees and other built-in advantages are hard for challengers to overcome.

**3. A**
Committee chairs are always members of the majority party. This proves to be a very important advantage for majority parties.

**4. E**
A candidate's political party identification is the most important factor in a presidential campaign. This is a bit surprising. In many ways, it goes against other trends toward independence; however, party identification still carries a great deal of influence.

**5. E**
Benjamin Franklin had no role in the writing of the *Federalist Papers*. Alexander Hamilton wrote the bulk of the *Federalist Papers*, with James Madison and John Jay helping to a lesser degree.

**6. D**
A closed primary requires voters to proclaim a party preference; they cannot cross over to opposing parties.

**7. D**
It is not true that the people of the South are accepting of gay marriage. Only 23 percent of people from the South responded that they favor gay marriages. This figure is substantially below the 42 percent favorable rating for people from the East.

**8. C**
The widest gap between those favoring and those opposing gay marriage occurs in respondents from rural areas. There is a 47 percent spread between those favoring and those opposing gay marriages in rural areas. This gap is by far the widest indicated by the chart.

**9. B**
A *writ of certiorari* is the formal proclamation that forwards a case to the Supreme Court. This Latin term means "made more certain." It requires the lower court to send up its records of a case for review. This is how most cases reach the Supreme Court. It requires that at least four justices feel the need for a case to be reviewed.

**10. E**
In fact, the Virginia Plan strongly favored the inclusion of a state's population as a determining factor for representation. This would have been a big advantage for a large state such as Virginia.

**11. D**
The officials directly elected by the people are House and Senate members. House members were always chosen by the people; the 17th Amendment changed the election of U.S. senators from state legislatures to the people of the various states. These are the only federal officials directly elected by voters.

**12. B**
Cases from the appellate jurisdiction contribute most of the workload of the Supreme Court. Cases from appellate jurisdiction tie into the answer to question 9 concerning the *writ of certiorari*.

**13. C**
The landmark decision *McCulloch v. Maryland* established the supremacy of the national government over the state governments.

**14. C**

Shay's Rebellion vividly illustrated the need for a strong national government because it showed how weak the government was under the Articles of Confederation. After this uprising, there was a consensus that something had to be done to strengthen the national government.

**15. B**

The 14th Amendment, passed shortly after the Civil War, had numerous aspects. One of those was that the rights stated in the Bill of Rights were extended to apply to the states. This interpretation evolved after a Supreme Court decision.

**16. B**

The president does not have the power to create Cabinet-level departments as he or she feels necessary. Only Congress can create new Cabinet-level positions. The president may request them, but it is Congress that creates them.

**17. C**

Due process protects a U.S. citizen from being imprisoned without a trial. Due process rights deal with the judicial system's treatment of accused criminals. This interpretation of an accused person's rights has been refined through several Supreme Court decisions.

**18. A**

When the House of Representatives debates a bill under a closed rule, no amendments to the bill can be offered.

**19. D**

The writers of the *Federalist Papers* saw political parties and interest groups as basically evil. There is little argument that they had a very dim view of political parties and interest groups.

**20. B**

Interest groups are bound together by common policy goals. Another aspect of interest groups is that they try to accomplish their goals through various means.

**21. A**

*Mapp v. Ohio* dealt with the exclusionary rule and illegally obtained evidence.

**22. E**

Statistically, an overwhelming majority of bills introduced in the House of Representatives simply die in committee.

**23. D**

*Iron triangle* is the term for the relationship among federal agencies, congressional committees, and interest groups. This working arrangement has proven to be advantageous to all three parties.

**24. D**

Important industries experiencing extreme problems might expect the government to intervene with subsidies, tax breaks, funding for product research, or guaranteed loans. However, one thing the federal government has refused to do to help struggling industries has been to establish fixed prices.

**25. C**

One of the most basic principles protected throughout U.S. history has been individual property rights.

**26. C**

Despite a popular belief that the media has a built-in liberal bias, a number of studies done by independent groups show no factual data to support this claim. The news has almost always been determined to be neutral in its coverage.

**27. A**

George Herbert Walker Bush had a 60 percent difference between his highest and lowest approval ratings. This is the biggest difference cited by the chart.

**28. E**

President Kennedy had a high of 83 percent and a low of 56 percent in his approval ratings. According to the chart, this is the most consistent approval rating of these presidents.

**29.  C**
The vast majority of criminal cases are handled by state and local courts. Crimes must fit particular parameters to be considered federal crimes and, therefore, handled in federal courts.

**30.  C**
The Preamble to the Constitution mentions the establishment of justice, the provision for the common defense, and the promotion of the general welfare. Education, while very important to our country, is not mentioned in the Preamble to the Constitution.

**31.  D**
Immediately following the decision in *Brown v. Board of Education* in 1954, there was a rapid growth of private schools in the South. This put public education in the South in peril.

**32.  E**
Presidential primaries have grown in importance during the last 40 years. Today, the majority of delegates to both major conventions are delegated through presidential primaries.

**33.  A**
A period of low inflation would most benefit those on fixed incomes. Low inflation means that prices are not rising. When prices rise, those on fixed incomes are essentially losing money.

**34.  E**
The government is the largest provider of health care dollars in the United States. Programs such as Medicare and Medicaid channel the government's output.

**35.  B**
Party loyalty has decreased over the past 40 years. There is more ticket splitting than ever before. While individuals identify with parties for presidential elections, they are very willing to step outside the party in elections below that level.

**36.  C**
If Congress disagrees with the Supreme Court's declaring a law unconstitutional, it may make the law an amendment to the Constitution.

**37.  D**
Inalienable rights are considered to be basic rights based on individual's natural rights granted through Providence. This implies that they are our rights as human beings based upon our existence and that government has no right to interfere with them.

**38.  A**
The 18-to-29-year-olds show the most support for *Roe v. Wade*. According to the chart, 66 percent of this group opposes the overturning of *Roe v. Wade*.

**39.  E**
It is not true that women support overturning *Roe v. Wade* more than men do. In fact, the answer is the opposite. The chart shows that 31 percent of men support overturning *Roe v. Wade* in comparison to 29 percent of women. Men favor overturning this decision more than women do.

**40.  C**
The Speaker of the House is chosen by the members of the majority party. This position is important and powerful.

**41.  D**
Historically, wartime has proven to be a period of bureaucratic growth. Once a bureaucracy has grown, it becomes very difficult to reduce its size.

**42.  B**
The size or number of delegates to a national party convention is determined by a party's national committee.

**43.  D**
*Brown v. Board of Education of Topeka* reversed the Supreme Court's earlier position stating that separate but equal was constitutional. This decision was reversed because separate was, in fact, very rarely even close to equal.

**44. D**

The Secretary of Defense serves as the president's chief civilian military advisor. With an office in the Pentagon, the secretary works very closely with the military and keeps the president apprised of military affairs.

**45. C**

The theory of Keynesian economics encourages the government to create jobs for people during periods of high unemployment. John Maynard Keynes, an English economist, believed it was beneficial for the government to create jobs during periods of high unemployment thereby stimulating economic growth.

**46. C**

As explained earlier, with increased ticket splitting, the former concept of presidential coattails has proven less and less to be the case.

**47. E**

Franking privilege is the right of members of Congress to send mail to their constituents free of charge. Members seem to use their franking privilege more during election years. This is only one of many reasons why it is difficult to defeat an incumbent.

**48. E**

Electors are not bound by the Constitution to vote the way the state they represent voted. There are numerous examples of an elector voting his or her conscience or otherwise deviating from the way the state he or she represented voted.

**49. D**

Only the national government can regulate trade with foreign countries. Sometimes, if a foreign government is at odds with the U.S. government, the national government will forbid trade with the offending country.

**50. B**

The 22nd Amendment limited the president to two terms. This was passed following Franklin Roosevelt's having been elected to four terms as president. Before FDR, presidential candidates had limited themselves to two terms by tradition. Many were afraid that having presidents remain in office for longer than two terms could lead to innumerable problems.

**51. A**

*Stare decisis* is a Latin term meaning "let the decision stand." The concept of basing judicial decisions on previously decided cases (precedent) comes from this term.

**52. D**

The membership of the Senate has always been made up of the rich elite. The Senate has at times in our history been known as the "Millionaires Club." Members of the Senate have tended to be wealthier than members of the House.

**53. E**

According to the graph, poverty for metro black children is lower than poverty for nonmetro Hispanic children.

**54. D**

This is the text of the 2nd Amendment. Its interpretation in recent years has been a dividing factor. Many people today support some form of gun control, while others refer to this amendment as supporting their unequivocal right to bear arms.

**55. D**

The concept of a progressive income tax (also called a graduated income tax) is that the more an individual makes, the higher that person's tax rate should be. The income tax system of the United States is a progressive income tax system; it has proven to be a very complex system for many individuals to understand.

**56. D**

It is the consensus opinion that print and broadcast media coverage of the news tends to be very superficial. Many believe this is because news coverage has become more and more ratings driven.

**57.  C**

Critical elections are those elections where party realignment of some type takes place. This term refers to the fact that a certain segment of votes will change their loyalty from one party to the other. One example would be the Democrats losing the "solid South" to the Republicans.

**58.  E**

A pocket veto occurs when the president simply holds onto a bill and takes no action during the last 10 days of a Congressional session, effectively killing that particular bill.

**59.  D**

The graph shows that the number of single-person households increased over five times over the period 1900 to 2000.

**60.  C**

According to the graph, the sharpest drop in housing with five or more persons after 1950 took place between 1970 and 1980.

## SECTION II: FREE-RESPONSE QUESTIONS

### RUBRIC FOR QUESTION 1: 5 POINTS TOTAL

**Part (A): 2 points** for defining gridlock.

- Gridlock occurs when there is a lack of movement or progress in the passage of legislation. Typically, this is the result of conflicts between the political parties inside of Congress or in partisan arguments between Congress and the president.

**Part (B): 1 point** for explaining that gridlock might exist between the House and the Senate when one chamber is controlled by one party and the other chamber is controlled by the opposite party.

**Part (C): 1 point** for explaining that gridlock exists between Congress and the president when one party has a majority in Congress and the opposite party controls the presidency. It may be noted that the opposing party may only need to control one chamber of Congress.

**Part (D): 1 point** for explaining that gridlock has happened more often recently because these conditions have occurred more frequently due to ticket splitting by voters. Also, there seems to have been a more partisan attitude and less of a spirit of compromise in recent years.

### RUBRIC FOR QUESTION 2: 5 POINTS TOTAL

**Part (A): 2 points** for describing the process for selection of Supreme Court justices.

- The president nominates a person for the Supreme Court, and the U.S. Senate ratifies that nominee.

**Part (B): 2 points** for discussing the reason why the process has been more difficult recently.

- The recent problems can be traced to the fact that the Senate has been from the opposite party to that of the president.
- Another valid reason would be that there has been an increase in partisanship within the Senate itself.
- A final possibility might be because as life expectancies have increased, everyone realizes this appointment might influence important decisions for many years to come.

**Part (C): 1 point** for explaining that a president's Supreme Court appointments can perpetuate his or her philosophies long after he or she has left office.

## RUBRIC FOR QUESTION 3: 7 POINTS TOTAL

**Part (A): 2 points** for identifying that the Swift Boat Veterans group had an important negative effect on Senator John Kerry's 2004 presidential campaign.

**Part (B): 2 points** for defining the term *independent expenditure*.

- An independent expenditure is money spent for a communication that expressly advocates the election of one candidate or the defeat of the other candidate. This money is not considered to be a campaign contribution, so independent expenditures are not limited. The individual or group making the expenditure cannot consult or coordinate with the campaign they are benefiting.

**Part (C): 1 point each (3 points total)** for one positive and two negatives.

### Possible positives:

- Individuals can spend their money to support candidates of their choice in any amount that they wish because technically, independent expenditures are not considered part of a candidate's campaign.
- Independent expenditures are another way for individuals to express their right of free speech as established in the 1st Amendment to the Constitution.

### Possible negatives:

- The Federal Regulatory Commission does not regulate these groups and expenditures.
- It is difficult to define the difference between the candidate's campaign, the candidate, and private spending.
- A candidate may not approve of or endorse the message of the ads.
- It is difficult to establish accountability if the ads are misleading.

### RUBRIC FOR QUESTION 4: 5 POINTS TOTAL

**Part (A): 1 point** for explaining either

- that the framers did not want Congress to elect the president because it would have caused the presidency to be too much under congressional influence; or
- that the framers did not want to leave the election of the presidency in the hands of the popular vote because they were concerned that would create many problems.

**Part (B): 1 point each** (2 points total) for discussing two of the following:

- Electors are not bound by the Constitution to vote for the candidate they were named to represent.
- As parties grew in strength, the process led to a president from one party and a vice president from the opposite party. (This was later corrected by the 12th Amendment.)
- The winner of the popular vote may not win the vote in the Electoral College.

**Part (C): 1 point each** (2 points total) for discussing two of the following:

- A district plan that would allocate electoral votes based upon results, congressional district by congressional district
- A proportional plan under which a presidential candidate would receive the same share of a state's electoral votes as he or she received of the state's popular vote
- A direct election of a president based entirely on the direct popular vote
- A national bonus plan where a presidential candidate would receive a number of bonus electoral votes for winning the national popular vote, helping to ensure that the winner of the popular vote would almost certainly win the election in the Electoral College

# Practice Test 2 Answer Grid

1. Ⓐ Ⓑ Ⓒ Ⓓ Ⓔ
2. Ⓐ Ⓑ Ⓒ Ⓓ Ⓔ
3. Ⓐ Ⓑ Ⓒ Ⓓ Ⓔ
4. Ⓐ Ⓑ Ⓒ Ⓓ Ⓔ
5. Ⓐ Ⓑ Ⓒ Ⓓ Ⓔ
6. Ⓐ Ⓑ Ⓒ Ⓓ Ⓔ
7. Ⓐ Ⓑ Ⓒ Ⓓ Ⓔ
8. Ⓐ Ⓑ Ⓒ Ⓓ Ⓔ
9. Ⓐ Ⓑ Ⓒ Ⓓ Ⓔ
10. Ⓐ Ⓑ Ⓒ Ⓓ Ⓔ

11. Ⓐ Ⓑ Ⓒ Ⓓ Ⓔ
12. Ⓐ Ⓑ Ⓒ Ⓓ Ⓔ
13. Ⓐ Ⓑ Ⓒ Ⓓ Ⓔ
14. Ⓐ Ⓑ Ⓒ Ⓓ Ⓔ
15. Ⓐ Ⓑ Ⓒ Ⓓ Ⓔ
16. Ⓐ Ⓑ Ⓒ Ⓓ Ⓔ
17. Ⓐ Ⓑ Ⓒ Ⓓ Ⓔ
18. Ⓐ Ⓑ Ⓒ Ⓓ Ⓔ
19. Ⓐ Ⓑ Ⓒ Ⓓ Ⓔ
20. Ⓐ Ⓑ Ⓒ Ⓓ Ⓔ

21. Ⓐ Ⓑ Ⓒ Ⓓ Ⓔ
22. Ⓐ Ⓑ Ⓒ Ⓓ Ⓔ
23. Ⓐ Ⓑ Ⓒ Ⓓ Ⓔ
24. Ⓐ Ⓑ Ⓒ Ⓓ Ⓔ
25. Ⓐ Ⓑ Ⓒ Ⓓ Ⓔ
26. Ⓐ Ⓑ Ⓒ Ⓓ Ⓔ
27. Ⓐ Ⓑ Ⓒ Ⓓ Ⓔ
28. Ⓐ Ⓑ Ⓒ Ⓓ Ⓔ
29. Ⓐ Ⓑ Ⓒ Ⓓ Ⓔ
30. Ⓐ Ⓑ Ⓒ Ⓓ Ⓔ

31. Ⓐ Ⓑ Ⓒ Ⓓ Ⓔ
32. Ⓐ Ⓑ Ⓒ Ⓓ Ⓔ
33. Ⓐ Ⓑ Ⓒ Ⓓ Ⓔ
34. Ⓐ Ⓑ Ⓒ Ⓓ Ⓔ
35. Ⓐ Ⓑ Ⓒ Ⓓ Ⓔ
36. Ⓐ Ⓑ Ⓒ Ⓓ Ⓔ
37. Ⓐ Ⓑ Ⓒ Ⓓ Ⓔ
38. Ⓐ Ⓑ Ⓒ Ⓓ Ⓔ
39. Ⓐ Ⓑ Ⓒ Ⓓ Ⓔ
40. Ⓐ Ⓑ Ⓒ Ⓓ Ⓔ

41. Ⓐ Ⓑ Ⓒ Ⓓ Ⓔ
42. Ⓐ Ⓑ Ⓒ Ⓓ Ⓔ
43. Ⓐ Ⓑ Ⓒ Ⓓ Ⓔ
44. Ⓐ Ⓑ Ⓒ Ⓓ Ⓔ
45. Ⓐ Ⓑ Ⓒ Ⓓ Ⓔ
46. Ⓐ Ⓑ Ⓒ Ⓓ Ⓔ
47. Ⓐ Ⓑ Ⓒ Ⓓ Ⓔ
48. Ⓐ Ⓑ Ⓒ Ⓓ Ⓔ
49. Ⓐ Ⓑ Ⓒ Ⓓ Ⓔ
50. Ⓐ Ⓑ Ⓒ Ⓓ Ⓔ

51. Ⓐ Ⓑ Ⓒ Ⓓ Ⓔ
52. Ⓐ Ⓑ Ⓒ Ⓓ Ⓔ
53. Ⓐ Ⓑ Ⓒ Ⓓ Ⓔ
54. Ⓐ Ⓑ Ⓒ Ⓓ Ⓔ
55. Ⓐ Ⓑ Ⓒ Ⓓ Ⓔ
56. Ⓐ Ⓑ Ⓒ Ⓓ Ⓔ
57. Ⓐ Ⓑ Ⓒ Ⓓ Ⓔ
58. Ⓐ Ⓑ Ⓒ Ⓓ Ⓔ
59. Ⓐ Ⓑ Ⓒ Ⓓ Ⓔ
60. Ⓐ Ⓑ Ⓒ Ⓓ Ⓔ

# PRACTICE TEST 2

## Section I: Multiple-Choice Questions

**Time: 45 Minutes 60 Questions**

**Directions:** Select the answer choice that best answers the question or completes the statement.

1. Which of the following **BEST** describes the concept of "reserved powers" of the states?

    (A) These are powers given to the states through the implied powers concept.

    (B) These are powers not specifically granted to the national government or denied to states.

    (C) These are powers given only to Congress and are not available to the executive branch.

    (D) These are powers given only to the Supreme Court.

    (E) These are powers, such as foreign trade agreements, over which states maintain only a small amount of control.

2. Candidates for president have been **LEAST** likely to come from which of the following sources?

    (A) The vice presidency

    (B) State governorships

    (C) The Cabinet

    (D) The House of Representatives

    (E) The Senate

3. Which of the following has the responsibility for creating additional federal courts and assigning the number of judges who will preside in them?

    (A) The secretary of the treasury

    (B) The attorney general

    (C) The secretary of the Department of Justice

    (D) The president

    (E) The Congress

4. Which of the following **BEST** describes the president's responsibilities under the War Powers Resolution?

    (A) The president must seek approval of Congress and the United Nations before committing troops for more than 10 days.

    (B) The president must propose a financial plan for financing a conflict within 30 days of committing troops.

    (C) The president must utilize National Guard units prior to asking Congress to reinstate a selective service system.

    (D) The president must bring troops home from hostilities within 60 to 90 days unless Congress extends the time.

    (E) The president must have approval of the Joint Chiefs of Staff before committing troops for over 30 days.

GO ON TO THE NEXT PAGE

5. Which of the following labels describes the principle under which our government does not meddle with the economy?

(A) Elitist economics policy

(B) Voodoo economics policy

(C) *Laissez-faire* economic policy

(D) Supply-side economic policy

(E) Monetarism

6. To create a balance of power without harming the independence of the presidency, which of the following measures did the framers of the Constitution take?

(A) They omitted the president as a power player in the area of national security.

(B) They created a weak position as a head of the executive branch.

(C) They checked or balanced what they believed to be the president's most dangerous powers.

(D) They intentionally established a vice presidency that would be from the opposite party.

(E) They created a presidency that had no powers over the military.

7. The Supreme Court decision in *Bakke v. California Board of Regents* dealt with which of the following issues?

(A) Segregation in student housing

(B) Censorship of a student newspaper

(C) Freedom of speech for college professors

(D) Affirmative action and reverse discrimination

(E) Fair salary schedules for female faculty members

8. Until the latter part of the 1800s, the primary method for government employees to secure their job was which of the following?

(A) Nepotism

(B) Military accomplishments

(C) Patronage system

(D) Merit system

(E) None of the above

9. Which of the following is a power that state legislatures have relating to the federal government?

(A) State legislatures recommend names of potential Supreme Court justices to the president.

(B) State legislatures determine the persons who will represent each state in the Electoral College.

(C) State legislatures redraw the boundaries of limited congressional districts following a census.

(D) State legislatures determine how often a national census should be conducted.

(E) State legislatures must independently vote on declarations of war following the vote from Congress.

10. Which of the following best describes the term *de facto segregation*?

(A) This is the type of segregation seen in the North, which is not caused by laws; rather, it is the result of residential segregation, preferred living patterns, and informal social forces.

(B) This is the type of segregation based in the South prior to the Civil War.

(C) This is the type of segregation founded in laws such as Jim Crow legislation.

(D) This is a type of segregation dealing only with economic issues, not social issues.

(E) This is segregation based only on Supreme Court decisions that were later reversed.

GO ON TO THE NEXT PAGE

*Using the table provided, answer questions 11 and 12.*

**News Media Viewed More Favorably Than Political Institutions**

| Favorable opinion of... | 2001% | 2005% | Change |
|---|---|---|---|
| Daily newspaper | 82 | 80 | −2 |
| Local TV news | 83 | 79 | −4 |
| Cable TV news* | 88 | 79 | −9 |
| Network TV news | 76 | 75 | −1 |
| Major national papers | 74 | 61 | −13 |
| Supreme Court | 78 | 66 | −12 |
| Democratic Party | 63 | 57 | −6 |
| Congress | 65 | 54 | −11 |
| George W. Bush** | 64 | 55 | −9 |
| Republican Party | 54 | 52 | −2 |

\* In 2001, the cable news question listed only CNN and MSNBC as examples. In 2005, Fox News Channel was added to the question.

\*\* Bush 2005 figure from March. Percentages based on those who could rate each.

Source: Pew Research, Center for People and Press

**11.** According to the table, which type of media was viewed most favorably in 2001?

(A) Major national newspapers

(B) Daily newspapers

(C) Cable TV news

(D) Local TV news

(E) Network TV news

**12.** According to the table, which of the following political institutions experienced the largest decline in the public's favorable opinion rating from 2001 to 2005?

(A) Congress

(B) Republican Party

(C) Democratic Party

(D) George W. Bush

(E) Supreme Court

**13.** Which of the following was viewed by the framers of the Constitution as the center of policy making in the United States?

(A) President's Cabinet

(B) Secretary of State

(C) President

(D) Congress

(E) Supreme Court

**14.** Presidents often have nicknames for their overall program for the American people. Which president called his plan the "Great Society"?

(A) John Kennedy

(B) Ronald Reagan

(C) Lyndon Johnson

(D) Jimmy Carter

(E) George H. W. Bush

**15.** Which of the following Cabinet departments has the largest annual budget?

(A) Treasury

(B) Education

(C) Health and Human Services

(D) Commerce

(E) State

**16.** Which of the following is the party that initiates a lawsuit?

(A) Prosecutor

(B) Plaintiff

(C) Defendant

(D) Advocate

(E) Jurist

GO ON TO THE NEXT PAGE

17. Which division of government was most responsible for expanding the rights of accused criminals during the 1960s?

(A) The president

(B) Congress

(C) The attorney general

(D) The Department of Justice

(E) The Supreme Court

18. Which committee in the House of Representatives is responsible for placing a bill on the legislative calendar and for establishing the time limits for debate and the types of amendments that will be allowed?

(A) Ways and Means

(B) Judiciary

(C) Rules

(D) Joint

(E) None of the above

19. Which of the following amendments to the U.S. Constitution was intended to overturn the Dred Scott decision by the Supreme Court?

(A) 18th

(B) 20th

(C) 19th

(D) 16th

(E) None of the above

20. Which of the following are Cabinet departments of the president?

I. Veterans Affairs

II. Agriculture

III. White House Counsel

IV. Transportation

(A) I and IV only

(B) I, II, and III

(C) I, II, and IV

(D) II, III, and IV

(E) III and IV only

21. Which of the following statements concerning the federal income tax system is **NOT** correct?

(A) When originally attempted, the federal income tax was declared unconstitutional by the Supreme Court.

(B) The federal income tax provides only a small portion of the national government's income.

(C) The federal income tax was created by the 16th Amendment to the U.S. Constitution.

(D) The federal income tax is generally a progressive tax; the higher your income, the higher the tax rate.

(E) Corporations as well as individuals pay income taxes.

GO ON TO THE NEXT PAGE

**22.** Which of the following definitions best defines the concept of full faith and credit?

(A) It deals with economic policy, stating that the Federal Reserve will protect deposits and checking accounts.

(B) It concerns Congress respecting the autonomy of the Supreme Court.

(C) It deals with the federal governments maintaining a strong military capacity.

(D) It deals with cooperation between the executive and legislative branches on budgetary issues.

(E) It concerns states being required to recognize the official documents and civil judgments rendered by the courts of other states.

**23.** Which of the following is most correct in describing the U.S. House of Representatives?

I. Members are elected every two years.

II. Known as a continuous body.

III. Members must be at least 21 years old.

IV. Members can only serve six terms.

(A) I, II, and III

(B) I and IV only

(C) II, III, and IV

(D) I, III, and IV

(E) I and III only

**24.** Which of the following definitions best describes the concept of eminent domain?

(A) It is the protection guaranteed in the Constitution that citizens will not have to keep soldiers in their houses.

(B) It is the idea that economic policy is best handled by government intervention.

(C) It is a belief held by the people of the United States that they are destined to spread the country's borders.

(D) It is the right of the government to take private property for public use as long as the individual is fairly compensated.

(E) It is the belief that no person may be held in jail unless the government shows just cause.

**25.** The president of the United States possesses the constitutional power to negotiate treaties with other nations, but the treaty is not considered final until which additional step is taken?

(A) Congress votes to accept it by simple majority.

(B) Congress votes to accept it by a two-thirds majority.

(C) The House of Representatives votes to accept it by a two-thirds majority.

(D) The Senate votes to accept it by a two-thirds majority.

(E) Congress votes to accept it by a simple majority, and the Supreme Court declares it constitutional.

GO ON TO THE NEXT PAGE ⟹

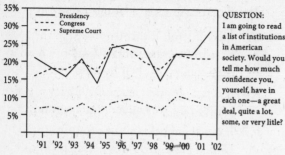

Confidence in Institutions

QUESTION:
I am going to read a list of institutions in American society. Would you tell me how much confidence you, yourself, have in each one—a great deal, quite a lot, some, or very litle?

Source: Surveys by the Gallup Organization latest trial of June, 2002

**26.** According to the chart provided, which of the following statements is **NOT** true?

(A) The confidence in the presidency sharply increased from 2001 to 2002.

(B) The trend in presidential confidence was declining between 1991 and 1994.

(C) Confidence in the Supreme Court was higher than that in the presidency in 1996.

(D) The confidence in the presidency dropped from 1999 to 2000.

(E) Confidence in the Supreme Court declined from 1996 to 1997.

**27.** At today's national party conventions, the majority of the delegates are chosen by which of the following methods?

(A) They are delegates to previous conventions.

(B) They are chosen by state party leaders.

(C) They are chosen in state presidential primaries.

(D) They are chosen through the caucus process.

(E) They are state and national office holders from that party.

**28.** Under the Articles of Confederation, the bulk of the power rested in which of the following entities?

(A) The national Congress

(B) The president

(C) State legislatures

(D) The military

(E) The U.S. Senate

**29.** Bureaucratic agencies are originally created by which of the following?

(A) Congress

(B) The president

(C) The federal courts

(D) The Supreme Court

(E) The president's Cabinet

**30.** Which of the following Supreme Court decisions established that an accused person has the right to be represented by a lawyer in felony cases and that if a person cannot afford an attorney, the state must provide one?

(A) *Miranda v. Arizona*

(B) *Bakke v. California*

(C) *Munn v. Illinois*

(D) *Buckley v. Valeo*

(E) *Gideon v. Wainwright*

GO ON TO THE NEXT PAGE

31. Which of the following statements is **NOT** true concerning the White House staff?

    (A) The press secretary is a member of the White House staff.

    (B) The president relies on the White House staff for information, policy options, and analysis.

    (C) The national security advisor is a member of the White House staff.

    (D) The White House staff size and responsibilities grew enormously in the latter half of the 1900s.

    (E) Appointments to the White House staff are confirmed by the Senate.

32. Which of the following committees in Congress is responsible for reconciling differences in bills passed by the House and Senate?

    (A) Ways and Means

    (B) Rules

    (C) Domestic Affairs

    (D) Conference

    (E) Appropriations

33. Which of the following elections legally uses federal money during campaigns?

    (A) Gubernatorial elections

    (B) Local elections

    (C) Presidential elections

    (D) Congressional elections

    (E) None of the above

34. Which historical events are generally blamed for ending the friendly relationship between the press and politicians?

    (A) World War I and World War II

    (B) The Great Depression and Prohibition

    (C) The Civil Rights Movement and the assassination of Martin Luther King Jr.

    (D) The presidential debates and television

    (E) The Vietnam War and Watergate

35. The term *establishment clause* refers to the part of the U.S. Constitution dealing with which of the following?

    (A) It is the part of the 2nd Amendment that establishes the right to bear arms.

    (B) It is the part of the 7th Amendment that establishes no excessive bail and no cruel and unusual punishment.

    (C) It is the part of the 1st Amendment that states that Congress shall make no law respecting establishment of religion.

    (D) It is the part of the 5th Amendment that establishes that no person shall be forced to testify against himself or herself.

    (E) It is the part of the 19th Amendment that establishes women's right to vote.

GO ON TO THE NEXT PAGE

**36.** The process of initiative is **BEST** described by which of the following?

(A) It is the formal expression of congressional opinion that must be approved by both houses of Congress.

(B) It is a procedure allowing voters to submit a proposed law to a popular vote by obtaining a required number of signatures.

(C) It is a congressional process by which the Speaker may send a bill to a second committee after the first committee is finished acting on the bill.

(D) It is a brief, unsigned opinion issued by the Supreme Court to explain its ruling.

(E) It is a phrase meaning action must be taken following a presidential veto.

*Use the following graph to answer questions 37 and 38.*

Percent Distribution of the Total Population
by Age: 1900 to 2000

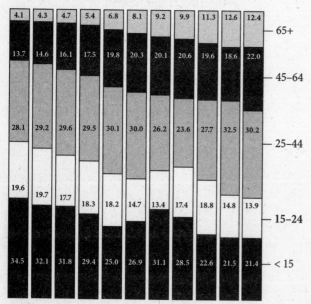

Source: U.S. Census Bureau, decennial census of population, 1900 to 2000.

**37.** According to the graph, which of the following groups decreased the most as a percentage of the population between 1900 and 2000?

(A) 65+

(B) 45–64

(C) 25–44

(D) 15–24

(E) < 15

**38.** According to the graph, which of the following statements is true?

(A) The 45–64 and 65+ age groups both grew by the same percentage between 1900 and 2000.

(B) The population of the 25–44 age group declined from 1980 to 2000.

(C) The 65+ age group increased its percentage of the population in every decade from 1900 to 2000.

(D) The 15–24 age group increased in every decade from 1900 to 1950.

(E) The 25–44 age group increased in every decade from 1900 to 1960.

**39.** Which of the following statements concerning the Speaker of the House is **NOT** correct?

(A) The Speaker presides over the House when it is in session.

(B) The Speaker exercises considerable control over which bills get assigned to which committees.

(C) The Speaker plays a major role in making committee assignments in the House.

(D) The Speaker is third in line for succession to the presidency following the vice president and the secretary of state.

(E) The Speaker appoints or plays a key role in appointing the party's legislative leaders and the party leadership staff.

GO ON TO THE NEXT PAGE

40. The War Powers Resolution, which requires the president to consult with Congress whenever possible prior to using military forces, was passed as a reaction to which historical action?

(A) The sinking of the *Lusitania*

(B) The bombing of Pearl Harbor

(C) American fighting in Vietnam and Cambodia

(D) The Korean War

(E) Operation Desert Storm

41. Bureaucratic agencies are initially created by which of the following governmental institutions?

(A) The presidency

(B) Federal court decisions

(C) Presidential Cabinet secretaries

(D) Congress

(E) None of the above

42. According to the Constitution, Congress is prohibited from passing a bill of attainder. Which of the following describes a bill of attainder?

(A) It is a bill forcing citizens to pay for their own legal representation in criminal trials.

(B) It is a law making something illegal "after the fact."

(C) It is a law that declares a person, without a trial, to be guilty of a crime.

(D) It is a law placing export tariffs on items that are completely manufactured in the United States.

(E) It is a bill forcing citizens to pay for the quartering of soldiers in their homes.

43. Which of the following statements concerning the U.S. Senate is **NOT** correct?

(A) The U.S. Senate is a continuous body.

(B) U.S. senators were elected by state legislatures until the ratification of the 17th Amendment.

(C) U.S. senators must be at least 30 years of age.

(D) The U.S. Senate confirms presidential nominees to the Supreme Court.

(E) The U.S. Senate, because of its size, has very strict rules and limitations concerning debate of proposed bills.

GO ON TO THE NEXT PAGE

*Use the graph to answer questions 44 and 45.*

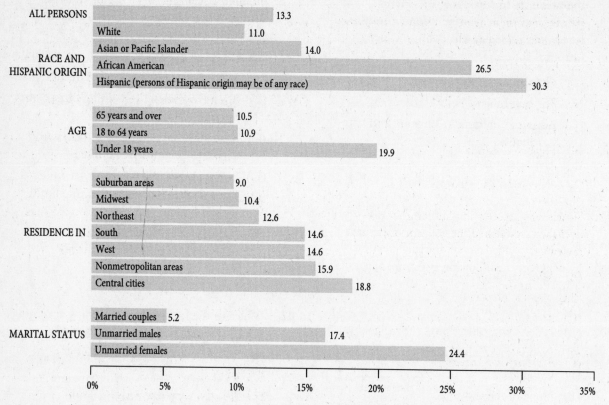

Source: U.S. Census Bureau (Poverty Rates for Persons with Selected Characteristics, 1997).

**44.** According to the graph, which of the following categories had the highest poverty rate in 1997?

(A) People 65 years and over

(B) People from the Midwest

(C) Married couples

(D) People from the South

(E) People from suburban areas

**45.** According to the graph, which category is not identified for its poverty rate?

(A) Race and Hispanic origin

(B) Age

(C) Education level

(D) Marital status

(E) Residence

GO ON TO THE NEXT PAGE

46. Which of the following describes the late-20th-century movement to reduce the influence of the federal government and other governments in general?

    (A) Client politics

    (B) Liberalism

    (C) Devolution

    (D) Elitism

    (E) Hyper-pluralism

47. Which of the following Supreme Court decisions established the concept of judicial review?

    (A) *Miller v. California*

    (B) *Mapp v. Ohio*

    (C) *McCulloch v. Maryland*

    (D) *Korematsu v. U.S.*

    (E) *Marbury v. Madison*

48. Primaries where voters are presented with a list of candidates from all parties and voters may switch back and forth between parties are called

    (A) closed primaries.

    (B) caucus primaries.

    (C) blanket primaries.

    (D) candidate primaries.

    (E) run-off primaries.

49. Which of the following definitions describes standing committees?

    (A) They exist in a few policy areas, and their membership is drawn from both the Senate and the House.

    (B) They are committees appointed for a specific purpose and a specific length of time.

    (C) They are the committees formed only when the Senate and the House pass a particular bill in different forms.

    (D) They are committees found only in the Senate that deal with continuous issues.

    (E) They are permanently established committees formed to handle bills in different policy areas.

50. Which of the following **BEST** describes the strict constructionist approach to judicial decisions?

    (A) It is the view that judges should consistently be harsh in the sentences they hand down.

    (B) It is the view that judges should decide cases on the basis of the language of the Constitution.

    (C) It is the view that judges should apply only acceptable local standards when deciding a case.

    (D) It is the view that judges should apply a broad interpretation of constitutional policies.

    (E) It is the view that judges should follow only judicial precedent and previous court decisions when deciding a case.

GO ON TO THE NEXT PAGE

51. According to the Constitution, which of the following has the power to pardon federal criminals?

(A) Congress

(B) The Senate

(C) The Supreme Court

(D) The president

(E) None of the above

52. The Great Compromise, which blended the Virginia and New Jersey Plans, is sometimes called by which other name?

(A) The Three-Fifths Compromise

(B) The Albany Plan

(C) The Rhode Island Compromise

(D) The Connecticut Compromise

(E) Pennsylvania Compromise

53. James Madison described political factions as undesirable but inevitable in which of the following?

(A) The Declaration of Independence

(B) The Preamble to the Constitution

(C) The *Federalist Papers*

(D) The body of the Constitution

(E) None of the above

54. Which of the U.S. minority groups has consistently been the least healthy and least educated and lived in the greatest poverty?

(A) African Americans

(B) Hispanic Americans

(C) Eastern-European Americans

(D) Asian Americans

(E) Native Americans

55. Which of the following groups make up the iron triangle?

I. Congressional subcommittees

II. Interest groups

III. Presidential Cabinet

IV. Bureaucracy

V. Joint Chiefs of Staff

(A) II, III, and V

(B) I, II, and IV

(C) II, III, and IV

(D) I, II, and III

(E) III, IV, and V

56. Which of the following statements concerning the position of the vice president is **NOT** true?

(A) In case of presidential disability, he assumes the position of president.

(B) He presides over the U.S. Senate.

(C) Since 1980, the role and activities of the vice president have been increased informally by presidents.

(D) His constitutional duties include serving as chairman of the Joint Chiefs of Staff.

(E) He only votes in the Senate if the Senate vote is tied.

57. Should the Supreme Court decide a case by a split decision, the justices on the losing side may write their reasons for disagreeing with the majority decision. This is called which of the following?

(A) *Writ of certiorari*

(B) *Per curiam* opinion

(C) *Writ of mandamus*

(D) *Writ of habeas corpus*

(E) Dissenting opinion

GO ON TO THE NEXT PAGE

**58.** Name the party position in Congress responsible for making certain that party members are present for a vote and that they vote the way the party wishes.

(A) President *pro tempore*

(B) Chairman of the caucus

(C) Minority leader

(D) Party whip

(E) None of the above

**59.** Which of the following types of federal grants do states prefer because they are for general areas and relatively unrestrictive?

(A) Categorical grants

(B) Grants-in-aid

(C) Block grants

(D) Mandates

(E) Class-action grants

**60.** Whenever the Supreme Court announces a decision *per curium,* it means which of the following?

(A) It signifies the decision was made by a unanimous vote of the Supreme Court.

(B) It signifies the decision was made by a split vote of the Supreme Court.

(C) It signifies the Supreme Court cannot decide the case and the lower court's decision stands.

(D) It signifies the Supreme Court decision is being announced without legal explanation or without a majority opinion.

(E) It signifies that the Supreme Court decision goes into effect immediately.

STOP

# Section II: Free-Response Questions

**Time: 100 Minutes**
**4 Questions**

**Directions:** You have 100 minutes to answer all four of the following questions. Unless the directions indicate otherwise, respond to all parts of all four questions. It is suggested that you take a few minutes to plan and outline each answer.

Spend 25 minutes to complete each question. In your response, use substantive examples where appropriate. Make certain to number/letter each of your answers as the question is numbered/lettered below.

1. Ever since the formation of the Constitution in 1787, the federal government has attempted to balance the notions of liberty and order.

   (A) Describe one of the following provisions of the Constitution and, using a specific historical example, explain how this provision has been used to enhance or diminish the balance between liberty and order.

   - The due process clause as described in the 5th and 14th Amendments

   - Freedom of expression clause of the 1st Amendment

   (B) Explain a key provision of each of the following laws and related court decisions and explain how each of these laws and decisions has enhanced the federal government's desire for order at the expense of liberty.

   - Executive Order 9066 (1942)—*Korematsu v. U.S.* (1944)

   - Espionage Act of 1917—*Schenck v. United States* (1919)

2. The two bodies of Congress, the House of Representatives and the Senate, operate in two very different manners.

   (A) Describe the role of each of the two listed institutional structures of the House of Representatives in terms of passing legislation. Explain how these structures make it difficult for the minority in the House of Representatives to have their ideas placed into action.

   - Committee structure

   - Speaker of the House

   (B) Describe one institutional process unique to the Senate in terms of passing legislation. Explain how this process enhances the power of the minority party to influence legislation.

GO ON TO THE NEXT PAGE

3. During the 1960s the Supreme Court experienced a very activist period under the leadership of Chief Justice Earl Warren.

   (A) Discuss the terms *loose constructionist* and *strict constructionist*.

   (B) Explain the specific rights gained by accused persons established in these three Supreme Court decisions:

   - *Miranda v. Arizona*

   - *Gideon v. Wainwright*

   - *Mapp v. Ohio*

   (C) Explain the reaction the public had to Earl Warren because of these and other decisions.

4. Iron triangles are an example of client politics. They are also a very important part of the governmental process of our country.

   - Identify the components of an iron triangle.

   - Explain the process of how iron triangles function.

   - Explain how this is an example of client politics.

GO ON TO THE NEXT PAGE

**STOP**

# ANSWERS AND EXPLANATIONS

## SECTION I: MULTIPLE-CHOICE QUESTIONS

**1.  B**

Reserved powers are discussed in the 10th Amendment to the Constitution. Essentially, reserved powers are any powers not given to the national government or prohibited to the states by the Constitution; these powers are reserved for the states.

**2.  C**

Candidates for the presidency have been least likely to come from the Cabinet. Cabinet secretary is not a position that has been seen as a stepping stone position to the presidency. In recent years, many presidents have come from state governorships. Many feel that coming from a state governorship might be an advantage because state governors are not seen as having executive experience.

**3.  E**

The Constitution grants Congress the power to create federal courts and to assign the number of judges who preside in them. If there were a movement to increase the number of justices on the Supreme Court, that increase would have to be accomplished by Congress.

**4.  D**

The War Powers Resolution requires the president to bring troops home within 60 to 90 days unless Congress extends the time.

**5.  C**

The principle under which our government does not meddle with the economy is called *laissez-faire*. This is a doctrine opposing governmental interference in economic affairs beyond the minimum interference required to maintain order and peace. The government for the better part of our country's history practiced this policy when it came to the economy.

**6.  C**

To create a balance of power without harming independence, the framers of the Constitution made sure to check what they believed to be a president's most dangerous powers. Probably the best example of this is the power to declare war. Only Congress can declare war. The framers clearly did not want the power to declare war in one person's hands.

**7.  D**

The Supreme Court decision in *Bakke v. California Board of Regents* dealt with a white man who had been denied entrance to the University of California. Because his scores exceeded those of some minority applicants, he argued that he was a victim of reverse discrimination. This has led to a trend with the Supreme Court that a quota or preference system cannot be used unless the rules are addressing an actual past or present pattern of discrimination.

**8.  C**

During the latter part of the 1800s, the primary method for government employees to secure their jobs was the patronage system. In the patronage system, which was sometimes referred to as the spoils system, government jobs were handed out as political favors. The controversy over changing from the patronage system to the presently used merit system was a bitter one. It led to the assassination of President Garfield and created many problems.

**9.  C**

Every 10 years, each state legislature redraws congressional districts if the state has been affected by reapportionment.

**10.  A**

De facto segregation was originally observed in the North. It was not in existence because of legislation. Rather, it was practiced as a result of housing patterns or social forces.

**11. C**

According to the table, cable TV news was reviewed most favorably in 2001. It had an 88 percent approval rating that year. This was 5 percent higher than local TV news, which ranked second.

**12. E**

The table shows that the approval ratings of the Supreme Court dropped by 12 percent between 2001 and 2005. Major national newspapers declined more, but they are not an answer choice.

**13. D**

The framers left no doubts that their desire was that Congress would be the center of policy making. Their concern over placing power in a single leader is well documented.

**14. C**

Lyndon Johnson called his overall program for the American people the "Great Society." The civil rights acts were central components of this program.

**15. C**

The Department of Health and Human Services is the Cabinet department with the largest annual budget; because of Social Security and Medicaid, it outspends all other departments.

**16. B**

The party that initiates a lawsuit is the plaintiff.

**17. E**

The Supreme Court is most responsible for expanding the rights of accused criminals in the 1960s; it made numerous decisions in the 1960s that dramatically expanded the rights of accused criminals.

**18. C**

The Rules Committee establishes the legislative calendar and sets the rules for debate and amending of a bill; it is a very powerful and important committee.

**19. E**

None of the amendments listed were intended to overturn the Dred Scott decision.

**20. C**

Veterans Affairs, Agriculture, and Transportation are all Cabinet-level departments. The White House counsel is a part of the White House staff, not a part of the Cabinet.

**21. B**

The federal income tax brings in approximately half of the government's income, definitely not a small portion.

**22. E**

Full faith and credit deals with each state recognizing official documents and civil judgments completed legally in another state.

**23. E**

Representatives are elected every two years and must be at least 21 years of age. The Senate, not the House of Representatives, is a continuous body; only one-third of the membership of the Senate is up for election every two years. There are no term limits for senators and representatives at the federal level.

**24. D**

Eminent domain is the right of the government to take private property for public use as long as the individual is fairly compensated. Eminent domain has been controversial lately due to a recent Supreme Court ruling.

**25. D**

The Senate must ratify treaties with other nations negotiated by the president with a two-thirds vote. This is part of the system of checks and balances.

**26. E**

It is not true that confidence in the Supreme Court declined from 1996 to 1997. Rather, the chart illustrates a sharp rise in confidence in the Supreme Court between 1996 and 1997.

**27. C**

Most delegates to today's national party conventions are chosen through state presidential primaries.

**28. C**

Under the Articles of Confederation, the bulk of the power rested with the state legislatures.

**29. A**

Bureaucratic agencies are originally created by Congress. Congress passes acts and then creates commissions to administer and enforce the acts.

**30. E**

*Gideon v. Wainwright* guaranteed accused felons the right to counsel during their trials.

**31. E**

Appointments to the White House staff do not require Senate approval. The White House staff works for and advises the president personally.

**32. D**

Conference committees work out the differences between the two houses of Congress on similar bills that both houses have passed with some differences. Bills must be passed by both chambers in identical form before becoming laws.

**33. C**

Federal money is legally used to help fund presidential campaigns only.

**34. E**

The Vietnam War and Watergate are responsible for adversely affecting the relationship between the press and politicians.

**35. C**

The establishment clause is part of the 1st Amendment that prohibits Congress from establishing a state religion.

**36. B**

Initiative is the process by which voters can petition to bring a law to a vote of the people.

**37. E**

According to the graph, the <15 group had the largest decline as a percentage of the population from 1900 to 2000. Their percentage dropped 13.1 percent over that period.

**38. A**

According to the graph, the 45–64-year-olds and the 65+ age group each grew by 8.3 percent.

**39. D**

The Speaker of the House is second in line for succession for the presidency behind only the vice president.

**40. C**

The War Powers Resolution was passed as a result of American soldiers being committed to Vietnam and Cambodia during the 1960s and 1970s without Congress being fully informed that this was happening.

**41. D**

Bureaucracies are created initially by Congress. Many times, this is a result of Congress passing an act that is administered by a commission. This commission requires a bureaucracy to carry out the requirements of the act.

**42. C**

A bill of attainder is defined as a law that declares a person guilty of a crime without benefit of a trial. The bill of attainder is unconstitutional.

**43. E**

It is not true that the U.S. Senate has strict rules and limitations concerning debate of proposed bills because of its size; in fact, because of its relatively small size (compared to the House of Representatives, for example), it has unlimited debate with a very few rules and limitations.

**44. D**

According to the graph, people from the South had the highest poverty rate in 1997 of the groups cited. (Be careful to only consider the groups that the question cites.)

**45. C**

Education level is not identified by this particular graph. This question requires you to study the graph carefully.

**46. C**

*Devolution* is a relatively recently coined term used to describe a movement to reduce the influence of the federal and other governments.

**47. E**

*Marbury v. Madison* is the landmark Supreme Court decision that established the court's right of judicial review.

**48. C**

Blanket primaries allow voters to switch back and forth between parties to select the candidate they want regardless of their political party.

**49. E**

Standing committees are permanently established committees designed to handle bills in specific policy areas.

**50. B**

Strict constructionists are judges who decide cases based upon the language of the Constitution. They do not impose their personal views when deciding cases, and they do not make broad interpretations of the intentions of the Constitution.

**51. D**

The Constitution places the power to pardon federal criminals solely in the hands of the president.

**52. D**

The Connecticut Compromise, also known as the Great Compromise, saved the constitutional process by blending aspects of both the New Jersey and Virginia Plans into one plan incorporating aspects of both.

**53. C**

James Madison expressed his views on factions in the Federalist Papers, which were written to help the ratification process for the Constitution.

**54. E**

Sadly, Native Americans have historically existed with the least pleasant conditions of any group.

**55. B**

Congressional subcommittees, interest groups, and bureaucracies form the important group known as the iron triangle.

**56. D**

The vice president does not serve as the chairperson of the Joint Chiefs of Staff. That position is filled by a person from the military.

**57. E**

Dissenting opinions are written by justices voting in the minority. These written opinions sometimes become the basis for overturning or revisiting similar cases.

**58. D**

The party whip is responsible for making sure that members of his or her party are present for votes and that party members vote according to the party's wishes.

**59. C**

Block grants are preferred by states because the state has flexibility in how to spend the money.

**60. D**

*Per curium* is a term the Supreme Court uses when it is issuing a decision without any legal explanation.

## SECTION II: FREE-RESPONSE QUESTIONS

### RUBRIC FOR QUESTION 1: 6 POINTS TOTAL

#### Part (A): 2 Points

**1 point** for describing one of the two provisions listed. **1 point** for a specific historical example.

Description for the first provision would include discussion of the meaning of due process under the 5th and 14th Amendments. *Due process* is defined as protection against arbitrary deprivation of life, liberty, or property (**1 point**). The second point would come from citing the Nisei during World War II and defendants' rights during the 1960s, among others.

Description for the second provision would include discussion of the meaning of freedom of expression. *Freedom of expression* is defined as the constitutional rights of Americans to "freedom of speech, or of the press, or the right of the people peaceably to assemble, and to petition the Government for a redress of grievances" (**1 point**). The **second point** for freedom of expression would come from citing examples such as burning the flag, wearing armbands, and arguments over defining obscenity, among others.

#### Part (B): 4 Points

A provision for Executive Order 9066—*Korematsu v. Japan* involved the internment of American citizens of Japanese descent during World War II (**1 point**). The **second point** would come from explaining that the U.S. government believed order prevented these citizens from committing possible acts of espionage and sabotage.

A provision for the Espionage Act of 1917—*Schenck v. United States* was that it prevented a citizen from advocating lawless acts, such as refusing the call to military service during World War I (**1 point**). The **second point** would come from explaining that the U.S. government believed this order prevented chaos and military problems.

### RUBRIC FOR QUESTION 2: 6 POINTS TOTAL

#### Part (A): 4 points

Discussion of committee structure could include references to the composition of committees being dominated by the majority party (**1 point**). The majority party can prevent legislation it does not approve of from being sent to the floor for a vote (**1 point**).

Discussion of the Speaker of the House could include that the Speaker is the most powerful position in the House and that the Speaker comes from the majority party. The Speaker controls appointments of majority members to committees (**1 point**). The Speaker can control whether or not a motion is relevant and has a great deal of power over the debate of bills (**1 point**).

**Part (B): 2 points**

Discussion of a Senate institutional process could include one of the following: filibuster, amendments not needing to be germane, and the fact that in the Senate legislation can bypass the committee hearing process altogether (**1 point**). Another point would be awarded for explaining how the minority might use the filibuster, nongermane amendments, or bypassing committee hearings to influence legislation (**1 point**).

## RUBRIC FOR QUESTION 3: 6 POINTS TOTAL

**Part (A): 2 points** for explaining that loose constructionists have a very broad interpretation of the Constitution, while strict constructionists interpret the Constitution very narrowly.

**Part (B): 1 point each (3 points total)** for explaining the result of each ruling.

1. *Miranda v. Arizona*—An accused person must be read his or her Constitutional rights at the time of arrest.

2. *Gideon v. Wainwright*—A person accused of a felony must be provided an attorney to represent him or her during trial.

3. *Mapp v. Ohio*—Establishes the exclusionary rule, which holds that illegally obtained evidence cannot be used in a trial.

**Part (C): 1 point** for explaining that Earl Warren was extremely unpopular because of these and other rulings, with many people calling for his impeachment.

## RUBRIC FOR QUESTION 4: 5 POINTS TOTAL

**Part (A): 1 point each (3 points total)** for identifying a federal agency, an interest group, and a congressional committee.

**Part (B): 1 point** for explaining that the three components develop a relationship that allows them to work together for the benefit of all three. The federal agency, the interest group, and the congressional committee are dependent upon each other, and all three benefit through their cooperation.

**Part (C): 1 point** for explaining that the iron triangle illustrates client politics in that the public at large bears the costs but the benefits are realized by a relatively small number of people.

# Part Five

# AP U.S. GOVERNMENT & POLITICS RESOURCES

# APPENDIX 1: **U.S. PRESIDENTS**

| # | President | Election Year/s | Term of Office (Years in Office) | | Party Affiliation |
|---|-----------|-----------------|--------------------|---|-------------------|
| 1 | George Washington | 1789, 1792 | 1789–1797 | (8) | Federalist |
| 2 | John Adams | 1796 | 1797–1801 | (4) | Federalist |
| 3 | Thomas Jefferson | 1800, 1804 | 1801–1809 | (8) | Democratic–Republican |
| 4 | James Madison | 1808, 1812 | 1809–1817 | (8) | Democratic–Republican |
| 5 | James Monroe | 1816, 1820 | 1817–1825 | (8) | Democratic–Republican |
| 6 | John Quincy Adams | 1824 | 1825–1829 | (4) | National–Republican |
| 7 | Andrew Jackson | 1828, 1832 | 1829–1837 | (8) | Democratic |
| 8 | Martin Van Buren | 1836 | 1837–1841 | (4) | Democratic |
| 9 | William H. Harrison | 1840 | 1841 | (1 month) | Whig |
| 10 | John Tyler | | 1841–1845 | (4) | Whig |
| 11 | James K. Polk | 1844 | 1845–1849 | (4) | Democratic |
| 12 | Zachary Taylor | 1848 | 1849–1850 | (1+) | Whig |
| 13 | Millard Fillmore | | 1850–1853 | (3) | Whig |
| 14 | Franklin Pierce | 1852 | 1853–1857 | (4) | Democratic |
| 15 | James Buchanan | 1856 | 1857–1861 | (4) | Democratic |
| 16 | Abraham Lincoln | 1860, 1864 | 1861–1865 | (4+) | Republican |
| 17 | Andrew Johnson | | 1865–1869 | (4) | Republican/ National Union |
| 18 | Ulysses S. Grant | 1868, 1872 | 1869–1877 | (8) | Republican |
| 19 | Rutherford B. Hayes | 1876 | 1877–1881 | (4) | Republican |
| 20 | James A. Garfield | 1880 | 1881 | (1–) | Republican |
| 21 | Chester A. Arthur | | 1881–1885 | (3+) | Republican |
| 22 | Grover Cleveland | 1884 | 1885–1889 | (4) | Democratic |
| 23 | Benjamin Harrison | 1888 | 1889–1893 | (4) | Republican |
| 24 | Grover Cleveland | 1892 | 1893–1897 | (4) | Democratic |

*(continued on next page)*

| # | President | Election Year/s | Term of Office (Years in Office) | | Party Affiliation |
|---|---|---|---|---|---|
| 25 | William McKinley | 1896, 1900 | 1891–1901 | (4+) | Republican |
| 26 | Theodore Roosevelt | 1904 | 1901–1909 | (7+) | Republican |
| 27 | William H. Taft | 1908 | 1909–1913 | (4) | Republican |
| 28 | Woodrow Wilson | 1912, 1916 | 1913–1921 | (8) | Democratic |
| 29 | Warren G. Harding | 1920 | 1921–1923 | (2+) | Republican |
| 30 | Calvin Coolidge | 1924 | 1923–1929 | (6+) | Republican |
| 31 | Herbert Hoover | 1928 | 1929–1933 | (4) | Republican |
| 32 | Franklin D. Roosevelt | 1932, 1936, 1940, 1944 | 1933–1945 | (12+) | Democratic |
| 33 | Harry Truman | 1948 | 1945–1953 | (7+) | Democratic |
| 34 | Dwight Eisenhower | 1952, 1956 | 1953–1961 | (8) | Republican |
| 35 | John F. Kennedy | 1960 | 1961–1963 | (2+) | Democratic |
| 36 | Lyndon B. Johnson | 1964 | 1963–1969 | (6+) | Democratic |
| 37 | Richard M. Nixon | 1968, 1972 | 1969–1974 | (5+) | Republican |
| 38 | Gerald Ford | | 1974–1977 | (2+) | Republican |
| 39 | James Carter | 1976 | 1977–1981 | (4) | Democratic |
| 40 | Ronald Reagan | 1980, 1984 | 1981–1989 | (8) | Republican |
| 41 | George H. W. Bush | 1988 | 1989–1993 | (4) | Republican |
| 42 | Bill Clinton | 1992, 1996 | 1993–2001 | (8) | Democratic |
| 43 | George W. Bush | 2000, 2004 | 2001–2009 | (8) | Republican |

## Notes on Party Labels for the Presidents:

- The Federalist Party was formed under the leadership of Alexander Hamilton during the administration of George Washington. The president hesitated to consider himself a member of a party.

- The label "Democratic-Republican" was attached to Jefferson's leadership after his presidency. During his service in the Washington and Adams administrations, Jefferson's opposition group was called "Republican" after the radicals in the French Revolution, "Democratic" as opponents to Federalists, and then later Democratic-Republican. None of these groups were related to the current Republican Party.

- The label "National Republican" was used during the campaign of 1824, when the party coalition of Jefferson to Monroe began to break apart. All four candidates of that campaign were nominally from the Democratic-Republican party, but J. Q. Adams ran a more "national" campaign, while his main opponent, Andrew Jackson, was forming the core of the new Western and Southern "Democratic" party.

- The Republican Party was originally a coalition of northern Whigs, Free Soil Party members, and other non-Democratic groups of the pre–Civil War crisis years. During the Civil War campaign of 1864, the Republicans invited some loyal Democrats of the border states to join with them. They officially ran that campaign as the "National Union" party and included Democratic Senator Andrew Johnson of Tennessee as the vice presidential candidate. Many history books list Johnson's presidency after Lincoln's murder as Republican, even though Johnson never thought of himself in those terms, nor was he welcome in the northern Republican circles.

- In the 1800s, the Republican Party took on the name "Grand Old Party," with propaganda connections to traditional and loyal leadership and philosophical connections to conservative politics then in control of England's Parliament.

- The Republican symbol of an elephant and the Democratic symbol of a donkey both started with political cartoons by famous journalists such as Thomas Nast. The symbols were used to make fun of elephants who rampaged and donkeys who were stubborn, but they stuck with party leadership as sources of pride.

# APPENDIX 2: UNIQUE PRESIDENTIAL ELECTIONS

| Year | Candidates (winner listed first) | Events |
|------|----------------------------------|--------|
| 1796 | Adams<br>Jefferson | Electors ended up making Adams the president and Jefferson the vice president, even though they were from opposing parties. |
| 1800 | Jefferson<br>Adams | Electors gave a tie to Jefferson and his vice presidential candidate (Aaron Burr), which threw the decision to the House of Representatives. The 12th Amendment was passed to redesign electoral voting. |
| 1824 | J. Q. Adams<br>Jackson<br>Clay<br>Crawford | Popular votes were reported for the first time. Jackson finished first with a plurality of popular and electoral votes, but the House had to decide the election. Adams was given the presidency with Clay's support. |
| 1844 | Polk<br>Clay<br>Birney | Key third-party votes in two states gave Polk the election. This was the first time a third party made the difference. Also, this was the first time an incumbent (Tyler) was denied the nomination. |
| 1860 | Lincoln<br>Breckinridge<br>Douglas<br>Bell | Lincoln received only 39.8 percent of the popular vote, yet he won the majority of the Electoral College votes. Douglas finished second in the popular votes but a distant third in the Electoral College. |
| 1872 | Grant<br>Greeley | The weak Democratic party joined with "Liberal" Republicans to nominate Greeley. Greeley died between the popular vote and the electoral vote. His 66 electors had no one to vote for, so they selected names of leaders who were not on the November ballot. |
| 1876 | Hayes<br>Tilden | Tilden seemed to have the popular vote won, but massive national vote fraud and confused electoral votes sent the election to the House. Instead of voting, the House created a commission to decide the election, and after many twists, the election was given to Hayes. |
| 1888 | B. Harrison<br>Cleveland | Cleveland won the popular vote but lost the electoral vote. |

*(continued on next page)*

| Year | Candidates (winner listed first) | Events |
|------|----------------------------------|--------|
| 1892 | Cleveland<br>B. Harrison<br>Weaver | Weaver's People's Party (Populist) won 1 million popular votes and shocked the two major parties into the beginnings of the Progressive Era. |
| 1912 | Wilson<br>T. Roosevelt<br>Taft | T. Roosevelt was rejected by the Republican Party. He finished second as a third-party candidate, and Republican Taft finished third. |
| 1948 | Truman<br>Dewey<br>Thurmond | Dixiecrats (States' Rights Party) started to split from the Democratic Party and won electoral votes in the South. |
| 1968 | Nixon<br>Humphrey<br>Wallace | Further splits by Dixiecrats (American Party) and the capture of Southern electoral votes signaled the gradual shift to Republican control of the South. |
| 1992 | Clinton<br>G. H. W. Bush<br>Perot | Perot captured 19 percent of the popular vote but no electoral votes. |
| 2000 | G. W. Bush<br>Gore | Gore won the popular vote, but Bush won the electoral vote. |

# APPENDIX 3: **MAJOR ELECTION SHIFTS**

| Year | Candidates (winner listed first) | Events |
|------|----------------------------------|--------|
| 1800 | Jefferson<br>Adams | Jeffersonian Democratic-Republicans removed Federalists and would control politics for the next three decades. |
| 1828 | Jackson<br>J. Q. Adams | The Jacksonian Democratic Party emerged and would dominate the national agenda until the Civil War. |
| 1860 | Lincoln<br>Breckinridge<br>Douglas<br>Bell | Republicans replaced the fractured Whigs and Democrats and would dominate U.S. politics for the rest of the 19th century. |
| 1892 | Cleveland<br>B. Harrison<br>Weaver | The People's Party shocked the two major parties into ending the *laissez-faire* attitude of the Gilded Age and begin addressing the needs of farmers and urban workers. |
| 1912 | Wilson<br>T. Roosevelt<br>Taft | A split in the Republican Party gave Democrats control until after WWI. |
| 1920 | Harding<br>Cox | Republicans controlled the agenda until the Great Depression. |
| 1932 | F. Roosevelt<br>Hoover | The rise of the New Deal and WWII gave Democrats control of much of the political agenda and most of the terms of Congress until the 1990s. |
| 1964 | L. Johnson<br>Goldwater | Republicans' attempts to find the most conservative possible candidate backfired with one of the biggest losses in political history. Liberalism was at its political height. |
| 1968 | Nixon<br>Humphrey<br>Wallace | The assassinations of liberal leaders Robert Kennedy and M. L. King, plus anti-Vietnam violence, doomed the Democrats. Republicans began their re-emergence. |
| 1980 | Reagan<br>Carter | Reagan's emergence as solidly, and proudly, conservative began the dominance of the Republicans, especially in Southern states. Congress shifted to a Republican majority in 1994. *Liberalism* went from a term of dominance to being openly derided by Republicans. |

# APPENDIX 4: CHIEF JUSTICES OF THE SUPREME COURT

| Cheif Justice | Tenure | Notable Achievements |
| --- | --- | --- |
| 1. John Jay | 1789–1795 (6 years) | Few decisions, mostly "rode circuit" |
| 2. John Rutledge | 1795 (Aug.–Dec.) | Interim service, turned down by Senate |
| 3. Oliver Ellsworth | 1796–1800 (4) | |
| 4. John Marshall | 1801–1835 (34) | Dominant leader of Supreme Court powers |
| 5. Roger Taney | 1836–1864 (28) | First great "restraint" leader |
| 6. Salmon Chase | 1864–1873 (9) | |
| 7. Morrison Waite | 1874–1888 (14) | |
| 8. Melville Fuller | 1888–1910 (22) | |
| 9. Edward White | 1910–1921 (11) | |
| 10. William Taft | 1921–1930 (9) | Former president turned Chief Justice |
| 11. Charles Hughes | 1930–1941 (11) | |
| 12. Harlan Stone | 1941–1946 (5) | |
| 13. Frederick Vinson | 1946–1953 (7) | |
| 14. Earl Warren | 1953–1969 (16) | Major civil rights activist |
| 15. Warren Burger | 1969–1986 (17) | |
| 16. William Rehnquist | 1986–2005 (19+) | Major "restraint" leader |
| 17. John G. Roberts Jr. | 2005–present | |

The original role of the Supreme Court was only briefly described in Article 3 of the Constitution. Supreme Court justices assumed that they would wait for rare federal challenges, decide those, and then move back to their more important jobs of riding from one federal district to another to give advice and hear circuit cases.

The *Marbury v. Madison* case was decided in 1803 and gave the court the power of judicial review of the Constitution. This, and interstate challenges during the John Marshall years, dramatically increased the powers and workload of the Supreme Court.

# APPENDIX 5: U.S. FEDERAL CONSTITUTION

WE THE PEOPLE of the United States, in Order to form a more perfect Union, establish justice, insure domestic Tranquility, provide for the common defence, promote the general Welfare, and secure the Blessings of Liberty to ourselves and our Posterity, do ordain and establish this Constitution for the United States of America.

## ARTICLE I

**Section 1.**      All legislative Powers herein granted shall be vested in a Congress of the United States, which shall consist of a Senate and House of Representatives.

**Section 2.**      The House of Representatives shall be composed of Members chosen every second Year by the People of the several States, and the Electors in each State shall have the Qualifications requisite for Electors of the most numerous Branch of the State Legislature.

No Person shall be a Representative who shall not have attained to the Age of twenty five Years, and been seven Years a Citizen of the United States, and who shall not, when elected, be an Inhabitant of that State in which he shall be chosen.

[Representatives and [direct Taxes] shall be apportioned among the several States [which may be included within this Union,] according to their respective Numbers, which shall be determined by adding to the whole Number of free Persons, including those bound to Service for a Term of Years, and excluding Indians not taxed, three fifths of all other Persons. (This clause was changed by section 2 of the Fourteenth Amendment.)] The actual Enumeration shall be made within three Years after the first Meeting of the Congress of the United States, and within every subsequent Term of ten Years, in such Manner as they shall by Law direct. The Number of Representatives shall not exceed one for every thirty Thousand, but each State shall have at Least one Representative; and until such enumeration shall be made, the State of New Hampshire shall be entitled to chuse three, Massachusetts eight, Rhode Island and Providence Plantations one,

Connecticut five, New York six, New Jersey four, Pennsylvania eight, Delaware one, Maryland six, Virginia ten, North Carolina five, South Carolina five, and Georgia three.

When vacancies happen in the Representation from any State, the Executive Authority thereof shall issue Writs of Election to fill such Vacancies.

The House of Representatives shall chuse their Speaker and other Officers; and shall have the sole Power of Impeachment.

**Section 3.**    The Senate of the United States shall be composed of two Senators from each State, [chosen by the Legislature thereof, (This provision was changed by section 1 of the Seventeenth Amendment.)] for six Years; and each Senator shall have one Vote.

Immediately after they shall be assembled in Consequence of the first Election, they shall be divided as equally as may be into three Classes. The Seats of the Senators of the first Class shall be vacated at the Expiration of the second Year, of the second Class at the Expiration of the fourth Year, and of the third Class at the Expiration of the sixth Year, so that one third may be chosen every second Year; [and if Vacancies happen by Resignation, or otherwise, during the Recess of the Legislature of any State, the Executive thereof may make temporary Appointments until the next Meeting of the Legislature, which shall then fill such Vacancies. (This clause was changed by section 2 of the Seventeenth Amendment.)]

No Person shall be a Senator who shall not have attained to the Age of thirty Years, and been nine Years a Citizen of the United States, and who shall not, when elected, be an Inhabitant of that State for which he shall be chosen.

The Vice President of the United States shall be President of the Senate, but shall have no Vote, unless they be equally divided.

The Senate shall chuse their other Officers, and also a President *pro tempore*, in the Absence of the Vice President, or when he shall exercise the Office of President of the United States.

The Senate shall have the sole Power to try all Impeachments. When sitting for that Purpose, they shall be on Oath or Affirmation. When the President of the United States is tried, the Chief justice shall preside: And no Person shall be convicted without the Concurrence of two thirds of the Members present.

Judgment in Cases of Impeachment shall not extend further than to removal from Office, and disqualification to hold and enjoy any Office of honor, Trust or Profit under the United States: but the Party convicted shall nevertheless be liable and subject to Indictment, Trial, Judgment and Punishment, according to Law.

**Section 4.**    The Times, Places and Manner of holding Elections for Senators and Representatives, shall be prescribed in each State by the Legislature thereof; but the Congress may at any time by Law make or alter such Regulations, except as to the Places of chusing Senators.

The Congress shall assemble at least once in every Year, and such Meeting shall be [on the first Monday in December, (This provision was changed by section 2 of the Twentieth Amendment.)] unless they shall by Law appoint a different Day.

**Section 5.**   Each House shall be the judge of the Elections, Returns and Qualifications of its own Members, and a Majority of each shall constitute a Quorum to do Business; but a smaller Number may adjourn from day to day, and may be authorized to compel the Attendance of absent Members, in such Manner, and under such Penalties as each House may provide.

Each House may determine the Rules of its Proceedings, punish its Members for disorderly Behaviour, and, with the Concurrence of two thirds, expel a Member.

Each House shall keep a journal of its Proceedings, and from time to time publish the same, excepting such Parts as may in their judgment require Secrecy; and the Yeas and Nays of the Members of either House on any question shall, at the Desire of one fifth of those Present, be entered on the journal.

Neither House, during the Session of Congress, shall, without the Consent of the other, adjourn for more than three days, nor to any other Place than that in which the two Houses shall be sitting.

**Section 6.**   The Senators and Representatives shall receive a Compensation for their Services, to be ascertained by Law, and paid out of the Treasury of the United States. They shall in all Cases, except Treason, Felony and Breach of the Peace, be privileged from Arrest during their Attendance at the Session of their respective Houses, and in going to and returning from the same; and for any Speech or Debate in either House, they shall not be questioned in any other Place.

No Senator or Representative shall, during the Time for which he was elected, be appointed to any civil Office under the Authority of the United States, which shall have been created, or the Emoluments whereof shall have been encreased during such time; and no Person holding any Office under the United States, shall be a Member of either House during his Continuance in Office.

**Section 7.**   All Bills for raising Revenue shall originate in the House of Representatives; but the Senate may propose or concur with Amendments as on other Bills.

Every Bill which shall have passed the House of Representatives and the Senate, shall, before it become a Law, be presented to the President of the United States; If he approve he shall sign it, but if not he shall return it, with his Objections to that House in which it shall have originated, who shall enter the Objections at large on their Journal, and proceed to reconsider it. If after such Reconsideration two thirds of that House shall agree to pass the Bill, it shall be sent, together with the Objections, to the other House, by which it shall likewise be reconsidered, and if approved by two thirds of that House, it shall become a Law. But in all such Cases the Votes of both Houses shall be determined by yeas and Nays, and the Names of the Persons voting for and against the Bill shall be entered on the journal of each House respectively. If any bill shall not be returned by the President within ten Days (Sundays excepted) after it shall have been presented to him, the Same shall be a Law, in like Manner as if he had signed it, unless the Congress by their Adjournment prevent its Return, in which Case it shall not be a Law.

Every Order, Resolution, or Vote to which the Concurrence of the Senate and House of Representatives may be necessary (except on a question of Adjournment) shall be presented to the President of the United States; and before the Same shall take Effect, shall be approved by him, or being disapproved by him, shall be repassed by two thirds of the Senate and House of Representatives, according to the Rules and Limitations prescribed in the Case of a Bill.

**Section 8.**      The Congress shall have Power To lay and collect Taxes, Duties, Imposts and Excises, to pay the Debts and provide for the common Defence and general Welfare of the United States; but all Duties, Imposts and Excises shall be uniform throughout the United States;

To borrow Money on the credit of the United States;

To regulate Commerce with Foreign Nations, and among the several States, and with the Indian tribes;

To establish an uniform Rule of Naturalization, and uniform Laws on the subject of Bankruptcies throughout the United States;

To coin Money, regulate the Value thereof, and of foreign Coin, and fix the Standard of Weights and Measures;

To provide for the Punishment of counterfeiting the Securities and current Coin of the United States;

To establish Post Offices and post Roads;

To promote the Progress of Science and useful Arts, by securing for limited Times to Authors and Inventors the exclusive Right to their respective Writings and Discoveries;

To constitute Tribunals inferior to the supreme Court;

To define and punish Piracies and Felonies committed on the high Seas, and Offences against the Law of Nations;

To declare War, grant Letters of Marque and Reprisal, and make Rules concerning Captures on Land and Water;

To raise and support Armies, but no Appropriation of Money to that Use shall be for a longer Term than two Years;

To provide and maintain a Navy;

To make Rules for the Government and Regulation of the land and naval Forces;

To provide for calling forth the Militia to execute the Laws of the Union, suppress Insurrections and repel Invasions;

To provide for organizing, arming, and disciplining, the Militia and for governing such Part of them as may be employed in the Service of the United States, reserving to the States respectively, the Appointment of the Officers, and the Authority of training the Militia according to the discipline prescribed by Congress;

To exercise exclusive Legislation in all Cases whatsoever, over such District (not exceeding ten Miles square) as may, by Cession of particular States, and the Acceptance of Congress, become the Seat of the Government of the United States, and to exercise like Authority over all Places purchased by the Consent of the Legislature of the State in which the Same shall be, for the Erection of Forts, Magazines, Arsenals, Dockyards, and other needful Buildings; And

To make all Laws which shall be necessary and proper for carrying into Execution the foregoing Powers, and all other Powers vested by this Constitution in the Government of the United States, or in any Department or Officer thereof.

**Section 9.**     The Migration or Importation of such Persons any of the States now existing shall think proper to admit, shall not be prohibited by the Congress prior to the Year one thousand eight hundred and eight, but a Tax or duty may be imposed on such Importation, not exceeding ten dollars for each Person.

The Privilege of the Writ of Habeas Corpus shall not be suspended, unless when in Cases of Rebellion or Invasion the public Safety may require it.

No Bill of Attainder or *ex post facto* Law shall be passed.

No Capitation, or other direct, Tax shall be laid, unless in Proportion to the Census or Enumeration herein before directed to be taken.

No Tax or Duty shall be laid on Articles exported from any State.

No Preference shall be given by any Regulation of Commerce or Revenue to the Ports of one State over those of another: nor shall Vessels bound to, or from, one State, be obliged to enter, clear, or pay Duties in another.

No Money shall be drawn from the Treasury, but in Consequence of Appropriations made by Law; and a regular Statement and Account of the Receipts and Expenditures of all public Money shall be published from time to time.

No Title of Nobility shall be granted by the United States: And no Person holding any Office of Profit or Trust under them, shall, without the Consent of the Congress, accept of any present, Emolument, Office, or Tide, of any kind whatever, from any King, Prince, or foreign State.

**Section 10.**     No State shall enter into any Treaty, Alliance, or Confederation; grant Letters of Marque and Reprisal; coin Money; emit Bills of Credit; make any Thing but gold and silver Coin a Tender in Payment of Debts; pass any Bill of Attainder, *ex post facto* Law, or Law impairing the Obligation of Contracts, or grant any Title of Nobility.

No State shall, without the Consent of the Congress, lay any Imposts or Duties on Imports or Exports, except what may be absolutely necessary for executing its inspection Laws: and the net Produce of all Duties and Imposts, laid by any State on Imports or Exports, shall be for the Use of the Treasury of the United States; and all such Laws shall be subject to the Revision and Controul of the Congress.

No State shall, without the Consent of Congress, lay any Duty of Tonnage, keep Troops, or Ships of War in time of Peace, enter into any Agreement or Compact with another State, or with a foreign Power, or engage in War, unless actually invaded, or in such imminent Danger as will not admit of delay.

# ARTICLE II

**Section 1.**     The executive Power shall be vested in a President of the United States of America. He shall hold his Office during the Term of four Years, and, together with the Vice President, chosen for the same Term, be elected, as follows.

Each State shall appoint, in such Manner as the Legislature thereof may direct, a Number of Electors, equal to the whole Number of Senators and Representatives to which the State may be entitled in the Congress: but no Senator or Representative, or Person holding an Office of Trust or Profit under the United States, shall be appointed an Elector.

[The Electors shall meet in their respective States, and vote by Ballot for two Persons, of whom one at least shall not be an inhabitant of the same State with themselves. And they shall make a List of all the Persons voted for, and of the Number of Votes for each; which List they shall sign and certify, and transmit sealed to the Seat of the Government of the United States, directed to the President of the Senate. The President of the Senate shall, in the Presence of the Senate and House of Representatives, open all the Certificates, and the Votes shall then be counted. The Person having the greatest Number of Votes shall be the President, if such Number be a Majority of the whole Number of Electors appointed; and if there be more than one who have such Majority, and have an equal Number of Votes, then the House of Representatives shall immediately chuse by Ballot one of them for President; and if no Person have a Majority, then from the five highest on the List the said House shall in like Manner chuse the President. But in chusing the President, the Votes shall be taken by States, the Representation from each State having one Vote; A quorum for this purpose shall consist of a Member or Members from two thirds of the States, and a Majority of all the States shall be necessary to a Choice. In every Case, after the Choice of the President, the Person having the greatest Number of Votes of the Electors shall be the Vice President. But if there should remain two or more who have equal Votes, the Senate shall chuse from them by Ballot the Vice President. (This clause was superseded by the Twelfth Amendment.)]

The Congress may determine the Time of chusing the Electors, and the Day on which they shall give their Votes; which Day shall be the same throughout the United States.

No Person except a natural born Citizen, or a Citizen of the United States, at the time of the Adoption of this Constitution, shall be eligible to the Office of President; neither shall any Person be eligible to that Office who shall not have attained to the Age of thirty five Years, and been fourteen Years a Resident within the United States.

[In Case of the Removal of the President from Office, or of his Death, Resignation, or Inability to discharge the Powers and Duties of the said Office, the Same shall devolve on the Vice President, and the Congress may by Law provide for the Case of Removal, Death, Resignation or Inability, both of the President and Vice President, declaring what Officer shall then act as President, and such Officer shall act accordingly, until the Disability be removed, or a President shall be elected. (This clause was modified by the Twenty-Fifth Amendment.)]

The President shall, at stated Times, receive for his Services, a Compensation, which shall neither be increased nor diminished during the Period for which he shall have been elected, and he shall not receive within that Period any other Emolument from the United States, or any of them.

Before he enter on the Execution of his Office, he shall take the following Oath or Affirmation: "I do solemnly swear (or affirm) that I will faithfully execute the Office of President of the United States, and will to the best of my Ability, preserve, protect and defend the Constitution of the United States."

**Section 2.**    The President shall be Commander in Chief of the Army and Navy of the United States, and of the Militia of the several States, when called into the actual Service of the United States; he may require the Opinion, in writing, of the principal Officer in each of the executive Departments, upon any Subject relating to the Duties of their respective Offices, and he shall have Power to grant Reprieves and Pardons for Offences against the United States, except in Cases of Impeachment.

He shall have Power, by and with the Advice and Consent of the Senate, to make Treaties, provided two thirds of the Senators present concur; and he shall nominate, and by and with the Advice and Consent of the Senate, shall appoint Ambassadors, other public Ministers and Consuls, judges of the supreme Court, and all other Officers of the United States, whose Appointments are not herein otherwise provided for, and which shall be established by Law: but the Congress may by Law vest the Appointment of such inferior Officers, as they think proper, in the President alone, in the Courts of Law, or in the Heads of Departments.

The President shall have Power to fill up all Vacancies that may happen during the Recess of the Senate, by granting Commissions which shall expire at the End of their next Session.

**Section 3.**    He shall from time to time give to the Congress Information of the State of the Union, and recommend to their Consideration such Measures as he shall judge necessary and expedient; he may, on extraordinary Occasions, convene both Houses, or either of them, and in Case of Disagreement between them, with Respect to the Time of Adjournment, he may adjourn them to such Time as he shall think proper; he shall receive Ambassadors and other public Ministers; he shall take Care that the Laws be faithfully executed, and shall Commission all the Officers of the United States.

**Section 4.**    The President, Vice President and all civil Officers of the United States, shall be removed from Office on Impeachment for, and Conviction of, Treason, Bribery, or other high Crimes and Misdemeanors.

# ARTICLE III

**Section 1.**    The judicial Power of the United States, shall be vested in one supreme Court, and in such inferior Courts as the Congress may from time to time ordain and establish. The judges, both of the supreme and inferior Courts, shall hold their Offices during good Behaviour, and shall, at stated Times receive for their Services, a Compensation, which shall not be diminished during their Continuance in Office.

**Section 2.**    The judicial Power shall extend to all Cases, in Law and Equity, arising under this Constitution, the Laws of the United States, and Treaties made, or which shall be made, under their Authority; to all Cases affecting Ambassadors, other public Ministers and Consuls; to all Cases of admiralty and maritime jurisdiction; to Controversies to which the United States shall be a Party; to Controversies between two or more States; between a State and Citizens of another State; between Citizens of different States, between Citizens of the same State claiming Lands under Grants of different States, and between a State, or the Citizens thereof, and foreign States, Citizens or Subjects.

In all Cases affecting Ambassadors, other public Ministers and Consuls, and those in which a State shall be Party, the supreme Court shall have original jurisdiction. In all the other Cases before mentioned, the supreme Court shall have appellate jurisdiction, both as to Law and Fact, with such Exceptions, and under such Regulations as the Congress shall make.

The Trial of all Crimes, except in Cases of Impeachment, shall be by jury; and such Trial shall be held in the State where the said Crimes shall have been committed; but when not committed within any State, the Trial shall be at such Place or Places as the Congress may by Law have directed.

**Section 3.**  Treason against the United States, shall consist only in levying War against them, or in adhering to their Enemies, giving them Aid and Comfort. No Person shall be convicted of Treason unless on the Testimony of two Witnesses to the same overt Act, or on Confession in open Court.

The Congress shall have Power to declare the Punishment of Treason, but no Attainder of Treason shall work Corruption of Blood, or Forfeiture except during the Life of the Person attainted.

# ARTICLE IV

**Section 1.**  Full Faith and Credit shall be given in each State to the public Acts, Records, and judicial Proceedings of every other State; And the Congress may by general Laws prescribe the Manner in which such Acts, Records and Proceedings shall be proved, and the Effect thereof.

**Section 2.**  The Citizens of each State shall be entitled to all Privileges and Immunities of Citizens in the several States.

A Person charged in any State with Treason, Felony, or other Crime, who shall flee from justice, and be found in another State, shall on Demand of the executive Authority of the State from which he fled, be delivered up, to be removed to the State having jurisdiction of the Crime.

[No Person held to Service or Labour in one State, under the Laws thereof, escaping into another, shall, in Consequence of any Law or Regulation therein, be discharged from such Service or Labour, but shall be delivered up on Claim of the Party to whom such Service or Labour may be due. (This clause was superseded by the Thirteenth Amendment.)]

**Section 3.**  New States may be admitted by the Congress into this Union; but no new State shall be formed or erected within the jurisdiction of any other State; nor any State be formed by the junction of two or more States, or Parts of States, without the Consent of the Legislatures of the States concerned as well as of the Congress.

The Congress shall have Power to dispose of and make all needful Rules and Regulations respecting the Territory or other Property belonging to the United States; and nothing in this Constitution shall be so construed as to Prejudice any Claims of the United States, or of any particular State.

**Section 4.** The United States shall guarantee to every State in this Union a Republican Form of Government, and shall protect each of them against Invasion; and on Application of the Legislature, or of the Executive (when the Legislature cannot be convened) against domestic Violence.

## ARTICLE V

The Congress, whenever two thirds of both Houses shall deem it necessary, shall propose Amendments to this Constitution, or, on the Application of the Legislatures of two thirds of the several States, shall call a Convention for proposing Amendments, which, in either Case, shall be valid to all Intents and Purposes, as Part of this Constitution, when ratified by the legislatures of three fourths of the several States, or by Conventions in three fourths thereof, as the one or the other Mode of Ratification may be proposed by the Congress; Provided that no Amendment which may be made prior to the Year One thousand eight hundred and eight shall in any Manner affect the first and fourth Clauses in the Ninth Section of the first Article; and that no State, without its Consent, shall be deprived of its equal Suffrage in the Senate.

## ARTICLE VI

All Debts contracted and Engagements entered into, before the Adoption of this Constitution, shall be as valid against the United States under this Constitution, as under the Confederation.

This Constitution, and the Laws of the United States which shall be made in Pursuance thereof; and all Treaties made, or which shall be made, under the Authority of the United States, shall be the supreme Law of the Land; and the judges in every State shall be bound thereby, any Thing in the Constitution or Laws of any State to the Contrary notwithstanding.

The Senators and Representatives before mentioned, and the Members of the several State Legislatures, and all executive and judicial Officers, both of the United States and of the several States, shall be bound by Oath or Affirmation, to support this Constitution; but no religious Test shall ever be required as a Qualification to any Office or public Trust under the United States.

## ARTICLE VII

The Ratification of the Conventions of nine States, shall be sufficient for the Establishment of this Constitution between the States so ratifying the Same.

DONE in Convention by the Unanimous Consent of the States present the Seventeenth Day of September in the Year of our Lord one thousand seven hundred and Eighty seven and of the Independance of the United States of America the Twelfth.

IN WITNESS whereof We have hereunto subscribed our Names.

[The first ten amendments (the Bill of Rights) were ratified December 15, 1791.]

## AMENDMENT I

Congress shall make no law respecting an establishment of religion, or prohibiting the free exercise thereof; or abridging the freedom of speech, or of the press, or the right of the people peaceably to assemble, and to petition the Government for a redress of grievances.

## AMENDMENT II

A well regulated Militia, being necessary to the security of a free State, the right of the people to keep and bear Arms, shall not be infringed.

## AMENDMENT III

No Soldier shall, in time of peace be quartered in any house, without the consent of the Owner, nor in time of war, but in a manner to be prescribed by law.

## AMENDMENT IV

The right of the people to be secure in their persons, houses, papers, and effects, against unreasonable searches and seizures, shall not be violated, and no Warrants shall issue, but upon probable cause, supported by Oath or affirmation, and particularly describing the place to be searched, and the persons or things to be seized.

## AMENDMENT V

No person shall be held to answer for a capital, or otherwise infamous crime, unless on a present-ment or indictment of a Grand Jury, except in cases arising in the land or naval forces, or in the Militia, when in actual service in time of War or public danger; nor shall any person be subject for the same offence to be twice put in jeopardy of life or limb, nor shall be compelled in any criminal case to be a witness against himself, nor be deprived of life, liberty, or property, without due process of law; nor shall private property be taken for public use, without just compensation.

## AMENDMENT VI

In all criminal prosecutions, the accused shall enjoy the right to a speedy and public trial, by an impartial jury of the State and district wherein the crime shall have been committed; which district shall have been previously ascertained by law, and to be informed of the nature and cause of the accusation; to be confronted with the witnesses against him; to have compulsory process for obtaining witnesses in his favor, and to have the Assistance of Counsel for his defence.

## AMENDMENT VII

In Suits at common law, where the value in controversy shall exceed twenty dollars, the right of trial by jury shall be preserved, and no fact tried by a jury, shall be otherwise reexamined in any Court of the United States, than according to the rules of the common law.

## AMENDMENT VIII

Excessive bail shall not be required, nor excessive fines imposed, nor cruel and unusual punishments inflicted.

## AMENDMENT IX

The enumeration in the Constitution, of certain rights, shall not be construed to deny or disparage others retained by the people.

## AMENDMENT X

The powers not delegated to the United States by the Constitution, nor prohibited by it to the States, are reserved to the States respectively, or to the people.

## AMENDMENT XI (RATIFIED FEBRUARY 7, 1795)

The judicial power of the United States shall not be construed to extend to any suit in law or equity, commenced or prosecuted against one of the United States by Citizens of another State, or by Citizens or Subjects of any Foreign State.

## AMENDMENT XII (RATIFIED JUNE 15, 1804)

The Electors shall meet in their respective states, and vote by ballot for President and Vice President, one of whom, at least, shall not be an inhabitant of the same state with themselves; they shall name in their ballots the person voted for as President, and in distinct ballots the person voted for as Vice President, and they shall make distinct lists of all persons voted for as President, and of all persons voted for as Vice President, and of the number of votes for each, which lists they shall sign and certify, and transmit sealed to the seat of the government of the United States, directed to the President of the Senate; The President of the Senate shall, in the presence of the Senate and House of Representatives, open all the certificates and the votes shall then be counted; The person having the greatest number of votes for President, shall be the President, if such number be a majority of the whole number of Electors appointed; and if no person have such majority, then from the persons having the highest numbers not exceeding three on the list of those voted for as President, the House of Representatives shall choose immediately, by ballot, the President. But in choosing the President, the votes shall be taken by states, the representation from each state having one vote; a quorum for this purpose shall consist of a member or members from

## POLICY DEVELOPMENT

### FEDERAL BUDGET/ECONOMIC POLICY

- Central task of federal government is to create **budget**
- **Office of Management and Budget** (federal agency) drafts budget, but Congress prepares final version
- Large mandatory spending limits discretionary spending
- Tension exists between open competition and government guidance for economy
- Twentieth century has seen expanded government role
- **Unfunded mandates** are rules Congress makes without allocating money for enforcement, creating conflict between federal and local/state governments

### DOMESTIC POLICY

- Public demands large-scale domestic policy to address retirement needs, bank and stock stability, needs of poor
- Federal policies:
  - Assist business and individuals directly
  - Create rules to encourage certain behaviors
  - Help those unable to help themselves
- Many federal priorities set through financial assistance to states and local governments in form of grants.
- Federal government often sets policy priorities based on cost-benefit analysis
- Domestic policy changes often brought about by responses to industrial developments, monopolies, abuses, economic crises, and civil rights

### FOREIGN POLICY: MILITARY/ECONOMIC

- Vast majority of military conflicts conducted without congressional declaration of war
- President plays role in foreign and military policy; relies on large staff/network
- Various agencies and entities involved in decision making
- Treaties often replaced by executive agreements that don't require Senate approval
- U.S. leader in United Nations/World Trade Organization

## POLITICAL BELIEFS (CONT'D)

- Role of government in setting national/news agenda
- Recent legal cases and court rulings have shown limits on freedom of speech for journalists
- Most media outlets owned by big corporations.
- Candidates and parties use media to get ideas out
- Technological advances have changed role of media and the way facts are presented/shared:
  - Radio    - Television    - Internet

## BRANCHES OF GOV'T (CONT'D)

- 1960s and '70s—many famous Supreme Court decisions
- Structured methods exist to decide cases, define rights, etc.
- Tension between judicial activism and judicial restraint

## POLITICAL BELIEFS & BEHAVIORS

- Overall—free participation, limited government controls
- Meaning/policy impact of liberal versus conservative has shifted throughout U.S. history
- Voter turnout low; voters tend toward moderate viewpoint
- Political spectrum relatively centrist
- Family and other factors influence political beliefs
- **Voting access** has often been restricted

### PUBLIC OPINION/POLLING

- **Public opinion data** has become important to leaders in pursuing agendas
- Most citizens focus on jobs and self-interests
- **Polls**—statistical samples, carefully crafted questions

### POLITICAL PARTIES

- U.S. system dominated by two parties: Democratic and Republican
- Policy positions of parties have switched from days of Founding Fathers, particularly regarding role of federal government
- Democrats tend to dominate in Northeast and West; Republicans have majorities in South and rural states
- Some typical **voting patterns** are changing
- **Money for parties is increasing**
- Current parties diverging, more polarized
- History of third parties and independent voters; role of independents in 2008 election

### CAMPAIGNS AND ELECTIONS

- **Elections** are frequent, time consuming, expensive
- Money is part of controversy, but few restrictions made or followed
- **Political Action Committees** (PACs), lobbyists, and special interests can be major influencers
- Changes in way presidential candidates are nominated, leading to rise of the primary system
- Functioning and history of **Electoral College system**
- Since 1896, significant political realignments have occurred

### MEDIA AND FREE SPEECH

- **Bias in media coverage**
  - Role of Watergate
  - Perceived bias

## DEVELOPMENT OF FEDERAL SYSTEM OF GOVERNMENT

### DECLARATION OF INDEPENDENCE
- List of freedoms
- Rights of citizens

### ARTICLES OF CONFEDERATION
- Initial road map for union
- Participation voluntary
- Local and state governments dominant
- No mechanisms for foreign threats
- Disagreements among states
- Financial chaos
- No tax collection

- No executive branch
- No judiciary

### CONSTITUTION
- Designed to correct flaws in Articles of Confederation, including amendment procedure
- Preamble—sets out six basic goals of new government
- Seven articles
- Article I is most detailed. Describes Congress; legislative powers:
  - Commerce Clause
  - Elastic Clause
- Article II lays out executive powers:
  - purposely vague
  - powers were to be checked by Congress
  - Judicial and State powers less detailed
- Bill of Rights—first 10 amendments that came out of ratification process; ratified in 1791; 17 additions since
- Constitutional themes include:
  - Representative govt.
  - Indirect democracy
  - Federalism
  - Separation of powers
  - Checks and balances
  - Civil liberties limit govt.

### FEDERALIST PAPERS
- Essays explaining U.S. system of government
- Central versus regional power
- Political parties took shape around this issue:
- Alexander Hamilton—Federalist
- Thomas Jefferson—Democratic-Republican (anti-federalist)
- Focus of debate throughout history—still important today

### FEDERALISM AND U.S. GOVERNMENT
- Powers not in Constitution are reserved for States
- Concept of federalism has changed dramatically since inception. Major points of change:
  - Civil War
  - Great Depression
  - World War II
- Shift over time from relative isolation between federal and state authority to domination of federal standards.
- Major shifts in federal power since the Great Depression include creation of:
  - Social Security
  - Medicare/Medicaid
  - Voting Rights Act
  - Civil Rights Act

## BRANCHES OF GOVERNMENT

### LEGISLATIVE BRANCH
- Constitution is mostly about Congress:
  - How each house is structured
  - How laws are made
  - Role of conference committees
  - Role of presidential veto in lawmaking
- Lawmaking is complex—hard to pass new laws or amend existing laws
- Creation of federal budget—major duty of Congress
- Party leaders central to control of issues, budgets
- Federal laws in 20th century expanded influence of federal government
- Incumbents usually win re-election

### EXECUTIVE BRANCH
- Executive authority expanded throughout history:
  - Expressed/Implied powers
  - Changes over time
- Presidential image shifts often based on events, media
- Executive branch large and powerful; high-level political executives have significant power
- When president makes unpopular decisions, Americans usually willing to accept them despite backlash
- Citizens expect members of government to behave/use influence appropriately
- History of power shifts between Congress and president

#### Federal Bureaucracy
- Most dramatic change in structure of government is growth of bureaucracy
- Powers similar to constitutional branches of government
- Controlled by interlocking groups that benefit from existence of federal programs
- Agencies have major role in policy-making and governing
- Plays key role in filling public needs
- 15 Cabinet departments work closely with president

### JUDICIAL BRANCH
- Structure of federal court system:
  - Circuit courts
  - Appeals courts
  - Supreme Court
- Judicial review began with Marbury v. Madison (1803)
- 14th Amendment created legal shifts
- Supreme Court hears small minority of cases sent to it
- Separation of powers and checks and balances continue to limit government
- Judicial review not in Constitution
- Federal government controls money; extends its powers

two-thirds of the states, and a majority of all the states shall be necessary to a choice. [And if the House of Representatives shall not choose a President whenever the right of choice shall devolve upon them, before the fourth day of March next following, then the Vice-President shall act as President, as in the case of the death or other constitutional disability of the President (This clause was superseded by section 3 of the Twentieth Amendment.)]. The person having the greatest number of votes as Vice-President, shall be the Vice-President, if such number be a majority of the whole number of Electors appointed, and if no person have a majority, then from the two highest numbers on the list, the Senate shall choose the Vice-President; a quorum for the purpose shall consist of two-thirds of the whole number of Senators, and a majority of the whole number shall be necessary to a choice. But no person constitutionally ineligible to the office of President shall be eligible to that of Vice President of the United States.

## AMENDMENT XIII (RATIFIED DECEMBER 6, 1865)

**Section 1.**   Neither slavery nor involuntary servitude, except as a punishment for crime whereof the party shall have been duly convicted, shall exist within the United States, or any place subject to their jurisdiction.

**Section 2.**   Congress shall have power to enforce this article by appropriate legislation.

## AMENDMENT XIV (RATIFIED JULY 9, 1868)

**Section 1.**   All persons born or naturalized in the United States, and subject to the jurisdiction thereof, are citizens of the United States and of the State wherein they reside. No State shall make or enforce any law which shall abridge the privileges or immunities of citizens of the United States; nor shall any State deprive any person of life, liberty, or property, without due process of law; nor deny to any person within its jurisdiction the equal protection of the laws.

**Section 2.**   Representatives shall be apportioned among the several States according to their respective numbers, counting the whole number of persons in each State, excluding Indians not taxed. But when the right to vote at any election for the choice of electors for President and Vice President of the United States, Representatives in Congress, the Executive and judicial officers of a State, or the members of the Legislature thereof, is denied to any of the male inhabitants of such State, being twenty-one years of age, and citizens of the United States, or in any way abridged, except for participation in rebellion, or other crime, the basis of representation therein shall be reduced in the proportion which the number of such male citizens shall bear to the whole number of male citizens twenty-one years of age in such State.

**Section 3.**     No person shall be a Senator or Representative in Congress, or elector of President and Vice President, or hold any office, civil or military, under the United States, or under any State, who, having previously taken an oath, as a member of Congress, or as an officer of the United States, or as a member of any State legislature, or as an executive or judicial officer of any State, to support the Constitution of the United States, shall have engaged in insurrection or rebellion against the same, or given aid or comfort to the enemies thereof. But Congress may by a vote of two-thirds of each House, remove such disability.

**Section 4.**     The validity of the public debt of the United States, authorized by law, including debts incurred for payment of pensions and bounties for services in suppressing insurrection or rebellion, shall not be questioned. But neither the United States nor any State shall assume or pay any debt or obligation incurred in aid of insurrection or rebellion against the United States, or any claim for the loss of emancipation of any slave; but all such debts, obligations and claims shall be held illegal and void.

**Section 5.**     The Congress shall have power to enforce, by appropriate legislation, the provisions of this article.

## AMENDMENT XV (RATIFIED FEBRUARY 3, 1870)

**Section 1.**     The right of citizens of the United States to vote shall not be denied or abridged by the United States or by any State on account of race, color, or previous condition of servitude.

**Section 2.**     The Congress shall have power to enforce this article by appropriate legislation.

## AMENDMENT XVI (RATIFIED FEBRUARY 3, 1913)

The Congress shall have power to lay and collect taxes on incomes, from whatever source derived, without apportionment among the several States, and without regard to any census or enumeration.

## AMENDMENT XVII (RATIFIED APRIL 8, 1913)

The Senate of the United States shall be composed of two Senators from each State, elected by the people thereof, for six years; and each Senator shall have one vote. The electors in each State shall have the qualifications requisite for electors of the most numerous branch of the State legislatures.

When vacancies happen in the representation of any State in the Senate, the executive authority of such State shall issue writs of election to fill such vacancies: Provided, That the legislature of any State may empower the executive thereof to make temporary appointments until the people fill the vacancies by election as the legislature may direct.

This amendment shall not be so construed as to affect the election or term of any Senator chosen before it becomes valid as part of the Constitution.

## AMENDMENT XVIII (RATIFIED JANUARY 16, 1919.)

**Section 1.** After one year from the ratification of this article the manufacture, sale, or transportation of intoxicating liquors within, the importation thereof into, or the exportation thereof from the United States and all territory subject to the jurisdiction thereof for beverage purposes is hereby prohibited.

**Section 2.** The Congress and the several States shall have concurrent power to enforce this article by appropriate legislation.

**Section 3.** This article shall be inoperative unless it shall have been ratified as an amendment to the Constitution by the legislatures of the several States, as provided in the Constitution, within seven years from the date of the submission hereof to the States by the Congress.

## AMENDMENT XIX (RATIFIED AUGUST 18, 1920)

The right of citizens of the United States to vote shall not be denied or abridged by the United States or by any State on account of sex.

Congress shall have power to enforce this article by appropriate legislation.

## AMENDMENT XX (RATIFIED JANUARY 23, 1933)

**Section 1.** The terms of the President and Vice President shall end at noon on the 20th day of January, and the terms of Senators and Representatives at noon on the 3d day of January, of the years in which such terms would have ended if this article had not been ratified; and the terms of their successors shall then begin.

**Section 2.** The Congress shall assemble at least once in every year, and such meeting shall begin at noon on the 3d day of January, unless they shall by law appoint a different day.

**Section 3.** If, at the time fixed for the beginning of the term of the President, the President elect shall have died, the Vice President elect shall become President. If a President shall not have been chosen before the time fixed for the beginning of his term, or if the President elect shall have failed to qualify, then the Vice President elect shall act as President until a President shall have qualified; and the Congress may by law provide for the case wherein neither a President elect nor a Vice President elect shall have qualified, declaring who shall then act as President, or the manner in which one who is to act shall be selected, and such person shall act accordingly until a President or Vice President shall have qualified.

**Section 4.** The Congress may by law provide for the case of the death of any of the persons from whom the House of Representatives may choose a President whenever the right of choice shall have devolved upon them, and for the case of the death of any of the persons from whom the Senate may choose a Vice President whenever the right of choice shall have devolved upon them.

**Section 5.** Sections 1 and 2 shall take effect on the 15th day of October following the ratification of this article.

**Section 6.** This article shall be inoperative unless it shall have been ratified as an amendment to the Constitution by the legislatures of three-fourths of the several States within seven years from the date of its submission.

## AMENDMENT XXI (RATIFIED DECEMBER 3, 1933)

**Section 1.** The eighteenth article of amendment to the Constitution of the United States is hereby repealed.

**Section 2.** The transportation or importation into any State, Territory, or possession of the United States for delivery or use therein of intoxicating liquors, in violation of the laws thereof, is hereby prohibited.

**Section 3.** This article shall be inoperative unless it shall have been ratified as an amendment to the Constitution by conventions in the several States, as provided in the Constitution, within seven years from the date of the submission hereof to the States by the Congress.

## AMENDMENT XXII (RATIFIED FEBRUARY 27, 1951)

**Section 1.** No person shall be elected to the office of the President more than twice, and no person who has held the office of President, or acted as President, for more than two years of a term to which some other person was elected President shall be elected to the office of the President more than once. But this Article shall not apply to any person holding the office of President when this Article was proposed by the Congress, and shall not prevent any person who may be holding the office of President, or acting as President, during the term within which this Article becomes operative from holding the office of President or acting as President during the remainder of such term.

**Section 2.** This article shall be inoperative unless it shall have been ratified as an amendment to the Constitution by the legislatures of three-fourths of the several States within seven years from the date of its submission to the States by the Congress.

## AMENDMENT XXIII (RATIFIED MARCH 29, 1961)

**Section 1.**     The District constituting the seat of Government of the United States shall appoint in such manner as the Congress may direct:

A number of electors of President and Vice President equal to the whole number of Senators and Representatives in Congress to which the District would be entitled if it were a State, but in no event more than the least populous State; they shall be in addition to those appointed by the States, but they shall be considered, for the purposes of the election of President and Vice President, to be electors appointed by a State; and they shall meet in the District and perform such duties as provided by the twelfth article of amendment.

**Section 2.**     The Congress shall have power to enforce this article by appropriate legislation.

## AMENDMENT XXIV (RATIFIED JANUARY 23, 1964)

**Section 1.**     The right of citizens of the United States to vote in any primary or other election for President or Vice President, for electors for President or Vice President, or for Senator or Representatives in Congress, shall not be denied or abridged by the United States or any State by reason of failure to pay any poll tax or other tax.

**Section 2.**     The Congress shall have power to enforce this article by appropriate legislation.

## AMENDMENT XXV (RATIFIED FEBRUARY 10, 1967)

**Section 1.**     In case of the removal of the President from office or of his death or resignation, the Vice President shall become President.

**Section 2.**     Whenever there is a vacancy in the office of the Vice President, the President shall nominate a Vice President who shall take office upon confirmation by a majority vote of both Houses of Congress.

**Section 3.**     Whenever the President transmits to the President *pro tempore* of the Senate and the Speaker of the House of Representatives his written declaration that he is unable to discharge the powers and duties of his office, and until he transmits to them a written declaration to the contrary, such powers and duties shall be discharged by the Vice President as Acting President.

**Section 4.**     Whenever the Vice President and a majority of either the principal officers of the executive departments or of such other body as Congress may by law provide, transmit to the President *pro tempore* of the Senate and the Speaker of the House of Representatives their written declaration that the President is unable to discharge the powers and duties of his office, the Vice President shall immediately assume the powers and duties of the office as Acting President.

Thereafter, when the President transmits to the President *pro tempore* of the Senate and the Speaker of the House of Representatives his written declaration that no inability exists, he shall resume the powers and duties of his office unless the Vice President and a majority of either the principal officers of the executive department or of such other body as Congress may by law provide, transmit within four days to the President *pro tempore* of the Senate and the Speaker of the House of Representatives their written declaration that the President is unable to discharge the powers and duties of his office. Thereupon Congress shall decide the issue, assembling within forty-eight hours for that purpose if not in session. If the Congress, within twenty-one days after receipt of the latter written declaration, or, if Congress is not in session, within twenty-one days after Congress is required to assemble, determines by two-thirds vote of both Houses that the President is unable to discharge the powers and duties of his office, the Vice President shall continue to discharge the same as Acting President; otherwise, the President shall resume the powers and duties of his office.

## AMENDMENT XXVI (RATIFIED JULY 1, 1971)

**Section 1.**   The right of citizens of the United States, who are eighteen years of age or older, to vote shall not be denied or abridged by the United States or by any State on account of age.

**Section 2.**   The Congress shall have power to enforce this article by appropriate legislation.

## AMENDMENT XXVII (RATIFIED MAY 7, 1992)

No law varying the compensation for the services of Senators and Representatives shall take effect until an election of Representatives shall have intervened.

# APPENDIX 6: **A GUIDE FOR TEACHERS**

## HOW CAN A REVIEW GUIDE HELP?

There are at least two major challenges facing a high school teacher when presenting a university-level curriculum. The first is the issue of time management. The second is mastering the higher level of analysis and vocabulary. In both of these areas, a well-designed guide can be of significant help. Use Kaplan's guide for creating an efficient calendar, monitoring your course's pace, and focusing on the most important pieces of the course.

The goal of this guide was to give a direct set of data without requiring the reading of another full text. Students already have that kind of resource, and they likely will not have the time or initiative to read the course text twice. The emphasis has been on making usable tables, notes, outlines, and definitions that will strengthen review and learning. These also are the kind of materials that can help a teacher present information succinctly and easily. The glossary selections have been chosen to reflect the kinds of issues likely to appear on the exams. They should be a central source of the materials students should master.

## USING THIS GUIDE AND BUILDING YOUR CALENDAR

The key to building priorities is the course outline given by the College Board. It is summarized in Chapter 1. The following table takes that data and matches the guide chapters to College Board's. In addition, a blank column allows the teacher to estimate the number of days to commit to the major topics. Whether you have a semester of one-hour-a-day classes, a block schedule of classes every other day, or even a full year, the building of a realistic timeline is essential. Don't forget to factor out school days lost to state/district testing and schoolwide activities such as rallies, etc.

Various texts and guides use slightly different sets of scope and sequence; therefore, the chapters of the work do not match the College Board outline exactly. However, they follow the sequence found in most college texts and are a close approximate for setting up a rough calendar.

| College Board Topics | Kaplan Guide Chapters | Percent of the Exam (approximate number of questions) | Total number of days you have to teach this course = _____. Take this number and multiply by the % in column 3 to estimate the number of days you should target for each topic. |
|---|---|---|---|
| I. Constitutional Underpinnings | 5 parts of 6 | 5% to 15% (3 to 9) | |
| II. Beliefs | 8 9 | 10% to 20% (6 to 12) | |
| III. Parties, Interests, Media | 10 11 12 13 | 10% to 20% (6 to 12) | |
| IV. Institutions | 6 14 15 16 parts of 17 | 35% to 45% (21 to 27) | |
| V. Public Policy | 18 19 20 | 5% to 15% (3 to 9) | |
| VI. Civil Rights | parts of 17 | 5% to 15% (3 to 9) | |

# BE SURE TO...

- Spend a class reviewing the test structure information given in this guide, the hints for success, and the ways to set up a study schedule.

- Allow time in class to discuss the practice questions; use them for quizzes and measures of student progress.

- Help students practice free-response rubric construction. (See Chapters 1 and 2.)

- Use Diagnostic Test questions as a pretest or in-class practice test.

- Be sure to discuss fully the ways to find the logic of correct answers.

- Focus on the chapter notes and charts as summative guides to materials given in class.

- Have students practice the vocabulary given in the glossary.

- Have students take the practice tests in structured settings and with time limits, giving them more opportunities to get comfortable with the pace of the exam.

## PRACTICE TEST QUESTIONS AND TEACHER'S USES

The materials developed in this volume have been specifically designed to copy the style used by the College Board's testing agency, ETS. As with the materials found in released tests and on the website, words of caution are given regarding the availability of answers. Rephrasing or selecting short sections for "in-class" practice may be the most useful approach. Once students get used to questions with five choices, multiple variants of choices, and the kinds of language required to score well, the actual AP exam will be less of a challenge.

# GLOSSARY

### 527 group
A tax-exempt organization, named after a section of the U.S. tax code, that can engage in election activities on behalf of causes or issues. Many interest groups have formed both PACs and 527 groups on behalf of their causes.

### advice and consent
The power of Congress to confirm or deny presidential nominations for executive and judicial posts and approve of international treaties.

### affirmative action
A policy aimed at helping those previously discriminated against to receive extra advantages and opportunities, such as economic, educational, and political positions. The first presidential use came during Lyndon Johnson's administration in 1965. Recent challenges have been based on the idea that affirmative action creates reverse discrimination against majority-group citizens.

### Aid to Families with Dependent Children (AFDC)
The main form of individual welfare payments until the mid-1990s. More recent programs come in the form of grants to states, where the state distributes the family assistance as needed.

### American Bar Association (ABA)
The organization that ranks judicial nominees as well qualified, qualified, or not qualified. These rankings are used to assess nominees prior to their hearings in the Senate.

### amicus curiae brief
Summary case arguments given by interested parties who may be affected by the outcome of a case. This "friend of the court" summary is supposed to give judges more information about the arguments and the possible outcomes.

### Anti-Federalists
Members of the opposition to the new Constitution; they lost the vote but forced the promise that a set of rights would be added as amendments by the new government. This became the Bill of Rights.

### apportionment
The division of representative seats according to population.

### appropriation
Legislation that concerns the raising of revenues by the government.

### appropriation bill
A bill that provides funding for a program that has been authorized, usually for one year at a time.

### approval rating
A measurement of how popular, or unpopular, a leader or program is among the public.

**back-bencher**
A nickname given to newer members of Congress who have few important positions or those more senior members who tend to avoid positions of power or controversy.

**balanced budget**
The goal of the federal government to spend only the amount of money collected from tax revenues. Previous efforts to legislate such spending limits or to create an amendment for this goal have failed.

**ballot initiative**
A form of direct democracy that allows citizens to petition for issues that will be decided by a direct ballot and not by the legislative branch. This system is popular in California, where it reduced and reorganized taxes. However, at the same time, California has experienced major problems when such initiatives stop an agency from functioning or when opposing initiatives are passed in the same election.

**beltway ("inside the beltway")**
A critical term referencing to the highway loop that surrounds the greater Washington, D.C. area and seems to isolate the leaders of the country. If leaders concern themselves only with lobby groups and the hallways of power and are not concerned with the general interests of the nation at large, they are said to be thinking "inside the beltway."

**bicameral**
The "two chambers" of Congress: the House of Representatives and the Senate.

**bilateral agreement**
The resulting agreement when two nations create a joint policy.

**bill**
A proposed law being debated in Congress.

**bipartisan**
A label given if support for something comes from members of both parties.

**bloc**
A voting group that tends to include those with common interests and views.

**block grants**
Monies given to communities and states for general programs, such as social services and development projects.

**blog**
A media outlet (most often on the Internet) that presents rumors, opinions, and some news. Blogs tend to be highly partisan. Criticisms include their lack of filtering and editing and their lack of responsibility toward facts. Blogs do have the power to investigate where mainstream media outlets might hesitate.

**blue states**
The label given to states where the Democratic Party wins the electoral votes.

**Boll Weevils**
Southern Democratic members of Congress who openly voted for conservative issues and with the Republican Party in the 1980s. Many have now officially switched over to the GOP.

**brief**
A summary of case arguments given to the judges and justices before a hearing to outline the parameters of the case.

**budget resolution**
A congressional resolution binding the legislature to a specific total budget amount for the fiscal year.

**bully pulpit**
The idea, named for Teddy Roosevelt's use of the term *bully*, that presidents can gather national public support more easily than the numerous members of Congress. With this national support, Congress is pushed to follow the priorities of the president. Modern popularity polls seem to show that presidents with support of at least 60 percent of the public have a powerful forum for political pressure with Congress.

**capitation**

A head count for tax purposes as part of a census.

**categorical grants**

Grants given to communities and states for very specific programs that require certain conditions or rules to be applied by the agencies spending the federal monies. If the federal rules are not followed, the monies can be withdrawn.

**caucus**

The arena in which some states select delegates as party candidate representatives through meetings where only party members are allowed to participate.

**caucuses**

Informal meetings in the Congress of groups with similar interests or constituencies.

**charter school programs**

A conservative reform where struggling public schools are replaced by more privately run academies with the hopes that these charter campuses will be more efficient and hold higher standards than publicly run systems.

**checks and balances**

The policy allowing each of the three branches of government to "check" the power of the other two and limit that power, if necessary, to maintain balance.

**civil liberties**

The limits of governmental powers over citizens, or the level of freedom citizens have from government.

**class action suits**

A lawsuit involving numerous defendants afflicted by the same law or action who are represented as a group.

**clear and present danger test**

The policy limiting the rights of free speech if the government deems certain forms of speech as a clear and present danger to the public. These limits were first defined in the case *Schenk v. U.S.,* 1919.

**client politics**

Policies developed to help specific, smaller groups, where the costs of the actions will be borned by the nation as a whole.

**closed primary system**

The regulation that voters must preregister with a party to cast ballots on primary day, or the system where voters can only vote in one party's primary.

**closed rule**

A procedure used by the House of Representatives to prohibit amendments from being offered in order to speed consideration of the bill.

**cloture**

Procedure developed in the Senate to end filibuster through votes. The current rules for cloture are based on approval of 60 senators. If cloture passes against a filibuster, those delaying must end their actions within a set amount of time and allow business to move forward.

**coattail**

A concept allowing congressional and other candidates to ride the popularity of a leader, such as the president, especially at election time.

**Code of Federal Regulations (CFR)**

A series of volumes comprising a list of rules for the various departments and bureaucracies.

**commerce clause**

Article 1, Section 8, Clause 3 gives Congress the power to "regulate Commerce with Foreign Nations, and among the several States...."

**commercial speech**

A form of speech regulated and restricted to uphold "truth in advertising." Deception for the sake of money gains is not legal. The Federal Trade Commission (FTC) is in charge of such regulations.

**community standards**

The ability of communities to ban certain language, art, or actions based on what they deem obscene or appropriate for their citizens.

**comparable worth**

A guide for decisions concerning the pay scales of employees of different sexes.

**concurrent opinion**

A document drafted by court justices who voted with the majority to explain how they differ in their beliefs about the meaning of the majority vote.

**"consent of the governed"**

Describes a government that derives its power from the governed and does not force its power on the citizens.

**constant campaign**

The manner in which presidential candidates and members of the House, who must face re-election every other year, continually campaign to the public to uphold their positions.

**constituent**

Voters from the district or state that elected that leader. House members' constituents are from their districts. Senators' constituents are from the entire state.

**containment**

The effort to control the spread of opposing groups or influences, as in attempts to limit the spread of communism.

**continuing resolution**

An action allowing the government to continue to be funded temporarily if Congress is unable to complete the new federal budget by the October 1 deadline.

**continuous body**

The Senate is a continuous body in that only one-third of the Senate is up for re-election at a time. All of the House is up for re-election every other year and all seats could be changed. Therefore, the House is not "continuous."

**"Contract with America"**

A list and book used during the congressional elections of 1994 by conservatives led by Newt Gingrich. The effort was to define the basic goals of a new Republican majority if, and when, Republicans gained control of the House of Representatives. The contract was a list of items that Republicans promised to bring to discussion, such as pushing for a balanced budget amendment, limited welfare programs, and other reforms.

**convention**

A summer gathering where the parties elect their nominees, establish the party issue platforms, and approve the vice-presidential nominees.

**cooperative federalism**

The act of federal and state governmental units working together to shape, fund, and enforce policy.

**cost-benefit analysis**

A financial guide used by many agencies to compare the cost of a project with the potential benefits.

**C-SPAN**

The development of cable television in the late 20th century created several news-only television outlets. This network shows congressional activities and debates on several different stations and has been used by members to gain immediate "face time" with the public.

**de-alignment**

The trend for fewer citizens to claim they loyally support of the major parties.

**debt/public debt**

The combined deficits of the federal government owed in the form of bonds sold to U.S. citizens, foreign investors, countries, and parts of government. The largest part of the debt of the United States is currently held by governmental agencies. In mid-2009, the total debt came to about $11.4 trillion.

**de facto segregation**

The segregation and discrimination perpetuated by factions of society through patterns of residence and economic conditions. The segregation is private and difficult to correct with legislation.

**deficit**

The amount of money created and loaned to the federal government in a given year if it spends more than it collects in revenues.

**de jure segregation**

A form of discrimination that occurs when laws segregate citizens based on religion, ethnicity, or other grounds.

**delegates**

Members of a political party selected by party caucuses, primary votes, or other party rules. The party nominee is the candidate who receives the majority of the delegates' votes at the convention.

**democracy**

A form of government where rule is established by all citizens through votes. Usually, majority votes create policy.

**demography**

The study of population patterns for polling.

**détente**

The policy of working with opposing nations in an attempt to avoid open conflicts.

**devolution**

The late-20th-century movement to reduce the influence of the federal government and other governments to return to a simpler form of governmental controls.

**discharge**

A petition rule in the House that can allow some bills to be released from committee without committee approval.

**discretionary spending**

The programs that Congress can choose to fund. Even though spending to run the government and keeping up the military are seen as given needs, such funding is considered discretionary due to possible changes in the level of funding.

**divided government**

One party controls the majority of one or both chambers of Congress, and the other party controls the executive. It is a by-product of the separate election of presidents. *Gridlock* is also used to describe such a condition.

**domino theory**

The idea that allowing countries to fall under the influence of communism would topple nearby democracies. This was a leading cause of U.S. reaction in Korea, Cuba, and Vietnam.

**dual federalism**

Federal and state governments are relatively equal and separate in areas of authority.

**earmarks**

The official term used in Congress for bills that contain pork legislation.

**Earned Income Tax Credit**

Credits calculated by the Internal Revenue Service to provide financial assistance to the poor that can be paid at tax time in April, or eligibility guidelines for items like food stamps.

**elastic clause**

Article 1, Section 8, Clause 18: Congress's power "To make all Laws which shall be necessary and proper…" continues to be a basis of Congress adapting to the needs of the times.

**Electoral College**

The process by which electors are selected by states and are "directed" by the popular vote to select the president.

### elitist theory of government

The general belief that governments will come to be ruled by those with elite status, usually determined by wealth, educational level, or other methods.

### Emily's List

A recent campaign movement to give soft money to improve women's voter turnouts and support women's issues.

### eminent domain

The power of the government to seize private property for the public good. The property owner must be given "just compensation" for the loss.

### emolument

A gift given to a government official, which must be limited to avoid committing bribery.

### entitlements

Spending that Congress has promised for the future and, in cases such as Social Security, is obligated to fund.

### environmental impact statement

A statement showing the possible adverse effects of work by government agencies or private industry receiving government assistance on the air, land, or water. The statement is then given public review, and decisions are made whether or not the damage can be avoided, repaired, or ignored.

### espionage

The practice of using spies or secret agents to receive secret information from foreign countries or other companies in a similar industry.

### establishment clause

A law based on the 1st Amendment's section about the status of religion. "Congress shall make no law respecting an establishment of religion…." Government cannot lead citizens in the practices of certain religions, thus giving preference to those religions or sects.

### exclusionary rule

The idea that evidence obtained in some illegal manner cannot be used in court against the defendant.

### exclusive jurisdiction

Powers given solely to the federal government.

### exit poll

Polls taken directly after voters are finished to develop an early prediction of the outcome.

### *ex post facto*

A law barring government agencies from inflicting punishment for events that occurred when something was legal but has since been made illegal.

### fast-track authority

Pieces of legislation that must be voted on "as is" without amendment attempts. Presidents are sometimes given this authority when beginning talks concerning treaties so that the Senate must take or leave them.

### federalism

The distribution of governmental power among federal, state, and local groups.

### Federalist

One who supported the new Constitution and the ultimate name of the party in power under Washington, Adams, and Hamilton.

### Federalist Number 10

Madison's essay on "factions" or the influence of political parties and interest groups is used today to discuss access and control.

### Federalist Number 51

Madison's essay on the proper structure of power within the Constitution is used to understand the balance of powers.

**Federalist Number 78**
Hamilton's discussion of the federal judiciary and the powers of such courts is used to debate the role of the courts.

**Federalist Papers (The Federalist)**
A book of essays by the Federalists that explain the hows and whys of the federal system of the Constitution.

**Federal Register**
The official publication of executive orders and the rules and regulations of the various executive agencies. These are codified in the "Code of Federal Regulations" (CFR) volumes.

**filibuster**
A strategy used in the Senate to speak a bill to death by delaying votes, stopping other legislation, etc., until the bill sponsors give up.

**fiscal**
Refers to the budget and the budget year (October 1 to September 30).

**flat tax**
A national tax level that would be the same for all income groups or would replace the IRS system with a national sales tax system.

**floor**
Open, full debates by either the House members or the Senate members that can occur after a committee has referred a bill to the full chamber.

**"fourth branch"**
An informal name given to the U.S. bureaucracy because many agencies have powers of creating rules, administering rules, and judging those who must follow those rules. This label is also sometimes applied to the media in describing its power to influence public opinions.

**franking**
A traditional privilege allowing members of Congress to send mail to constituents for free.

**Freedom of Information Act, 1966**
A law created by Congress to help ensure that agencies were acting in the most open manner available. Citizens can petition to see files of agencies through this act.

**frontloading**
The process of determining candidates earlier in the presidential campaign because of more key primaries and caucuses in January–March.

**full faith and credit**
The practice of states giving the different laws of other states credit. An example is how marriage laws are different in various states but states usually recognize marriages from one state to another.

**gender gap**
A trend in U.S. voting where women have given a slight edge to Democrats and men to Republicans.

**general jurisdiction**
A label for the law allowing states the right to decide which cases will be heard in their courts.

**General Schedule Rating (GS Rating)**
The salaries of members of the civil service are set in levels, ranging from GS1 to GS18, thus eliminating pay disparities in different parts of government.

**gerrymandering**
The division of voting districts with the goal of guaranteeing seats for one party stronger.

**glass ceiling**
The difficulty women have had in gaining positions of high authority, power, and pay in industry and government.

### good faith exception

The concept that evidence collected by police can still be used in court, even if it is based on incorrect procedures, false testimony, or has other possible flaws, if it was collected by the police in "good faith." The key is often whether or not the police knew of the evidence's problems or were themselves misled by someone lying.

### graduated income tax

The progressive ideal that people with higher levels of income should pay higher percentages of tax.

### grassroots

Local efforts to raise money, raise awareness of certain issues, or influence political leaders.

### Great Compromise (Connecticut Plan, Sherman Plan)

The plan that created the modern Congress, where the House is dominated by populated states and the Senate is divided equally for all states.

### gridlock

A collapse of cooperation between the House and Senate or between Congress and the president. It is also used to describe the condition that arises under "divided" government.

### government corporations

The U.S. Postal Service and the Federal Deposit Insurance Corporation are the two most famous examples of governmental agencies that create revenue and are expected to run like businesses.

### hold

A request for a delay in the discussion of a bill in the Senate. If the leadership agrees, this hold can be a permanent block to the bill.

### honeymoon

The general tradition that Congress, and the public, will be very supportive of a president during the first 100 days of the first term.

### House Un-American Activities Committee

The investigative committee that gained notoriety during the late 1940s for its hunts of communists in the United States.

### hyper-pluralist theory

The general contention that strong groups within societies will weaken the overall control of governments.

### impeach

The act of charging a public official (often the president) with criminal acts or misconduct while in office. The House can impeach, and the Senate must decide whether to remove a person as a result of an impeachment.

### inalienable rights

The goals and duties of government and society to provide things such as "life, liberty, and the pursuit of happiness," according to Jefferson. Locke used the terms "life, liberty, and the pursuit of property."

### incite/incitement

The illegal action of causing violence or dangerous commotion through language.

### incorporation

The ability of constitutional rights to be applied to state governments through the requirements of the 14th Amendment.

### incumbent

A person already holding an office, often seeking re-election.

### indictment

A grand jury's determination that sufficient evidence has been presented in a criminal case.

### inflation

The overall rising of price in the economy. Inflation is caused by excessive consumer demand or spikes in the costs of producing goods.

### informal amendments

An adjustment to one of the amendments to the Constitution without formally passing the change. This concept also covers important changes in powers of parts of the government that occur through acts of Congress or other branches that are not challenged or incorporated into amendments.

### interest group

People who support a cause and work together for that cause or political interests.

### interest payments on the debt

The payments required each budget year for at least the owed interest on the public debt of the United States.

### Jim Crow

The various laws and practices of segregation, primarily in the South, installed after Reconstruction ended in 1876–1877.

### judicial review

The power of the Supreme Court to evaluate the constitutional status of laws and lower court rulings, established as a result of the case *Marbury v. Madison*, 1803.

### junkyard function

Media attacks that expose flaws, secrets, and scandals and are used to keep an eye on government leaders and sell stories.

### jurisdiction

Powers of the court set within the limits of specific areas of law or location.

### lame duck

A person who has been defeated in a recent election or has announced that he or she is retiring and has not yet been replaced. His or her power usually becomes severely limited.

### lapdog function

The idea that the press is at the mercy of news sources such as the White House staff. News is parceled out to those who but will give the story the requested emphasis.

### leaks (news leaks)

Intentional slipping of key pieces of news to supportive members of the press.

### Lemon Test

A test for the level of financial involvement of government agencies in religious schools based on *Lemon v. Kurtzman*, 1971. The government might assist religious entities if (1) there is a legitimate secular purpose for the help, (2) the help does not have the primary effect of advancing or prohibiting religion, and (3) the help does not create "excessive entanglement" between the government and the religion.

### libel

Any malicious or false content written about a person with the intention of causing ridicule and public derision.

### limited government

The notion that government can only use certain powers and these powers must be given by the people.

### limited jurisdiction

The federal government has only those powers given to it by the Constitution.

### linkage institutions

The groups and agencies that connect the average citizens with the political leadership.

### litigation

Presenting a lawsuit in court.

### litmus test

Issues such as abortion, gay rights, and gun control that are important enough to determine where voters will give their support or how certain elected officials will vote.

### lobby/lobbyist

Registered professionals who work at political centers on behalf of interest groups.

### majority

The requirement that the winner of any vote must have 50 percent of the vote plus one more to win.

### majority opinion

The decision written by the majority of the justices of the Supreme Court describing the meaning of the announced decision for the legal community.

### mandatory spending

Budget items that Congress is required to fund. Most noted is Social Security because these funds are based on previous contributions from the public that are owed back.

### margin of error

A positive or negative percentage attached to all polls to determine their levels of accuracy. If a candidate's support is 45 percent with a margin of error of 2 percent, then the prediction is that the support is between 43 percent and 47 percent.

### markup

The action made when correcting or revising a bill.

### means testing

The proof of need, usually based on low income levels, provided to the government for special program funding.

### midterm elections

The period of elections for all members of the House of Representatives and one-third of the senators when the presidency is not up for election.

### minority opinion

When the one to four justices who did not vote with the majority give their reasons for opposing the majority opinion. The legal community uses minority opinions as a guide to the power of the majority opinion and possible future challenges to that decision.

### Miranda warning

An advisement of one's rights that must take place before police can question someone they intend to arrest.

### muckraking

The practice of journalists to expose the inappropriate actions of public officials, government organizations, or corporations.

### narrowcasting

The mail and email campaigning toward certain demographics to gain support in Congress for specific issues. The term also describes the rise of media outlets that focus only on specific political events or target specific audiences. Examples include cable channels and Internet sites.

### NASCAR dads

Conservative male voters, often from the South, named after the race car organization because of its popularity in that faction of society.

### national chairperson

The director of the party organization. The leader can be critical in the development of party issues, advertisements, and reactions to other party actions.

### national committee

The committee group for a political party that focuses on elections, money-raising activities, party building, and the development of party platforms.

### natural rights

John Locke's idea that all societies are given basic rights by God and that these cannot be removed by governments. This was included in Jefferson's reasoning for the Declaration of Independence.

### naturalization

The process of becoming a citizen for someone born outside of the country.

### New Federalism

A conservative movement designed to return more power and control of money to the states. The term was coined during the Nixon presidency and expanded by the Reagan administration.

**New Hampshire primary**

Traditionally, these are the first of the public votes for the new presidential election. In 2008, it was held January 8.

**New Jersey Plan (Paterson Plan)**

The smaller states' counter to the Virginia Plan. It gave the unicameral (one chamber) Congress equal representation for all states.

**Nuclear Test Ban Treaty**

A document signed to limit the above-ground testing of nuclear weapons. The United States, the United Kingdom, and the Soviet Union were the main signers.

**"off the record"**

Information given to journalists with the understanding that the information is not for publication. This condition must be stated before a source divulges the information.

**omnibus**

Legislation that covers many different parts of government, subjects, or law in one bill.

**open primary system**

A primary that allows a voter to decide on election day which party list to select. Some states also allow voters to go to primaries for more than one party.

**open seat**

The relatively rare event when no incumbent is running for a post.

**original jurisdiction**

Rare court cases "affecting Ambassadors, other public Ministers and Consuls, and those in which a State shall be Party," where only the federal Supreme Court hears the issue.

**patronage (or the "spoils system")**

The act of doling out political positions to supporters of a party and its candidates, often used as incentive to gain that support. The system was so corrupt that major reforms now limit such appointments to very few positions, such as ambassadorships.

**penumbra rights**

Rights not clearly defined but existing in the "shadow" of formal Constitutional rights. An example would be privacy rights in the shadow of 1st Amendment rights.

***per curium* decisions**

Supreme Court decisions that are announced without legal explanation or without a majority opinion.

**petition for redress**

The right to request that the government restore the rights of the governed.

**platform**

A list of issues that each state party group and the national parties draw up, outlining all the issues they would like to address if voted into office.

**Plum Book**

The list of federal positions, published by Congress, that are open to presidential appointments. The list includes about 400 upper policy-making positions and about 2,500 assistant positions.

**pluralism**

The guiding principle that access to government should be open and widespread. Interest group proliferation is evidence of this in action.

**plurality**

Winning an election by finishing first, without regard to the percentage of the vote won, as in the U.S. presidential popular votes. A large number of presidents have won a majority of the electoral votes but only a plurality of the national popular votes.

**political action committee (PAC)**

A registered group that raises funds for candidates and campaigns.

**poll**

A sampling of opinions, political affiliations, or voting patterns used to predict outcomes or trends.

### pork/pork-barrel

Legislation that is often local and intended to help districts with contracts and money. This is known as pork and is used by members of Congress to gain favors from home constituents and pad voting support.

### poverty line

The amount of income a family in the United States needs to earn annually to maintain only an "austere" standard of living. Those with incomes below this line are the targets of many assistance programs.

### press corps/White House press corps

The journalists invited to represent their news companies at presidential press conferences and other events.

### price controls

The efforts led by the Nixon administration in the 1970s to freeze prices of products and try to keep inflation to a minimum.

### primary

A public election of delegates for party candidates run by states.

### probable cause

The requirement that police must have sufficient proof of evidence or suspicion of criminal acts before searching a suspect's personal property or possessions.

### Publius

The name used by Alexander Hamilton as a pseudonym for the *Federalist Papers* essays, derived from the name of a famous Roman consul. Publius was noted as a supporter of citizens' rights and as an opponent of kings. Hamilton used this name to hint at the power of the new Constitution to protect rights and to cover his contributions to the essays, because many would ignore them if his name were attached. Opponents to the Constitution fought back by writing essays under the name Cato or Brutus. These Roman names were symbols of opposition against governments that became too centralized.

### pure speech

Spoken or printed words and the extent of freedom involved. See also *symbolic speech*.

### quorum

The number of members needed to hold an official meeting or conduct binding votes. The traditional number in the U.S. Congress is half of members plus one.

### random polling

Polling conducted by selecting people from random phone and address lists. The poll data may not reflect actual intent to vote.

### realignment

The major regrouping of support within political parties. The New Deal was a source of realignment for Democrat support, and the Reagan election did the same for Republicans.

### reapportionment

The law created by Congress in 1929 that banned the addition of new seats to Congress, adding a cap of 435 seats. After the census, seats would be redistributed instead. Faster-growing states would gain seats from declining states or less rapidly growing states.

### recess appointments

The ability of the president to fill vacant federal positions, such as federal court judgeships, without senatorial approval if the Senate is in recess. These appointee can serve for almost a year before approval must be considered. After that period, it is difficult for the Senate to remove the person from the position. It is considered a significant way for a president to put in controversial leaders.

### reciprocity

The pattern of collecting vote promises from other members of Congress in exchange for vote support for their bills and projects.

**red states**

States where the Republican Party won the electoral votes during a presidential election and those that have a tendency to support the conservative position.

**red tape**

The general label of paperwork and procedures often required for actions to be completed in bureaucracies.

**reprieves and pardons**

The powers of the president to set a sentence aside or even declare that the crime is fully erased.

**republic**

The preferred form of government for the Founding Fathers because the public would guide the selection of some of the leaders, who would then make the laws. Other parts of government might be selected by educated elites.

**restraining order**

A court order restricting the actions and movements of persons or the press toward other individuals and their premises. Often used for the protection of one person from another who poses a severe threat.

**revenue bills**

Legislation concerning taxation or the use of tax dollars is a primary congressional duty.

**revolving door**

The practice of major lobby groups hiring recently retired members of Congress for high-paying lobby positions. The advantage of having a person who knows all the secret maneuvers of policy, has long experience with the key power brokers, and has made lasting friendships with those creating laws is seen as a major, and sneaky, advantage for those lobby groups with large amounts of money for such salaries.

**rider**

The name of an amendment, usually not of national import, attached to a larger and more important bill to allow the amendment to pass more easily.

**safe seat**

A term used when a representative appears to have an overwhelming level of local support in the home district. With greater uses of gerrymandering to ensure party domination, safe seats have become more common, thus allowing representatives to be more partisan and less willing to compromise.

**safety net**

A term that describes the idea of giving the elderly, jobless, and poor some assistance in order to avoid economic catastrophe.

**sample/target polling**

Polls that recruit specific groups that have certain ethnic, economic, or voting patterns to see how these groups react toward issues or candidates.

**search warrant**

An element of the 4th Amendment requiring that citizens be given a court-ordered document telling them what the police are searching for and the area being searched.

**self-incrimination**

An element of the 5th Amendment giving citizens protection from testifying against themselves. The police must prove the case without assistance of the defendant.

**senatorial courtesy**

The tradition that the president is expected to gather names of potential nominees from the senators of the states involved. This term also is used to refer to the tradition that the senior senator of the state of that nominee can block the approval of that person.

**seniority**

Those with the longest amount of service in Congress get the committee chairperson positions. Reforms in the seniority system allow some chair positions to be given to those with less seniority, but this is rare. Seniority positions on committees go to the discretion of the majority party.

**separations of power**
The powers specific to the different branches of government.

**session**
The annual meetings of Congress, starting in January and now usually ending in the late fall.

**school voucher programs**
The reform initiative by conservative groups to reallocate tax funds normally given to large school systems to parents in the form of refunds. This tax voucher allows parents to use the money to send their children to public schools or use it as tuition help for private schools. Recent challenges to such programs have focused on the possible use of public tax dollars to enrich church-run schools. In 2002, the Supreme Court held in the case of *Zelman v. Simmons-Harris* that some vouchers could be used for private schools.

**shield laws**
Laws passed by state governments giving the press protection from revealing sources of information.

**Silent Majority**
The term used by the Nixon administration for the citizens who preferred traditional values, supported the U.S. government, and would not openly criticize leaders the way some were doing during the Vietnam War.

**slander**
Spoken words that are intended to injure a party and are knowingly false.

**spin**
The manner in which a news story is emphasized or explained, often by administrative representatives, to try to ensure a certain interpretation of information.

**split-ticket voting**
A trend where voters select different candidates of different parties for various offices from the same long ballot. These are more independent voters.

**soccer moms**
A label given to stay-at-home moms who tend to vote more conservatively and usually base their opinions on family issues and religious affiliations.

**social contract/social contract theory**
An idea from Rousseau and Locke stating that the government's powers are given by agreement of the citizens and the government is required to follow only these powers.

**stare decisis**
Major precedent-setting cases in the Supreme Court, where the decisions were made with strong majority votes. These decisions are the most powerful precedents, whereas votes of 5 to 4 are the weakest in terms of likely future challenges.

**statutory law**
Fixed laws determined as such based on a certain statute or recognized rule.

**straight-ticket voting**
The ability of voters to choose all of the members of the same party with only one vote.

**Strategic Arms Limitations Talks treaties (SALT treaties)**
A set of agreements that began the process of reducing the numbers of missile and nuclear weapons held by the United States and the Soviet Union.

**Strategic Defense Initiative (SDI) or "Star Wars weapons"**
The policy of the Reagan administration to begin a series of plans to place antimissile weapons in space orbit.

**street-level (bureaucrats)**
The government employees who work directly with the public in the implementation of federal and local programs. They often have the responsibility of determining access to federal funds.

**subsidies**
Money assistance given to farmers and businesses aimed at protecting against monopolies, helping struggling companies, and providing sufficient resources for future growth.

**suffrage**
The constitutional term, coined during the Women's Rights Movement, for the right to vote.

**summit diplomacy**
A series of efforts made in the Cold War period to have the leaders of major powers sit down together and work on issues and conflicts.

**super delegates**
The members of Congress and members of the national committee given a certain set of votes at the Democratic National Convention. These delegates were created as part of Democratic Party reforms of the 1970s.

**Superfund**
Gasoline and chemical tax revenues set aside by the federal government in 1980 for a special trust fund used to clean up toxic waste sites around the country. The Love Canal site led to development of this fund.

**super majority**
A proposal that any legislation to increase taxes would need a vote percentage of two-thirds, or 66 percent, to pass, considered a "super" majority.

**surplus**
The amount of money left over in the budget when the government spends less than it collects in taxes. Rapid economic expansions of incomes created brief surpluses in the late 1990s, but these were eliminated by the crisis of 9/11, the recession of late 2001, tax cuts of 2001 and 2002, and the conflicts in Afghanistan and Iraq.

**swing voters**
Key voters who tend to be independent, or less loyal to the party system, and have a significant influence on close elections.

**symbolic speech**
Forms of speech outside of spoken or written words that have political meaning, such as flag burning or sit-in protests. *See also pure speech.*

**talking heads**
The name given to press shows dedicated to media representatives analyzing events or leaders. A famous example is the weekly television program *Meet the Press.*

**term**
The amount of time an elected official serves in that position.

**think tank**
A group or company whose main purpose is to research, develop, propose, and lobby for types of policies that favor liberal or conservative causes. One of the most powerful is the conservative Heritage Foundation.

**Three-Fifths Compromise**
The compromise over slavery in Philadelphia. A federal ban was placed on interference in slave cases before 1808, and slaves were as only part of the population for census and representation numbers.

**transfers**
The economic term used to describe the movement of tax money from those who pay to those who need. It is a form of wealth distribution.

**trial balloons**
A tactic of giving information about possible policy decisions and checking the reaction of the public and other governmental groups. If the reaction is extremely positive or negative, then further plans can be developed.

**unilateral policies**
A term defining the efforts of a single country to change policies and align those changes with their relations with other countries.

**vested**
The power held by an authority.

**Virginia Plan (Randolph Plan, Madison Plan)**
An outline of a constitution drafted by Madison before the formal meetings began. Governor Randolph presented the list. It proposed a bicameral legislature (two chambers) but gave populated states the most representation in both houses. The general outline was used by the convention delegates to build the basic framework of the Constitution, thus giving Madison the nickname "Father of the Constitution."

**wall of separation**
A phrase used by Jefferson in 1802 in a letter to describe his opinion about the relationship between church and state. Jefferson's emphasis, and that of modern supporters, was that government controls actions but not the opinions of religion.

**war chest**
The amount of money a candidate has created for the next campaign. This is usually a tremendous advantage for incumbents.

**watchdog function**
The idea that it is a duty of the media to keep the public informed of political events and to ensure that the rules of government are being followed.

**whip**
A traditional name of the assistant to the House Majority and Minority Leaders.

**"Whip Inflation Now" (WIN)**
A program by the Ford administration to curb inflation by putting pressure on businesses to lower prices and deter consumers from hording goods.

**whistleblowers**
A name given to government employees who reveal waste or fraud within their own agencies. They are often attacked by superiors, the press, and the general public for their actions.

**white-collar**
A term denoting careers and jobs in business and office management. These positions usually do not involve any manual labor.

**workfare**
A reform initiative of the welfare system to require recipients to find employment in order to receive governmental assistance.

**writ of mandamus**
The power given to federal courts to require action by citizens or governmental agencies.

**writ of habeas corpus**
A decree that laws cannot be created to have persons seized by authorities and held without charges being presented. The accused has the right to defend himself or herself against all charges.

**yellow journalism**
A late 1800s trend of sensationalist news, often centered in New York, that helped influence policy. The best example is the Hearst papers that helped create the Spanish-American War crisis.

# INDEX

# A SPECIAL NOTE FOR INTERNATIONAL STUDENTS

If you are an international student considering attending an American university, you are not alone. Nearly 600,000 international students pursued academic degrees at the undergraduate, graduate, or professional school level at U.S. universities during the 2004–2005 academic year, according to the Institute of International Education's Open Doors report. Almost 50 percent of these students were studying for a bachelor's or first university degree. This number of international students pursuing higher education in the United States is expected to continue to grow. Business, management, engineering, and the physical and life sciences are particularly popular majors for students coming to the United States from other countries.

If you are not a U.S. citizen and you are interested in attending college or university in the United States, here is what you'll need to get started.

- If English is not your first language, you'll probably need to take the TOEFL® (Test of English as a Foreign Language) or provide some other evidence that you are proficient in English. Colleges and universities in the United States will differ as to what they consider to be an acceptable TOEFL score. A minimum TOEFL score of 213 (550 on the paper-based TOEFL) or better is often required by more prestigious and competitive institutions. Because American undergraduate programs require all students to take a certain number of general education courses, all students—even math and computer science students—need to be able to communicate well in spoken and written English.

- You may also need to take the SAT® or the ACT®. Many undergraduate institutions in the United States require both the SAT and TOEFL for international students.

- There are over 3,400 accredited colleges and universities in the United States, so selecting the correct undergraduate school can be a confusing task for anyone. You will need to get help from a good advisor or at least a good college guide that gives you detailed information on the different schools available. Since admission to many undergraduate programs is quite competitive, you may want to select three or four colleges and complete applications for each school.

- You should begin the application process at least a year in advance. An increasing number of schools accept applications year-round. In any case, find out the application deadlines and plan accordingly. Although September (the fall semester) is the traditional time to begin university study in the United States, you can begin your studies at many schools in January (the spring semester).

- In addition, you will need to obtain an I-20 Certificate of Eligibility from the school you plan to attend if you intend to apply for an F-1 Student Visa to study in the United States.

# KAPLAN ENGLISH PROGRAMS*

If you need more help with the complex process of university admissions; assistance preparing for the SAT, ACT, or TOEFL; or help building your English language skills in general, you may be interested in Kaplan's programs for international students.

Kaplan English Programs were designed to help students and professionals from outside the United States meet their educational and career goals. At locations throughout the United States, international students take advantage of Kaplan's programs to help them improve their academic and conversational English skills; raise their scores on the TOEFL, SAT, ACT, and other standardized exams; and gain admission to the schools of their choice. Our staff and instructors give international students the individualized attention they need to succeed. Here is a brief description of some of Kaplan's programs for international students.

### General Intensive English

Kaplan's General Intensive English course is the fastest and most effective way for students to improve their English. This full-time program integrates the four key elements of language learning—listening, speaking, reading, and writing. The challenging curriculum and intensive schedule are designed for both the general language learner and the academically bound student.

### TOEFL and Academic English

Our world-famous TOEFL course prepares you for the TOEFL and also teaches you the academic language and skills needed to succeed in a university. Designed for high-intermediate to advanced-level English speakers, our course includes TOEFL-focused reading, writing, listening, speaking, vocabulary, and grammar instruction.

### General English

Our General English course is a semi-intensive program designed for students who want to improve their listening and speaking skills without the time commitment of an intensive program. With morning class times and flexible computer lab hours throughout the week, our General English course is perfect for every schedule.

## OTHER KAPLAN PROGRAMS

Since 1938, more than 3 million students have come to Kaplan to advance their studies, prepare for entry to American universities, and further their careers. In addition to the above programs, Kaplan offers courses to prepare for the ACT, GMAT®, GRE®, MCAT®, DAT®, USMLE®, NCLEX®, and other standardized exams at locations throughout the United States.

### Applying to Kaplan English Programs

To get more information, or to apply for admission to any of Kaplan's programs for international students and professionals, contact us at:

**Kaplan English Programs**
700 South Flower, Suite 2900
Los Angeles, CA 90017, USA
Phone (if calling from within the United States): (800) 818-9128
Phone (if calling from outside the United States): (213) 452-5800
Fax: (213) 892-1364
Website: kaplanenglish.com
Email: world@kaplan.com

*Kaplan is authorized under federal law to enroll nonimmigrant alien students. Kaplan is accredited by ACCET (Accrediting Council for Continuing Education and Training).

---

## FREE Services for International Students

Kaplan now offers international students many services online—**free of charge!**
Students may assess their TOEFL skills and gain valuable feedback on their English
language proficiency in just a few hours with Kaplan's TOEFL Skills Assessment.
Log onto kaplaninternational.com today.

# THINKING ABOUT BECOMING A LAWYER SOMEDAY?

Have you ever watched *Law & Order*, and imagined yourself standing at the front of the courtroom summing up your heartfelt argument to the jury? Has a teacher ever suggested you join your high school debate team? Perhaps someone has told you that you "are really good at arguing your point," and you've wondered what that might mean for your future. Well, what *does* that mean for your future? What will you do—or become—after high school, after college? Such questions, while you're just hoping to make it through the next project, paper, midterm, or AP exam!

You don't need to know what you want to do "for the rest of your life" right now. Keep an open mind about all the possibilities that lie before you. But if the thought of going into the legal profession *has* crossed your mind or if you feel that you were born to be a lawyer, know this: no matter what you think or feel or hope your future holds, now is the time to start getting ready for it!

You might be thinking, "Great! I'm ready to start getting ready...but now what do I do?" Well, that's where we come in. At Kaplan, we are committed to helping students at every step of their way toward academic and professional success. This book that you are holding right now is the result of that commitment and passion for your success. In addition to preparing you for tests, you can rely on us to help you figure out the application process, learn about the ins and outs of financial aid, and—once you're in—help you maximize your opportunities in law school.

But there we go again—talking about law school—and your only immediate concern is for that upcoming AP exam. Let's not get ahead of ourselves. You've got a lot of time to plan for the upcoming years. At the same time, it never hurts to be aware of what's on the academic horizon and whom you're competing with.

## WHO'S THINKING ABOUT GOING TO LAW SCHOOL?

More than 140,000 people sit for the Law School Admissions Test (LSAT) every year, and that number is trending upward—in June 2008, the number of people who took the LSAT rose by 15.8 percent compared to June 2007. But that's not the whole story—more than 80,000 people apply to law school every year, and only about 56,000 get in. That's just a little more than half!

So what does this mean for you? While many have the drive to succeed, only a chosen few get a spot in the next law school class. That's why your success in undergrad is so critical to your admission to law school: it helps demonstrate that you have what it takes to make it through the rigorous academic demands of a top law school.

## WHAT CAN I DO NOW TO HELP MY CHANCES OF GETTING IN TO LAW SCHOOL?

As an AP student, the advanced courses you're taking and demanding workload you are doing are a great way to prepare not only for success in college but in law school and in your career as well. But don't forget about extracurriculars! Join the school newspaper as a staff writer or editor to show off your strong writing skills. Consider working on the yearbook, too—those proofreading and organizational skills will come in handy later. And don't forget about volunteering for worthy causes! Whatever you do, try to get into a leadership role, which will look really great on your undergraduate applications.

First things first: you've got to finish high school and apply to colleges. You may have already taken the SAT or ACT, or maybe you're anticipating a test date in the near future. By the time you're a junior, your high school GPA is pretty set. The one number that you still have total control over is your SAT or ACT score. Take the test—and prepare for the test—with the seriousness and attention that it deserves.

Now, even if your GPA is pretty much determined by the time you are a junior or senior, that doesn't mean that you should give yourself permission to slack off in those last semesters of your high school career. In fact, one way to get colleges to pay attention to you is to finish out high school with an academic bang! Keep working hard to keep that GPA as high as possible. Take advantage of independent study courses, more APs, or other advanced courses if your school offers them. Broaden your academic horizons by taking classes in psychology, art, music, history, sociology, or economics. If your high school doesn't offer these courses, talk to your academic advisor about taking classes at a local college.

## WHAT SHOULD I STUDY IN COLLEGE? WHERE SHOULD I GO?

The great thing about law school is that it doesn't matter what your undergraduate major is, as long as you do well in your classes. Keep in mind though, that while it's just fine to major in English, a lot of other applicants will have liberal arts majors, too. Complement it with something that might set you apart from the pack, such as a minor in Economics or Spanish.

If you know what kind of lawyer you want to be, that can play a big part in what classes you choose. For example, if you really want to help save the environment, trying putting a few biology, geography, or natural sciences classes under your belt. If politics is your ultimate career path, focus on political science, history, or economics. Or if you want to work in the corporate world, classes in economics, accounting, or business are the way to go. Bottom line: Pick a major and classes you love. You'll get good grades because you are excited about the classes and learning new things.

There are many factors to consider when applying to college and choosing the one that's right for you. Academic reputation, international recognition, history, prestige, elite status, family legacy, and others are all fine to consider, but they shouldn't be at the very top of your list. Rather, consider primarily the "fit" of the school with your learning style, personality, interests, and goals.

Once you're in college, consider joining a pre-law chapter of a national law fraternity or sorority, like Phi Alpha Delta (PAD) or Sigma Alpha Nu (SAN). If you join in your freshman or sophomore year, you could become an officer in your junior or senior year. You'll have the option to continue your membership once you're in law school.

## WHOM SHOULD I TALK TO ABOUT MY LAW SCHOOL ASPIRATIONS?

Once you're in college, you may be assigned a Pre-Law Advisor—one who provides guidance to current and former students seeking a career in law. Pre-Law Advisors can be found in your undergraduate University Advising Center or Career Center or in academic departments, such as Political Science and History. Your Pre-Law Advisor will help you research and identify law schools to which you may want to apply. Another helpful resource is the Internet. There are hundreds of organizations, associations, and forums dedicated to providing helpful guidance along the path to law school. The LSAC (lsac.org) and ABA (aba.net) websites provide a wide variety of information about everything you need to get ready for a career in law school. They will also provide links for information on other topics, such as financial aid and nontraditional career choices for law school graduates.

## WHAT IS THE LSAT, AND WHEN DO I TAKE IT?

The LSAT is unlike any test you've ever taken. Sure, there are an essay and some multiple-choice questions, but you're not going to regurgitate memorized facts. Instead, the LSAT is going to test the critical reading, logical reasoning, and analytical thinking skills that you've picked up gradually in school.

If you plan to attend law school right after you graduate, expect to take the LSAT in your junior year of college (but start studying the summer between sophomore and junior year). Typically, you want to give yourself 18 months from when you first start studying for your LSAT until you have mailed off the last application to the school of your choice. Visit **kaptest.com/LSAT** for more information on how we can help you achieve a score that will get you into the school of your choice and on the path to a successful career in law.

**Carolyn Landis**
Pre-law Product Manager
Kaplan Test Prep and Admissions